IMAGES
of Rail

WATERBURY TROLLEYS

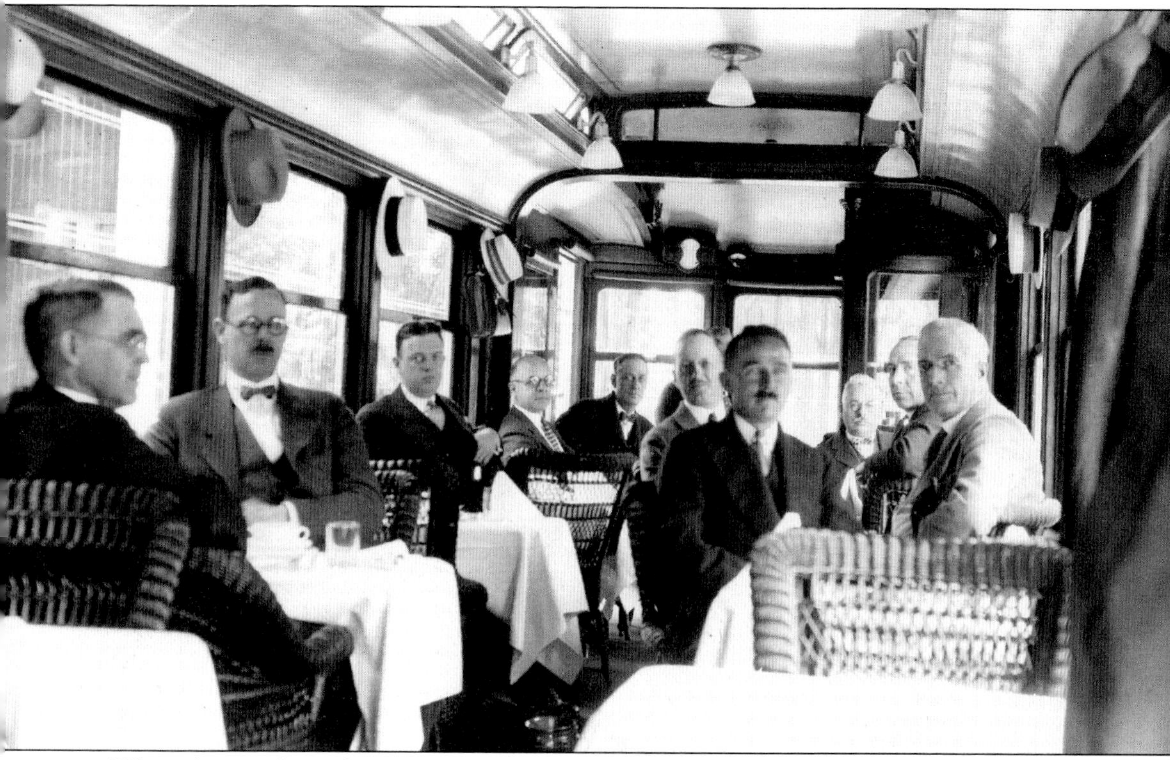

When the members of Connecticut's Public Utilities Commission made their annual inspection of trolley properties, they traveled in comfort aboard Connecticut Company parlor car 500. In June of 1927, when this picture was taken, air-conditioning was not yet available. The three-piece suits, standard business attire at that time, must have been uncomfortable, but the refreshments probably helped. Note the mandatory polished cuspidor in the aisle.

IMAGES
of Rail

WATERBURY TROLLEYS

Connecticut Motor Coach Museum

ARCADIA
PUBLISHING

ISBN 978-0-7385-3811-2

Published by Arcadia Publishing,
Charleston, South Carolina

Printed in the United States of America

Library of Congress Catalog Card Number: 2005922057

For all general information, contact Arcadia Publishing:
Telephone 843-853-2070
Fax 843-853-0044
E-mail sales@arcadiapublishing.com
For customer service and orders:
Toll-free 1-888-313-2665

Visit us on the Internet at www.arcadiapublishing.com

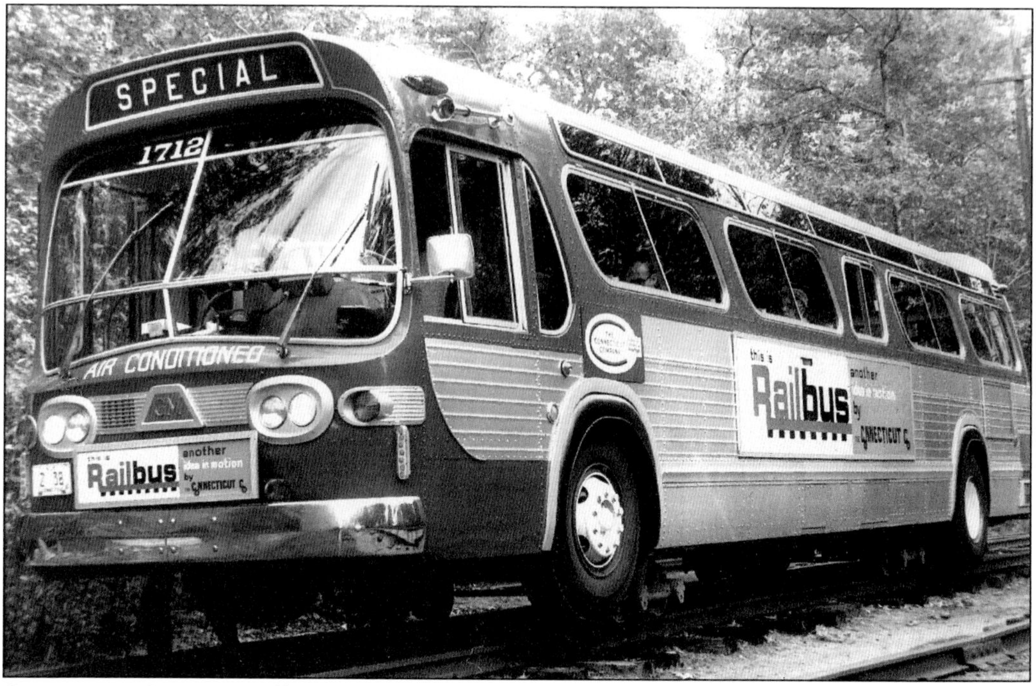

Connecticut Company railbus No. 1712, seen here in 1975 at Hancock Siding, at the Connecticut Trolley Museum in East Windsor, was to have been the first of a fleet of 50 buses that would be used in the Hartford area. The plan was for the buses to transport riders in and out of the city during the rush hour using the highway system and existing rail lines, thus decreasing traffic on the highway system during peak times. The proposal never got beyond the test stage due to a number of problems, especially concerning union work rules and the inability of the buses to operate in heavy snow. Proceeds from this book will go directly to the Connecticut Motor Coach Museum to restore railbus No. 1712 to operation.

Contents

ACKNOWLEDGMENTS

From 1907 to 1909 there was a rapid expansion of the electric trolley system in Waterbury and the suburbs, transforming public transportation from the era of the horse-drawn stagecoach and horse car into the modern age of the electric streetcar. The expansion of the electric streetcar system was a major factor in the growth of the cities and towns throughout the region. While much praise has gone to the "captains of industry" whose leadership led to the planning, designing, and financing of the lines, little has been said of the many "laborers" who accomplished great and indispensable jobs that enabled those captains to produce great things. It was the Reverend C. A. Dinsmore, D.D., in his toast at the Curtis House celebrating the opening of the Woodbury line on September 1, 1908, who made mention of this when he quoted a poem by Kipling. "It is the sons of Mary, the poets, and the artists, who get the praise and fame; but it is on the shoulders of the sons of Marth, the road builders, who accomplish the great things, that the brunt of the work falls. Yet they are unrecognized and forgotten."

This book is dedicated to those "unrecognized and forgotten" laborers, motormen, conductors, and workers who were instrumental in building, operating, and maintaining the early transit systems. We also want to acknowledge photographs from the collections of Fred Bennett and the late Horace Bromley, which supplemented those from the archives of the Motor Coach Museum. The proceeds from the sale of this book will go directly to the Connecticut Motor Coach Museum in East Windsor to restore unique railbus No. 1712 to operation.

Alan J. Walker
President
Connecticut Motor Coach Museum
P.O. Box 297
East Windsor, CT 06088

INTRODUCTION

Stretching from Shelton in the south to Winsted in the north, Connecticut's Naugatuck Valley attracted Yankee entrepreneurs quick to see the potential for industrial power in the Naugatuck River and its tributaries. Lacking waterways suitable for canals, the area quickly embraced the new technology of the railroad to replace primitive roads as the primary means of transportation. Waterbury, by far the largest community in the valley, enjoyed the north-south service of the Naugatuck Railroad and the east-west route of the New York and New England Railroad. A further, though short-lived, line to Meriden was opened via Cheshire, and a short branch was built to service the industrial and commuting needs of Oakville and Watertown.

As the long-distance train service grew steadily, the valley towns of Shelton, Derby, Ansonia, Seymour, Beacon Falls, Naugatuck, Waterbury, Thomaston, Torrington, and Winsted saw a gradual metamorphosis of local transit from single-livery services to horse omnibuses, and horse cars to the revolutionary new electric trolley car.

Following the first successful application of electric power to street transit in Montgomery, Alabama, in June 1887, the first large-scale introduction of the new technology was established in Richmond, Virginia, by Frank Julian Sprague in 1888, when the entire horse car system was electrified. The first electric trolley car to operate in New England was in Derby in 1887, with the electrification of the Derby Horse Railroad. This was a bold move because in 1887 there were fewer than 12 operating electric railways in the United States. The early electrification was for the movement of freight in the Derby dock area only. Later, passenger operations were electrified. In 1889 the line became the Derby Street Railway; in 1900 the company was merged with Connecticut Lighting and Power Company The first passenger-carrying electric street railway in Connecticut was in Meriden in 1888. However, this line was not a success, largely due to inadequately designed equipment, and it was converted back to horse cars within a year.

Most early electric street railways either evolved from horse operations or were started new by local visionaries anxious that their communities not be left behind in the new era of technology. As local systems grew, mergers with connecting and/or competing lines were inevitable. The rapid growth of street railways caught the eye of the mighty New Haven Railroad, which was then busy assembling its vast Southern New England network of railroads and coastal steamship companies. As the turn of the 20th century approached, the consolidations began.

Transit service first came to Waterbury in the form of horse cars on November 3, 1886. The Waterbury Horse Railroad Company had been chartered over two and a half years previous, on March 18, 1884, and it is believed that horse omnibuses of some sort operated for at least 20 years prior to the installation of rails.

On June 14, 1893, the Waterbury Traction Company was chartered by the state legislature and thereafter became the predominant factor in Waterbury public transportation. The new company ran its first electric cars on July 28, 1894, beginning an era that would not be concluded until the last local trolley ran on May 22, 1937. Torrington and Winsted operations were started in 1897 by the Torrington & Winchester Street Railway, which merged with the New

Haven Railroad in 1907. In 1910 the isolated 12-mile Torrington division was merged with the Connecticut Company. All operations were discontinued on January 5, 1929. Torrington was served by streetcars only, and its operations were not converted to bus as had been done in other divisions. New England Transportation, a New Haven Railroad subsidiary, provided bus service to Hartford and Waterbury but did not provide any local service like the streetcars.

By 1899 the Connecticut Lighting and Power Company, chartered on March 1, 1897, to operate streetcars and provide electric power to the public, had streetcar operations not only in Waterbury but also in New Britain, some 20 miles to the east. Operations consisted of four formerly independent companies running 103 cars of all types on 29.5 miles of track. Waterbury alone had 13 miles of track and 61 cars.

On January 10, 1901, the superior court ordered that the Connecticut Lighting and Power Company's name be changed to Connecticut Railway and Lighting Company, marking a more transit-oriented path for the company. (Note: While its name is similar, the present Connecticut Light and Power Company, formed in 1917, is not related to the Connecticut Railway and Lighting Company, although it does lease rights-of-way from that company.) Connecticut Railway and Lighting Company's valley properties were in Shelton, Derby, Naugatuck, and Waterbury.

On May 18, 1904, the Consolidated Railway Company was chartered under the jurisdiction of the New Haven Railroad and began its program of street railway acquisitions statewide. On August 1, 1906, Connecticut Railway and Lighting Company leased its properties to the Consolidated for 999 years.

Meanwhile, on July 18, 1905, the Thomaston Tramway Company was incorporated to build a line from Waterbury to Thomaston. Then, on May 31, 1907, the Thomaston Tramway Company's name was changed to the Connecticut Company and it was authorized by the state legislature to take over all street railway properties in the state that were owned by or leased to the New Haven Railroad. In the ensuing years, and backed by the seemingly limitless financial resources of the New Haven Railroad, the Connecticut Company added more properties and extended and improved the entire system. Beginning on July 8, 1907, residents of the Naugatuck Valley could ride from Waterbury to New Haven via Naugatuck and Derby. On August 3, 1908, service to Thomaston via Waterville began, more than three years after the Thomaston Tramway had been incorporated. However, the big event was the beginning of service from Waterbury to Woodbury via Middlebury. As was the practice of many street railway companies at that time, the Connecticut Company built a recreation area—Lake Quassapaug Park—to provide an enjoyable destination for its patrons on the weekends, thereby generating business during a time period when the railway would otherwise not have riders.

The next few years formed the golden age of trolleys in Connecticut: 1913 saw the largest fleet, with a total of 2,598 cars of all types statewide; and the greatest mileage of the system, measuring 1,138 miles, was reached in 1918.

Buses were an early part of the Waterbury scene, with jitney service started before the First World War. Many of the independent operators later consolidated to form the North East Transportation Company, which in 2005 still operates the Waterbury city lines, and other properties as well, as a contractor for the Connecticut Department of Transportation. The first bus line in Waterbury was the Hamilton Avenue line, which began operations in 1921, running from Exchange Place in the center of town to St. Joseph's cemetery in the eastern part of the city. Soon thereafter motorization of various other lines was undertaken, with buses largely instituting new services over new routes. These new routes brought transit service mainly to multidwelling neighborhoods, whose residents, workers in the brass mills and factories, had theretofore walked to work or to the nearest car line for their transportation.

The first conversion of an existing rail line came on January 5, 1929, when the Thomaston interurban route was abandoned completely. Never replaced by bus service, the line had suffered from competition with its parent—the New Haven Railroad's Winsted line paralleled its right-of-way. Nearly two years elapsed before the next abandonment. This time the interurban line to

Woodbury, 13.2 miles west of Waterbury, was the victim of low ridership and high right-of-way maintenance costs. Always lightly patronized except for seasonal crowds traveling to and from the Connecticut Company's amusement park at Lake Quassapaug, the line's discontinuance actually brought an extension of service; buses were now run past Woodbury Center to Hotchkissville, two miles to the northwest. Other conversions continued throughout the early 1930s. Beginning with Baldwin Street in January 1931, East Main Street, Naugatuck, the lines through Cheshire and Milldale to New Haven, and the Lakewood, Watertown, Waterville, and valley lines were converted to bus operations. June 19, 1937, saw the final car leave Waterbury for New Haven, closing the last remaining trolley service (city service having ceased on May 22, 1937). All local service in Derby was converted to motor coach operation on March 21, 1937. Finally, on June 20, 1937, all streetcar operations of the Connecticut Railway and Lighting Company converted to bus operation.

For many years, stockholders of the Connecticut Railway and Lighting Company had wanted to exit the transit business and depend on power-line right-of-way leases (dating back to the early 1900s) for revenue. In the early 1970s, with a major strike in the making and no possible financial relief from the state or local governments, the entire Connecticut Railway and Lighting Company system, including Bridgeport, New Britain, and Waterbury, shut down on October 10, 1972. Public transportation in Waterbury today is provided by North East Transportation, under contract to the Connecticut Department of Transportation.

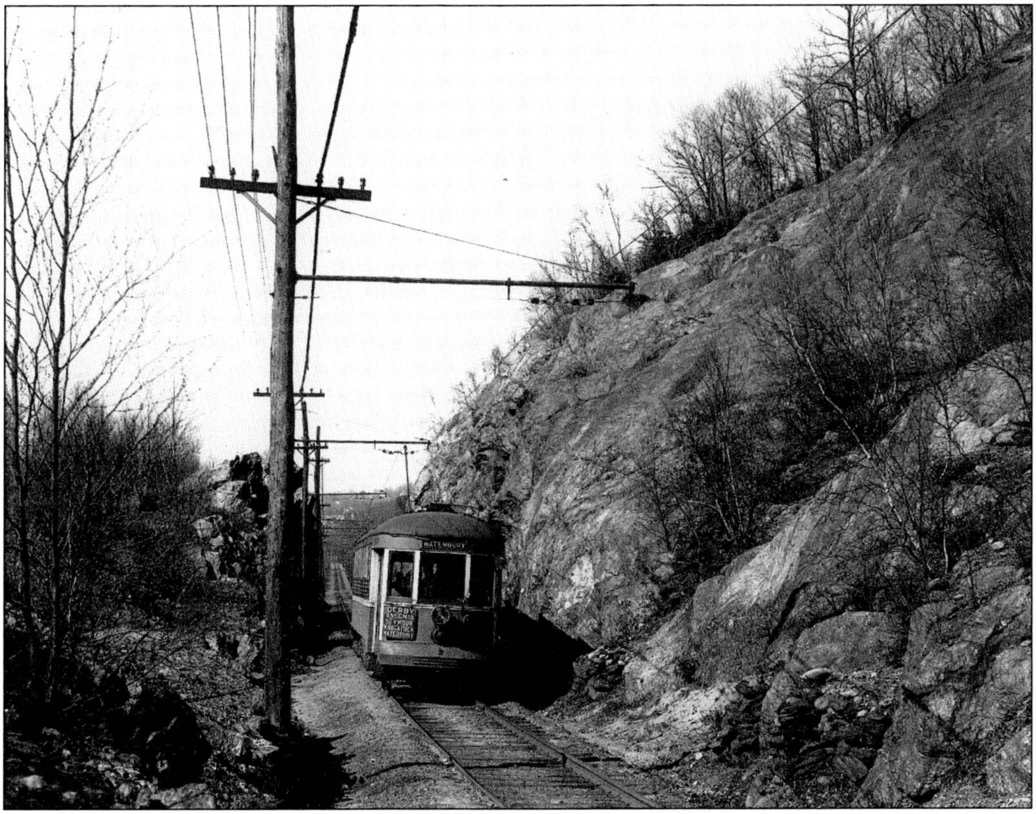

Connecticut Railway and Lighting car No. 1914 is heading northbound on the line between Derby and Waterbury in this 1937 view. One can just imagine the whir of the electric motors and the scenery flying by with the controller on full speed.

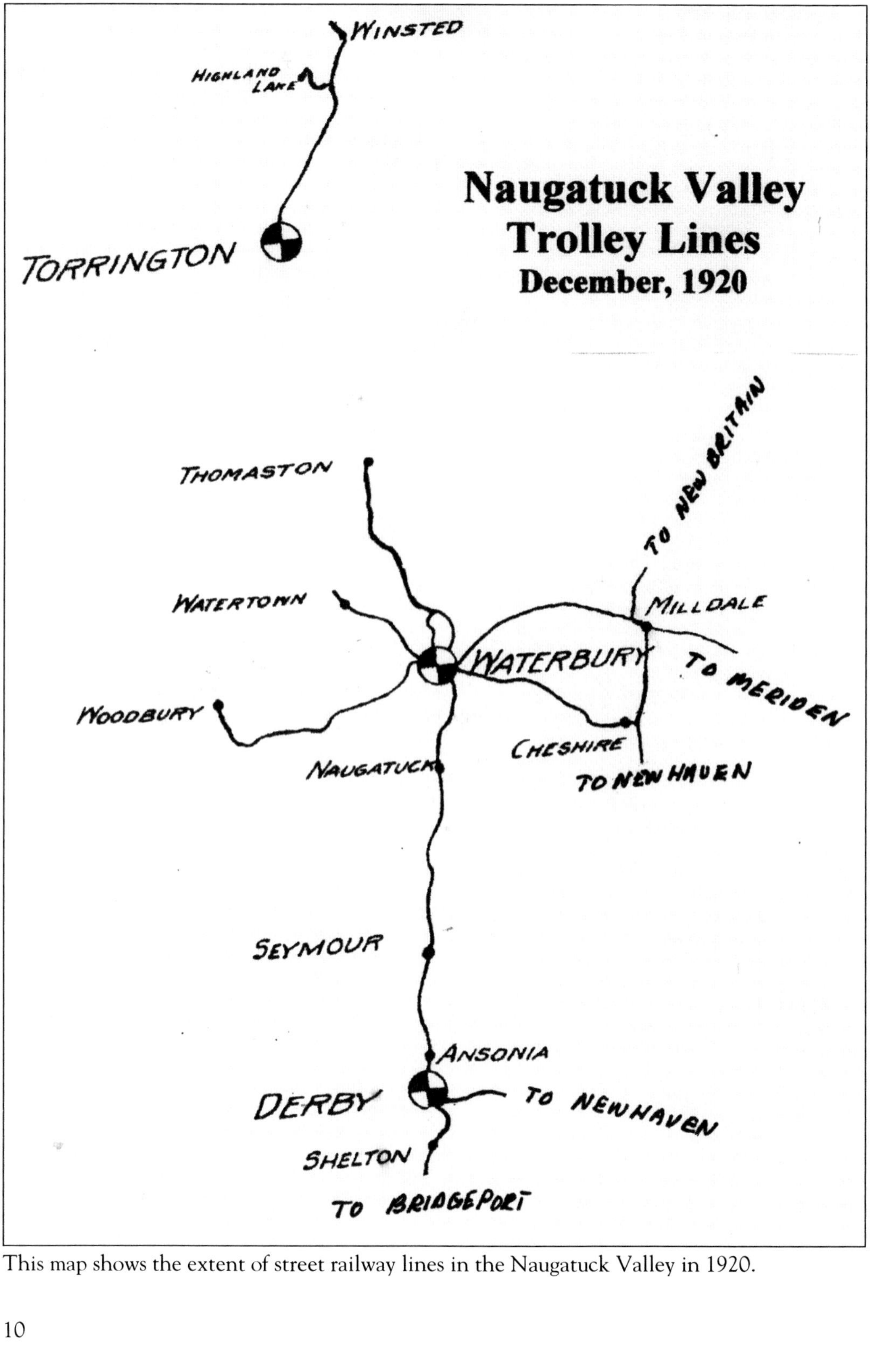

This map shows the extent of street railway lines in the Naugatuck Valley in 1920.

One

Early Days in Waterbury

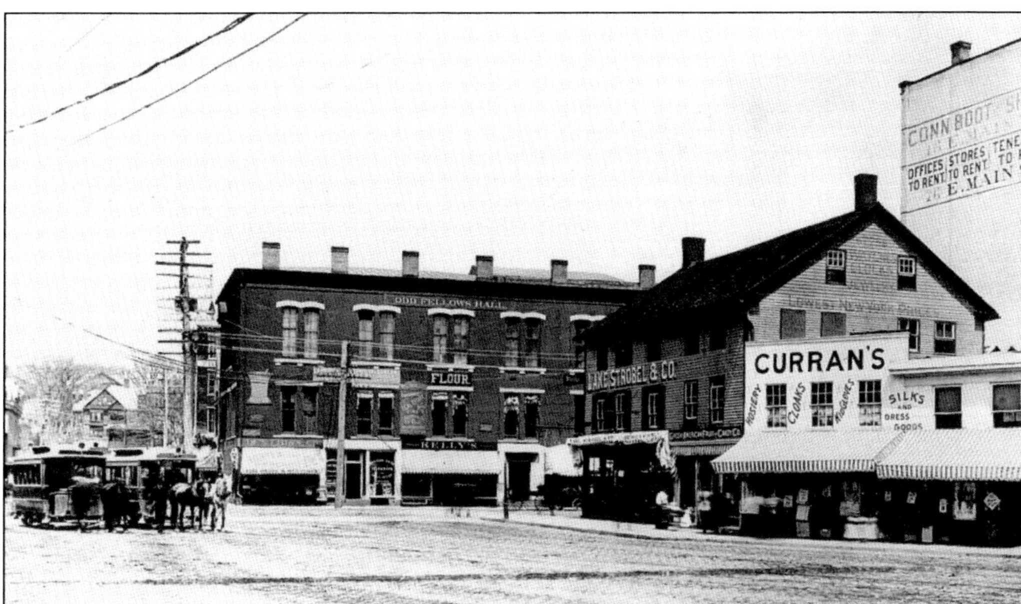

This view of Exchange Place, looking north in 1888, shows North Main Street behind the cars and East Main Street to the right. The image at the top of page 44 provides a 1922 view of the same area. By 1886 there were 300 cities in the United States with horse railways, which altogether employed more than 100,000 horses to power the vehicles. In Boston alone, more than 3,600 horses were owned by the Metropolitan Railroad. (F. S. Bennett Collection.)

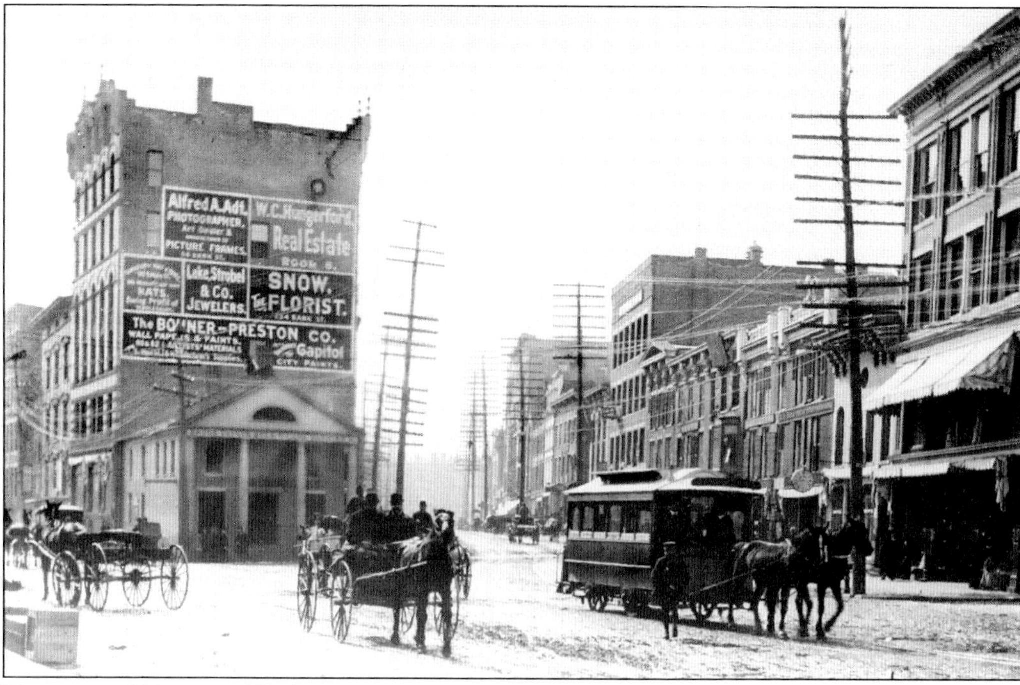

This is an 1888 view of Exchange Place in Waterbury, looking south; Bank Street is to the right, and South Main Street to the left. Wages for horse car drivers were quite low even for the 1880s, with the average driver working 16 hours to make one dollar per day. (F. S. Bennett Collection.)

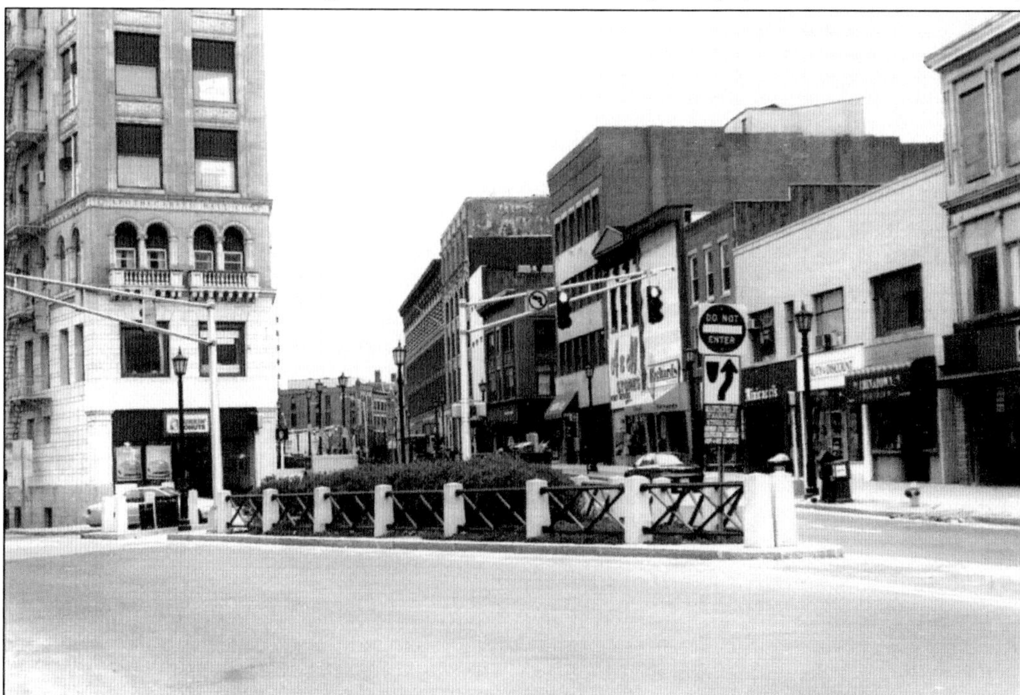

Here, Exchange Place is pictured in 2005, in a view looking south. Notice that some of the buildings seen in the 1888 photograph still stand.

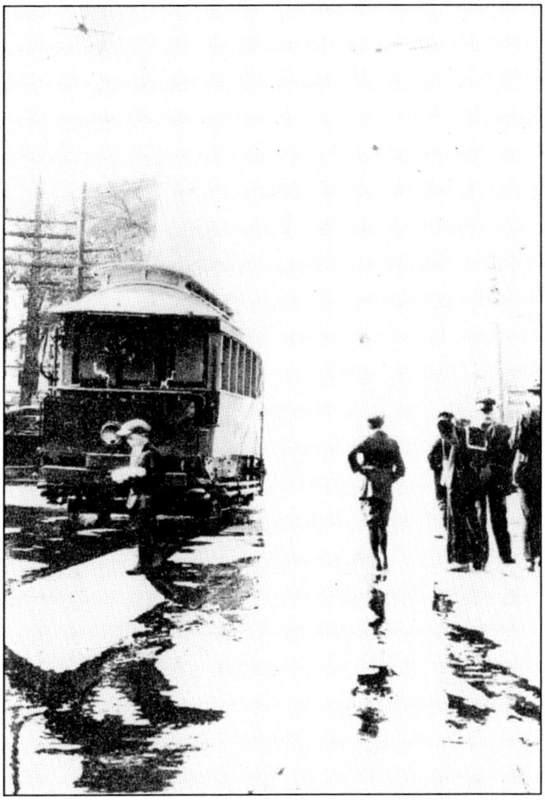

In the era when horses were still very much a part of the everyday traffic in Waterbury, sprinkler cars were used to clean the streets of horse droppings and sprinkle water on the dusty streets on dry days. These cars were owned by the American Sprinkler Car Company of Worcester, Massachusetts, but were operated by street railway personnel.

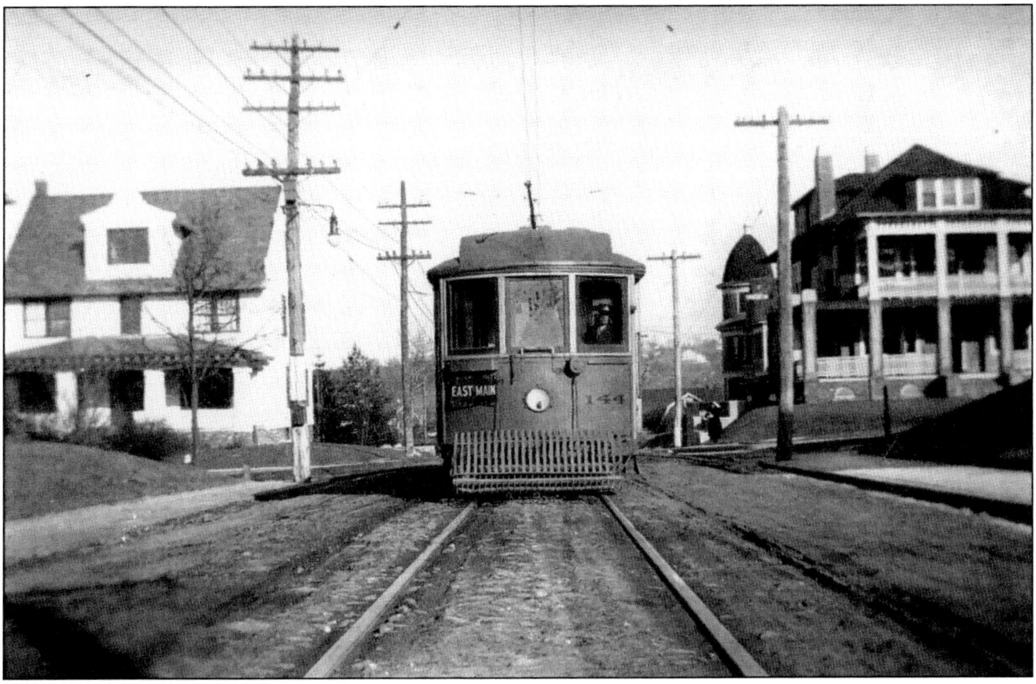

This view of car 144 on the East Main Street line was a common sight when this picture was taken in 1914.

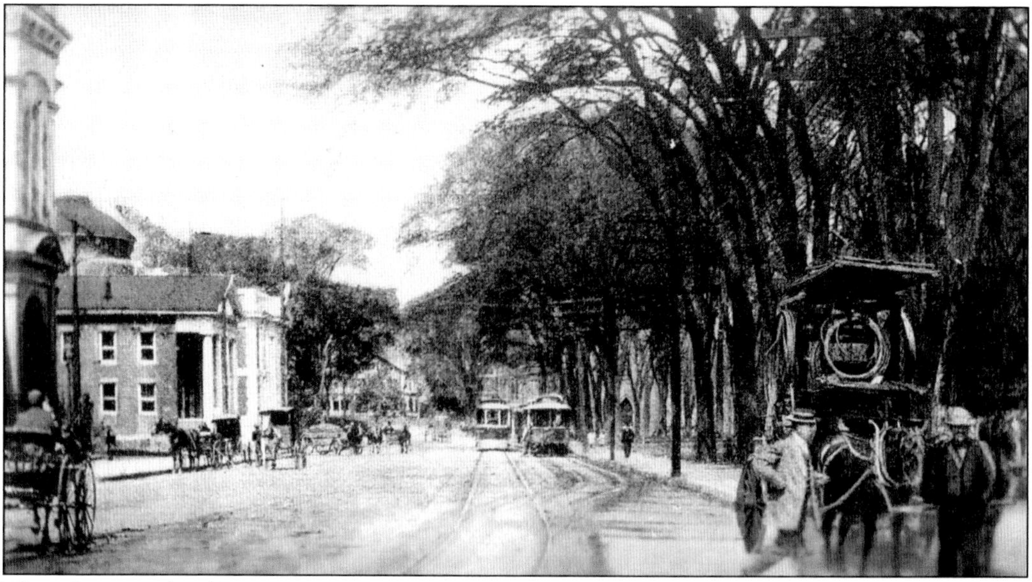

This photograph of West Main Street and the Waterbury Green, taken before the Great Fire of 1902, shows the Connecticut Railway and Lighting Company's horse-drawn line wagon, its crew ready to work on the overhead wire. These wagons, and the line trucks that replaced them, were available on a moment's notice to respond to any power emergency that may have struck the streetcar line. These units also responded to multiple-alarm fires to assist the fire department if any streetcar overhead wires caused an obstruction to the fire department's ladder trucks or water towers at the scene. These wagons also carried "hose jumpers" that were used to allow the streetcars to cross over any hose line stretched across the tracks.

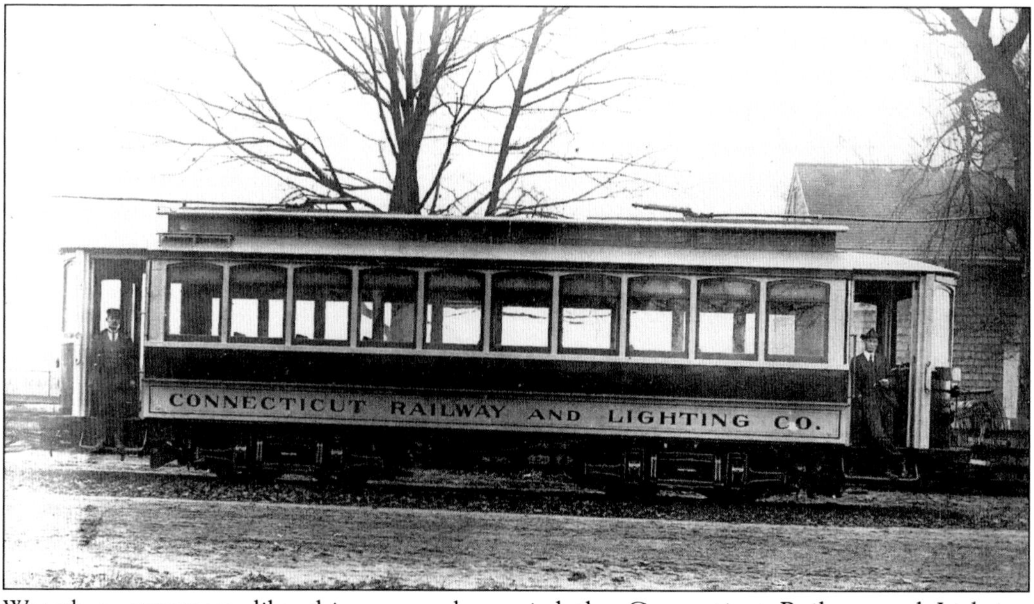

Waterbury streetcars, like this one, only carried the Connecticut Railway and Lighting Company name for five years, from 1901 until 1906. In 1906 the equipment and lines were leased to Consolidated Railway. (F. S. Bennett Collection.)

Waterbury division motorman Atwood Caswell, Badge No. 5449, is shown on Mitchell Avenue just a few blocks west of the green. Notice that the street was not yet paved; however, sidewalks had been installed. The apartment house to the right and the building under construction on Willow Street in the background still stand today. Wages had improved since the horse car days, and Mr. Caswell, as an experienced motorman working *only* 12 hours a day, six days a week, would probably be making $2 or more per day.

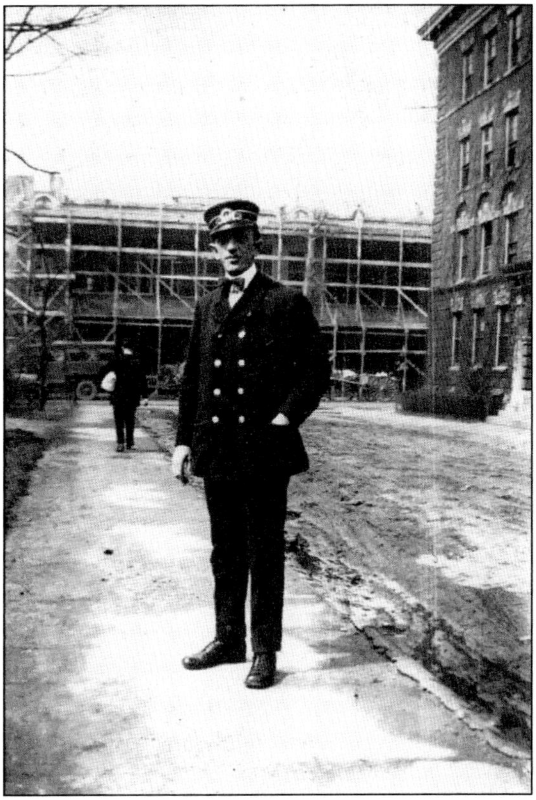

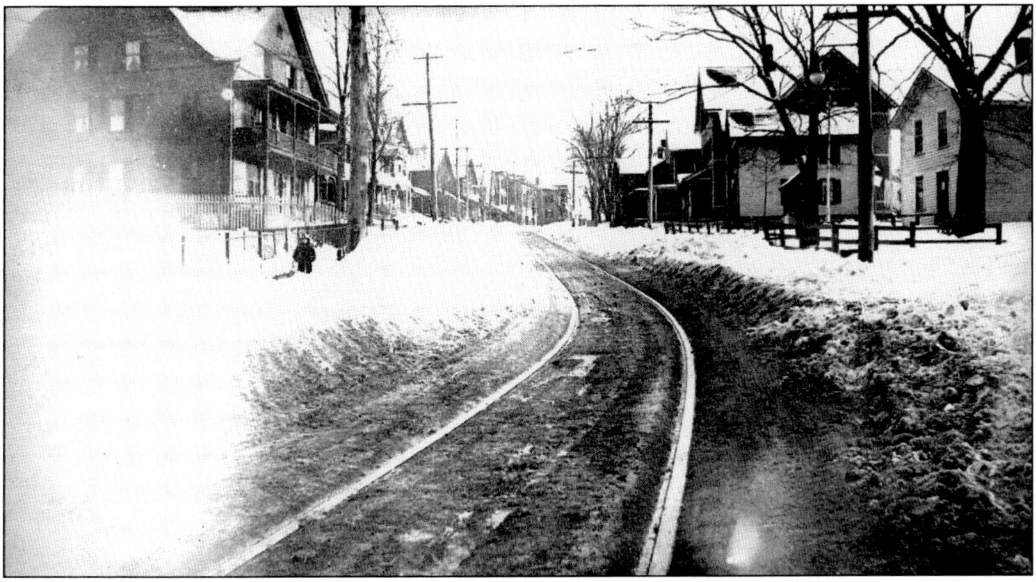

Unfortunately for residents of Baldwin Street in 1914, snow removal was limited to the area of the streetcar tracks. The streetcar company was required, as part of its charter, to clear snow on all the streets it operated on. Snow removal by the city was still some years away.

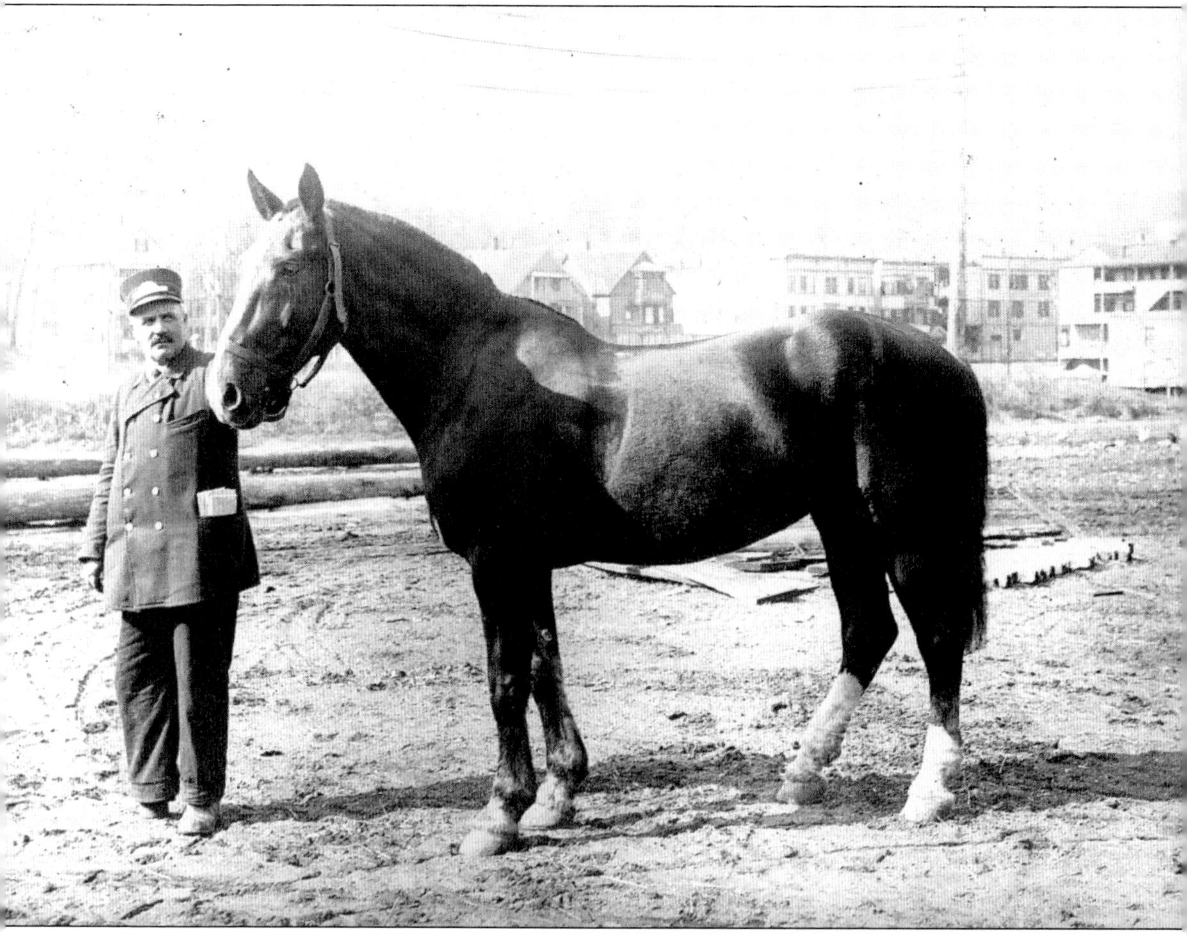

This picture shows one of the horses used in Waterbury to pull the tower wagon for crews working on the overhead wire. These animals were well cared for, working only a few hours per day. They munched down 25 to 30 pounds of grain per day, along with carrots and other horse "goodies" added to their diet. The horses were examined by a veterinarian on a regular basis to assure that they were fit for work. These horses were also very valuable. Evidence of this fact may be found in a notation in the Connecticut Company 1922 report to the Public Utilities Commission, under expenses, "To write off the value of two horses killed during the year: $462.50."

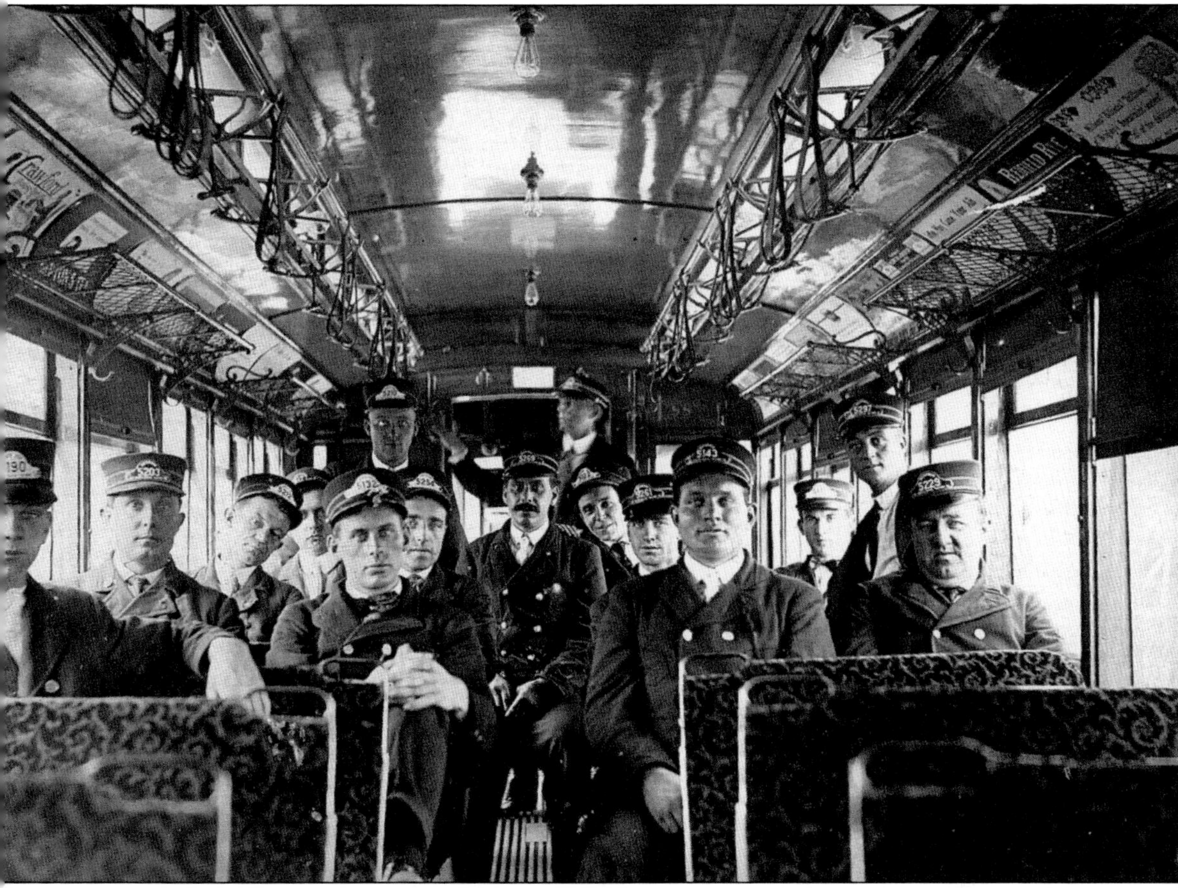

Connecticut Railway and Lighting car 88, seen here in 1906, had a deluxe interior with carpet-covered seats. Most cars in this era had seats that were either rattan covered or just plain wood. Compared to thc horse cars they replaced, these cars were equipped with electric heat and lights and were truly deluxe vehicles. Car 88 became Connecticut Company No. 969 in 1915 and was scrapped in 1929. Some of the operators on the Waterbury division are posing for a collective portrait in this car. (F. S. Bennett Collection.)

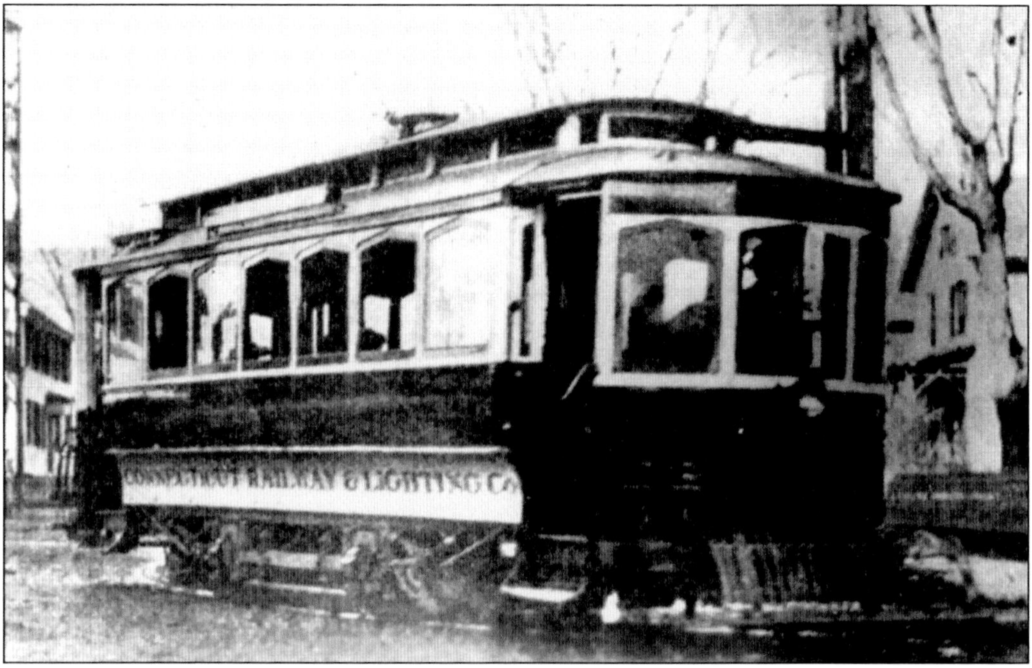

One of the Brill-built, single-truck Connecticut Railway and Lighting Company cars, No. 72, is shown running on a residential street. The earlier cars were built with outward-curving sides, similar to the earlier horse cars, which allowed the cars to pass bulky wagons and other horse-drawn vehicles on narrow streets without colliding. Later-model cars did away with this feature.

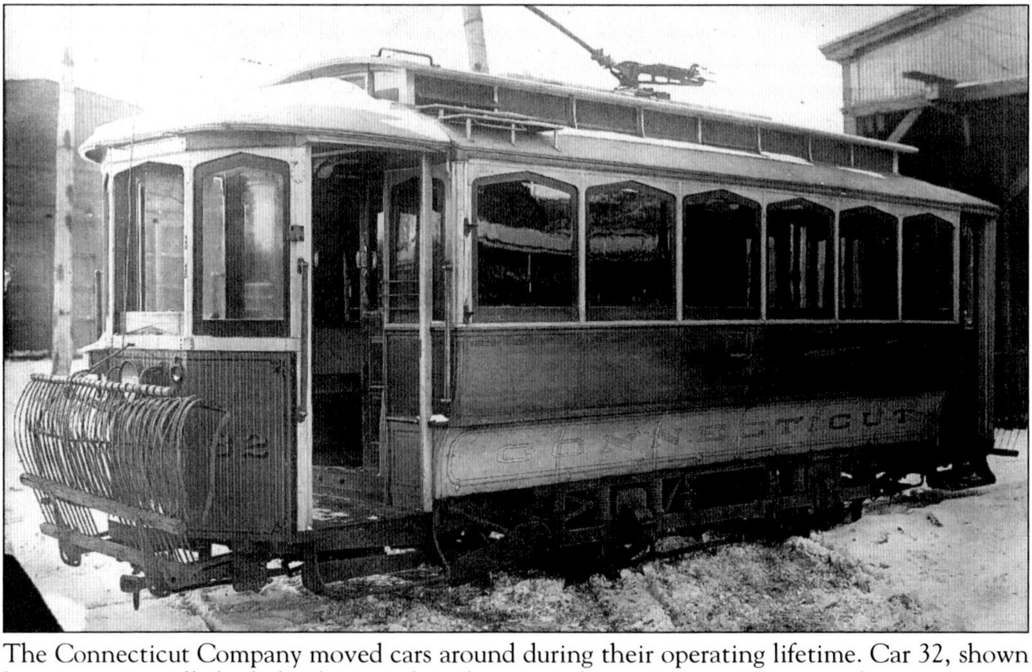

The Connecticut Company moved cars around during their operating lifetime. Car 32, shown here, was originally built for the Meriden Electric Railway in 1893 as No. 66. The Connecticut Company acquired the Meriden Electric Railway and renumbered the car. It ran in Waterbury until it was scrapped in 1920.

Two

DOWNTOWN WATERBURY LINES

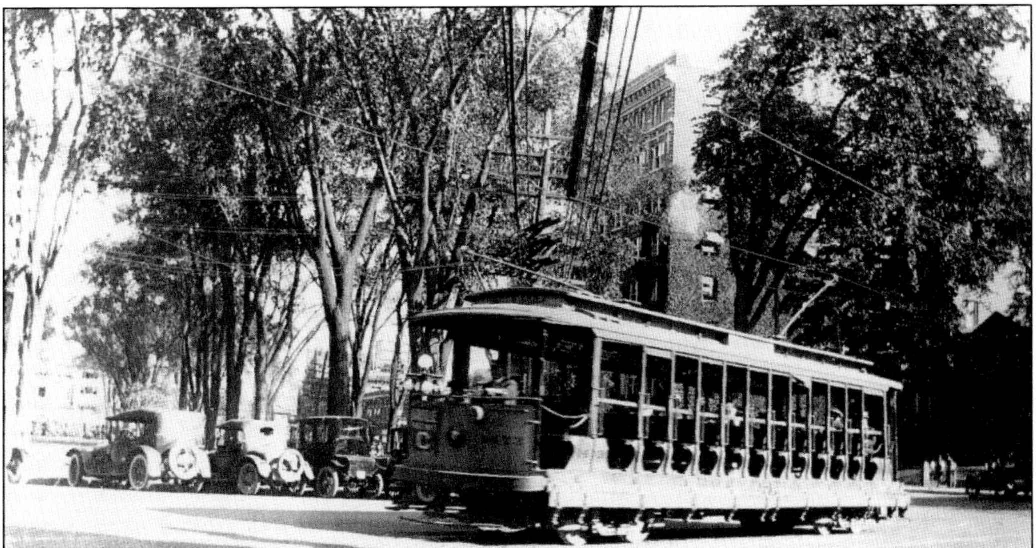

Open car 1473 is leaving Exchange Place en route to Oakville in this 1920 view. The riding public loved open cars, but for the railway companies they were not economical. The open cars could only be operated in warmer weather, meaning additional closed cars needed to be available for cold-weather use. Also, the accident rate for open cars was much higher since people tended to jump off the open cars while they were still moving because of the open sides. (F. S. Bennett Collection.)

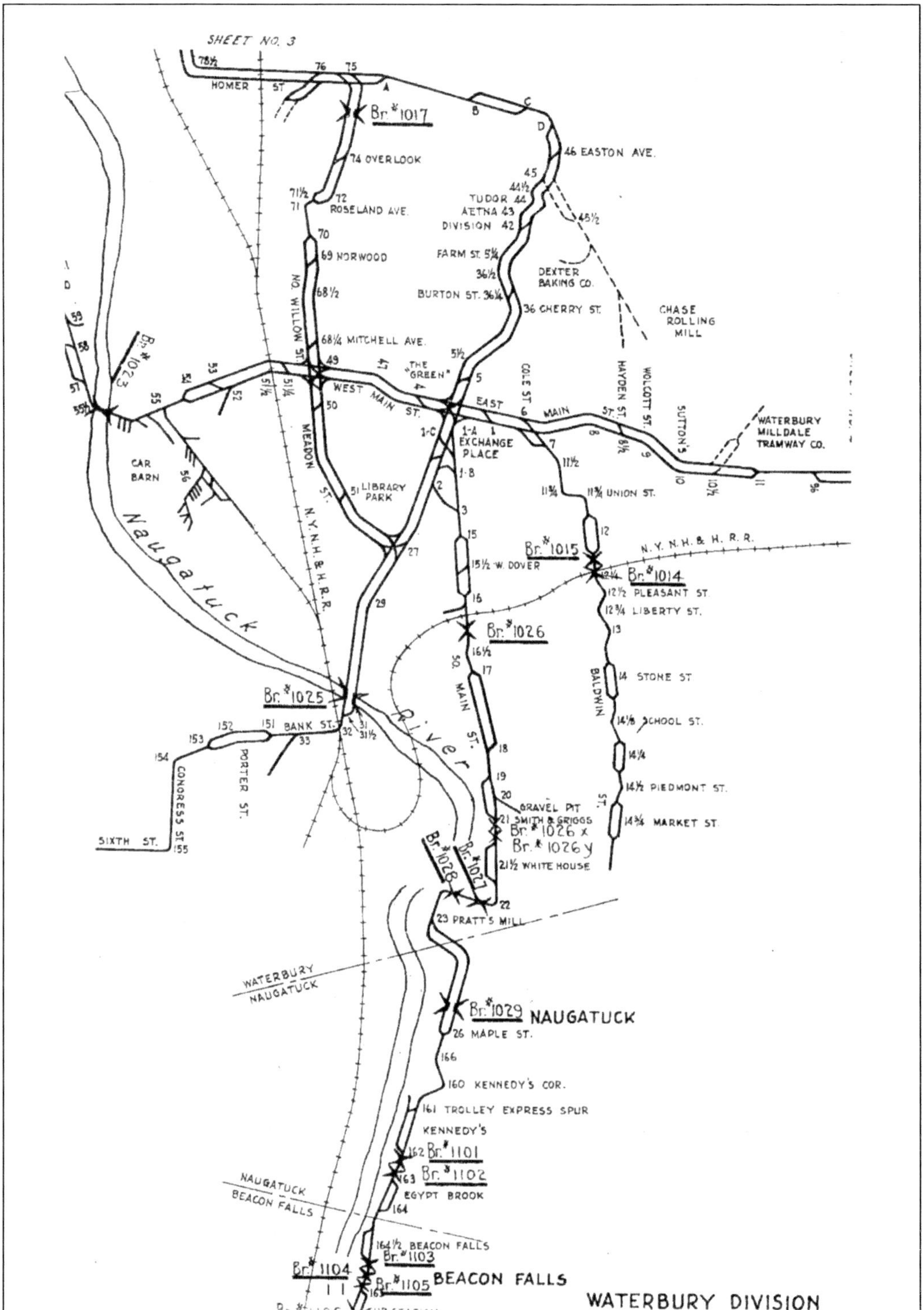

This 1920 map shows the lines in downtown Waterbury, as well as some of the suburban lines in the area.

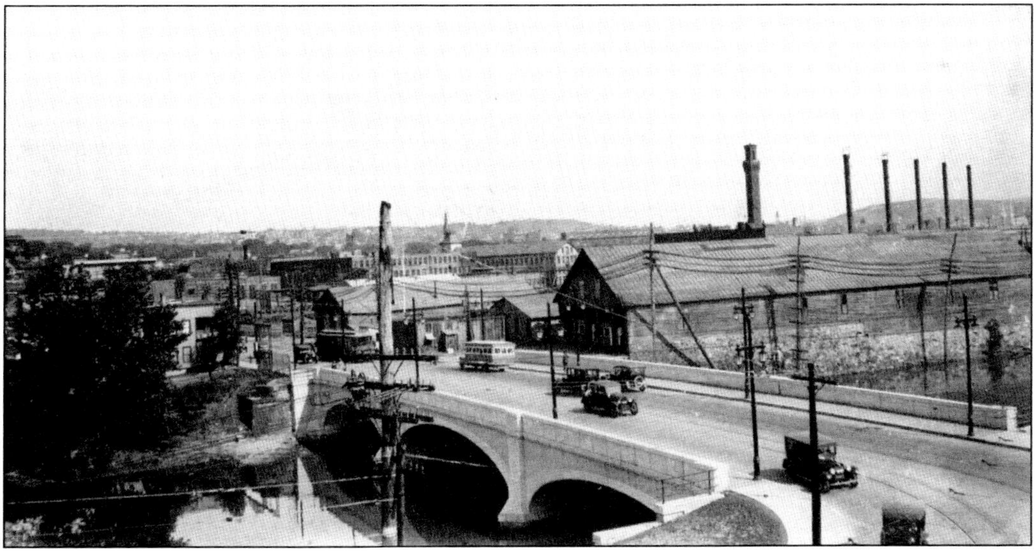

The new bridge carrying West Main Street over the Naugatuck River was designed for both trolley car and automobile/truck traffic. Still visible are the abutments from the original single-track trolley bridge to the left of the new bridge, and the soon-to-be-replaced Waterbury Traction Company carbarn complex to the right of the bridge. In 1922 the Connecticut Company paid bridge contractor C. W. Blakeslee & Sons $25,000 to to cover its portion of the cost of the new concrete bridge on West Main Street. The early bus on the bridge is a precursor of things to come.

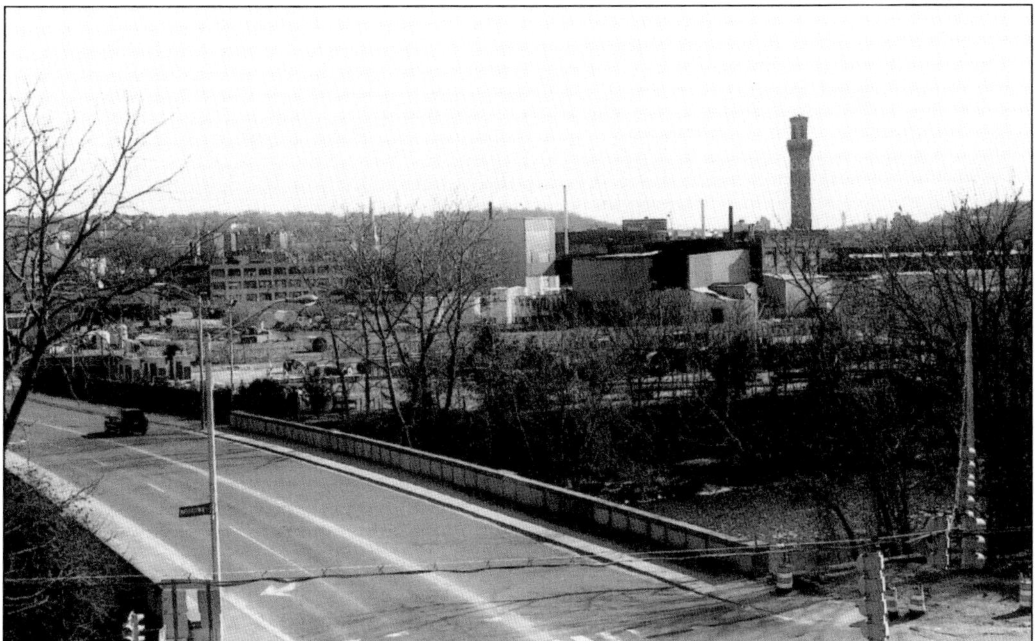

After eight decades, a major flood, redevelopment, and highway construction, the West Main Street Bridge today still carries traffic across the Naugatuck River.

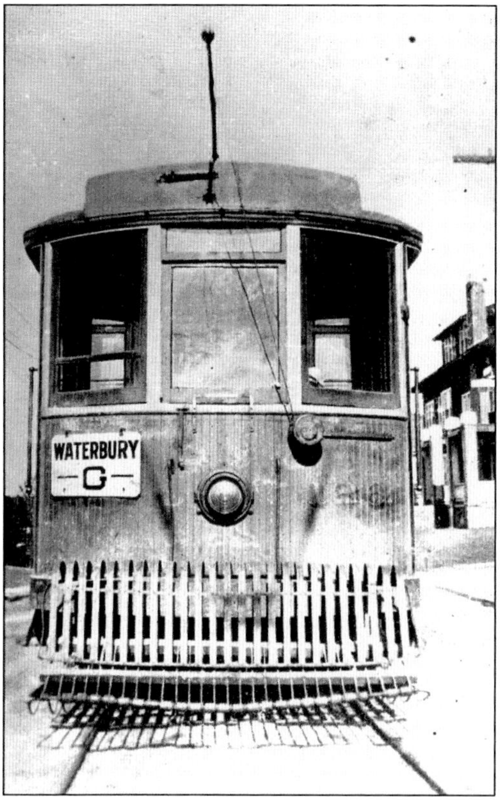

On the Waterbury lines, the letter "G" denoted cars that ran to or from Thomaston. Car 128 ended up as No. 1209 in Hartford, where it ran until it was scrapped in 1941. While in Hartford, 1209 ran on the interurban high-speed line from East Hartford to Rockville; after the interurban line closed in 1924, the car operated on Hartford city lines until streetcar service ended in July 1941.

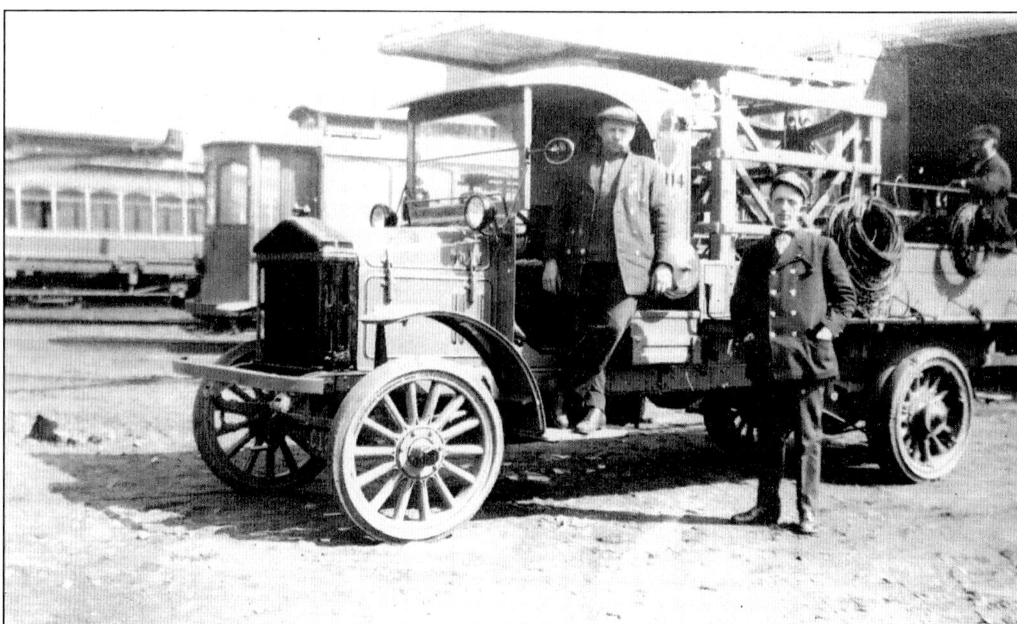

This line truck in Waterbury looks ready to roll to solve any mechanical or electrical problem that may arise on the line. This truck was surely chosen for this duty because of its capability to maneuver the many hills in Waterbury.

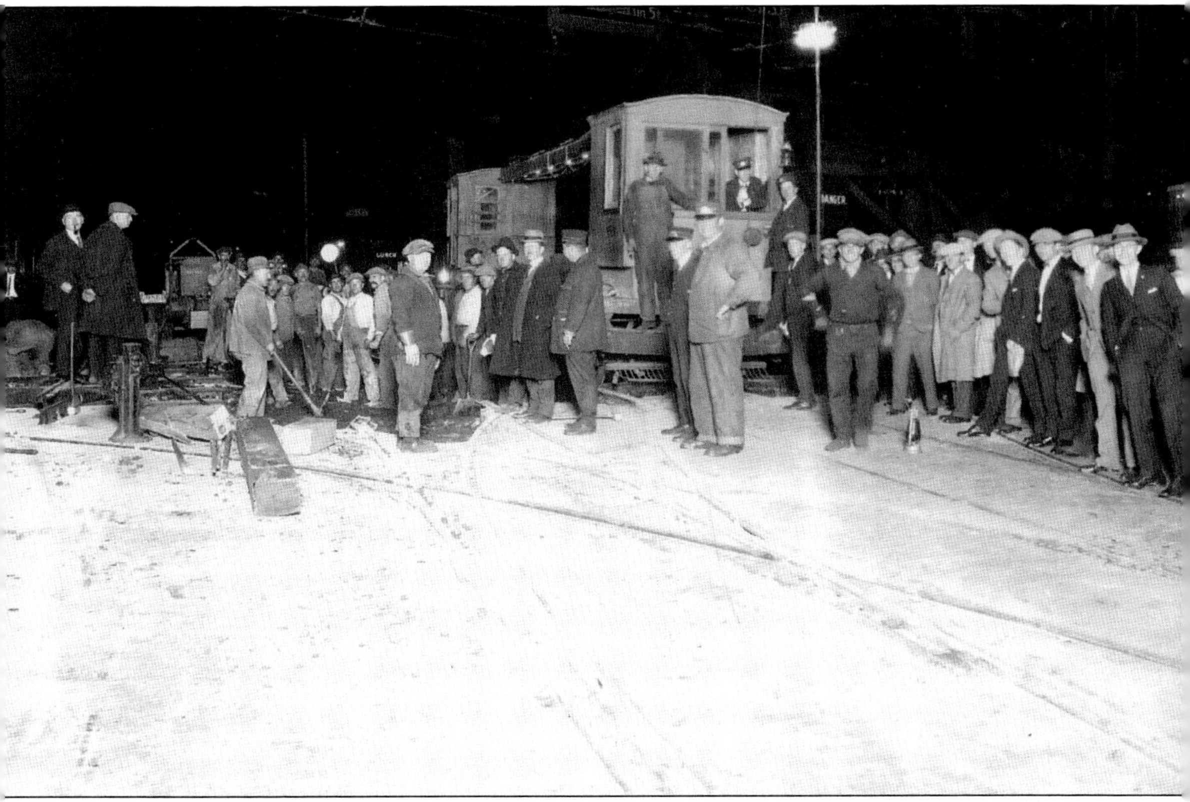

It is a cold night at Exchange Place in downtown Waterbury, where an enthusiastic crowd has gathered to watch a large track gang and its heavy equipment rebuilding some switches at this prime junction. The picture shows East Main Street. The wooden structure just visible in the background to the right will soon be replaced by the art deco–style Brown Building.

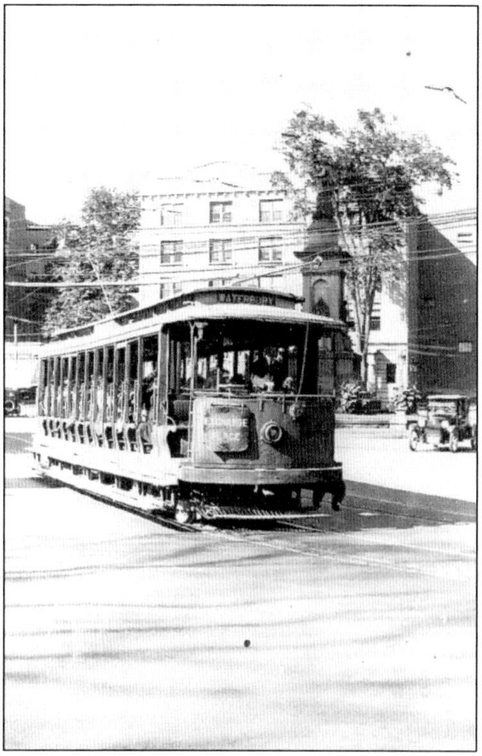

Transit companies had other reasons for not liking open cars, beyond the obvious added expense that went with needing two sets of equipment—one for warm weather and another for cold weather. Fare collection was also a problem. Without the convenience of a middle aisle, the conductor had to collect the fares by walking along the running boards while the car was in motion. On a typical open car with 15 benches, 80 people or more could be riding, and even the best conductor had a difficult time collecting the nickel fare from all the passengers who got on and off the car during a typical trip. Transit companies also employed "street railway police" to ride the cars and check up on the conductors' honesty. Even with an honest conductor, open cars made fare collection very difficult.

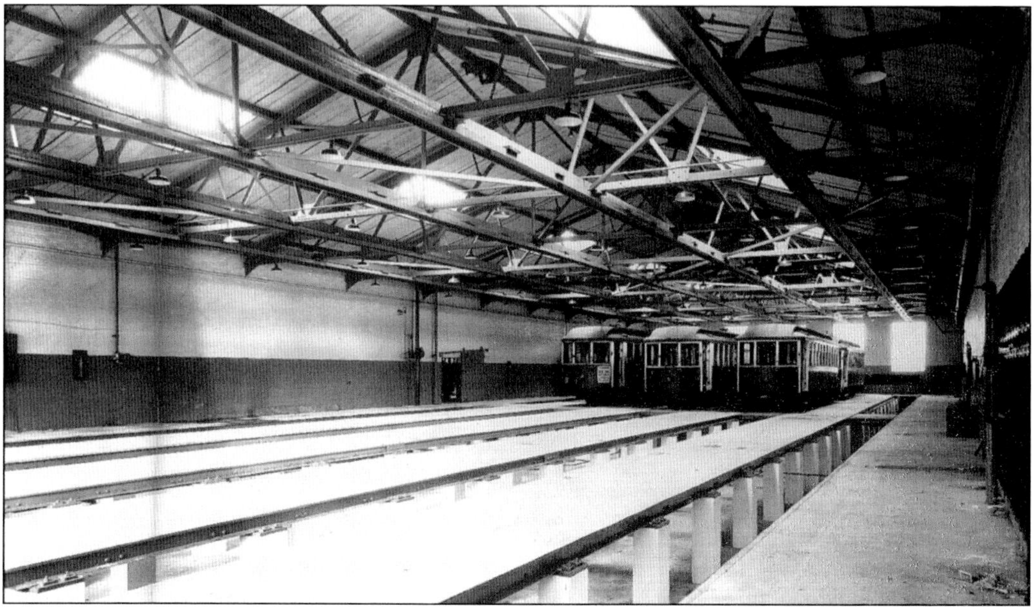

Carbarns were in such demand that often the railway companies began using the facilities before all the debris from the builders had been cleaned up. Here, part of a fleet is already inside a just-constructed carbarn.

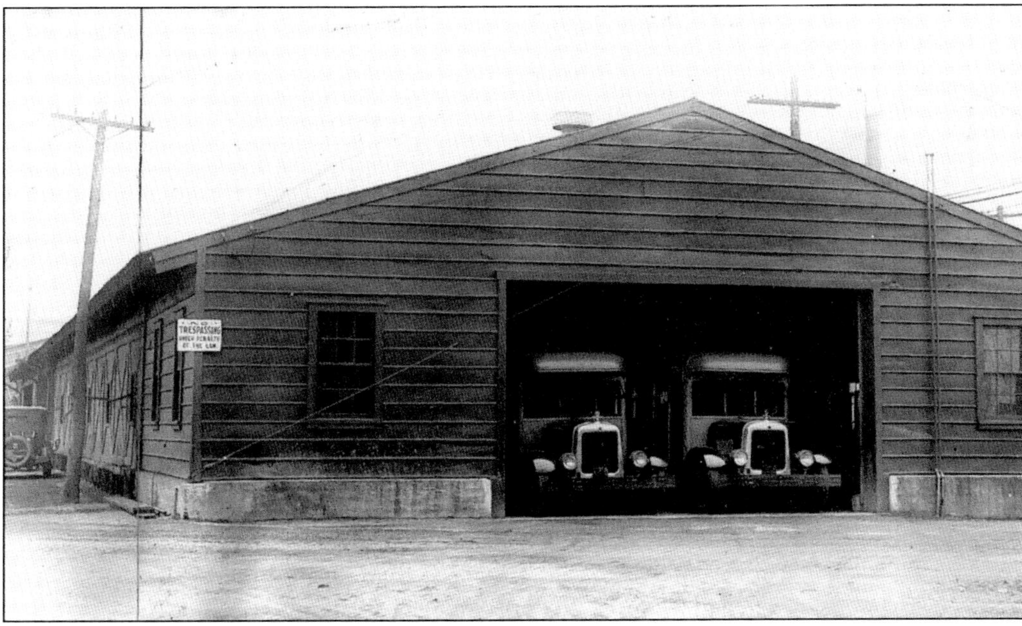

In the early years of transition from trolley cars to buses, it was common for trolley companies to utilize existing carbarns, such as the Waterbury Traction Company building shown here (with two Yellow Coach buses peering out). Shortly after this photograph was taken the structure was replaced, but bus transportation was here to stay in Waterbury.

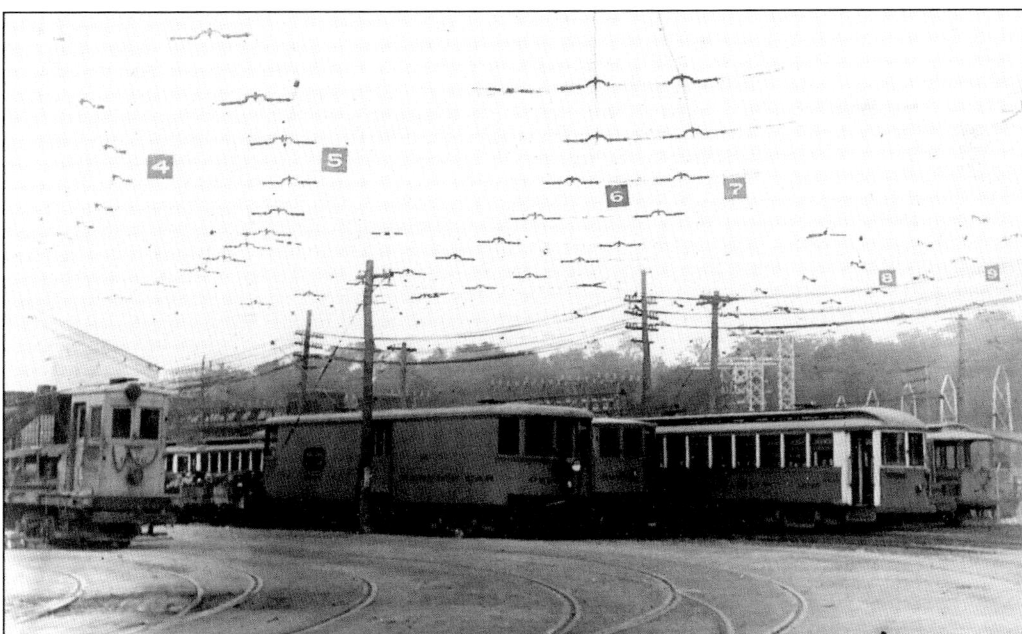

During the trolleys' finest hour, in the 1920s, it was not unusual to see a scene like this one at the West Main Street shops. The wide variety of equipment pictured here was typical of what it took to operate a street railway.

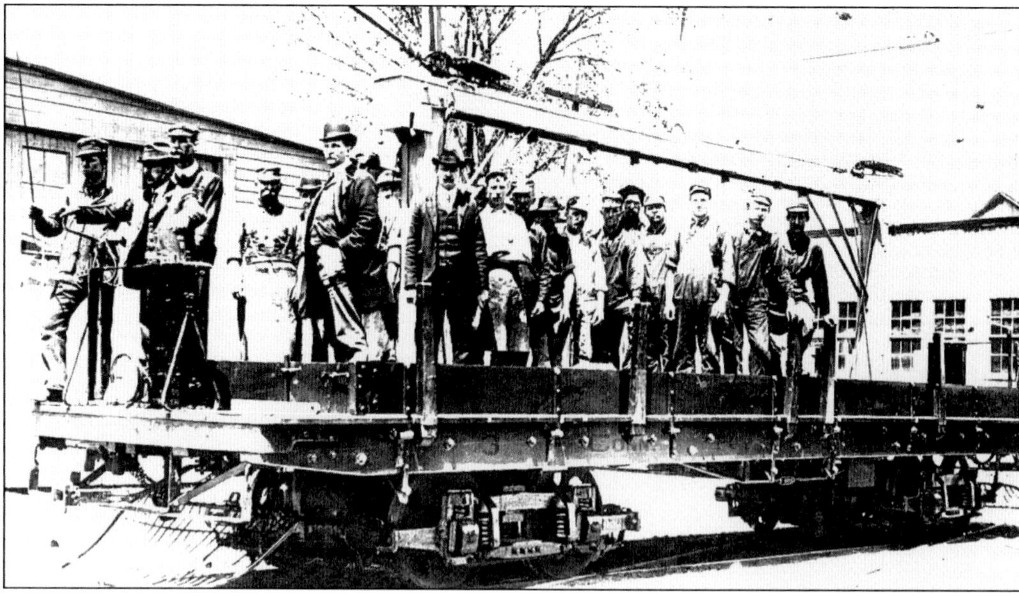

Trolley cars often had a number of different uses. Here, Connecticut Railway and Lighting motor flat car No. 3 serves as a platform for a group photograph of the Waterbury car shop crew in 1903. This car was built the previous year in the Waterbury car shops. This shop facility was one of the largest in Connecticut (after Hartford), and built many work cars. Most were converted from obsolete passenger cars into work equipment used in maintaining the track and overhead line. (F. S. Bennett Collection.)

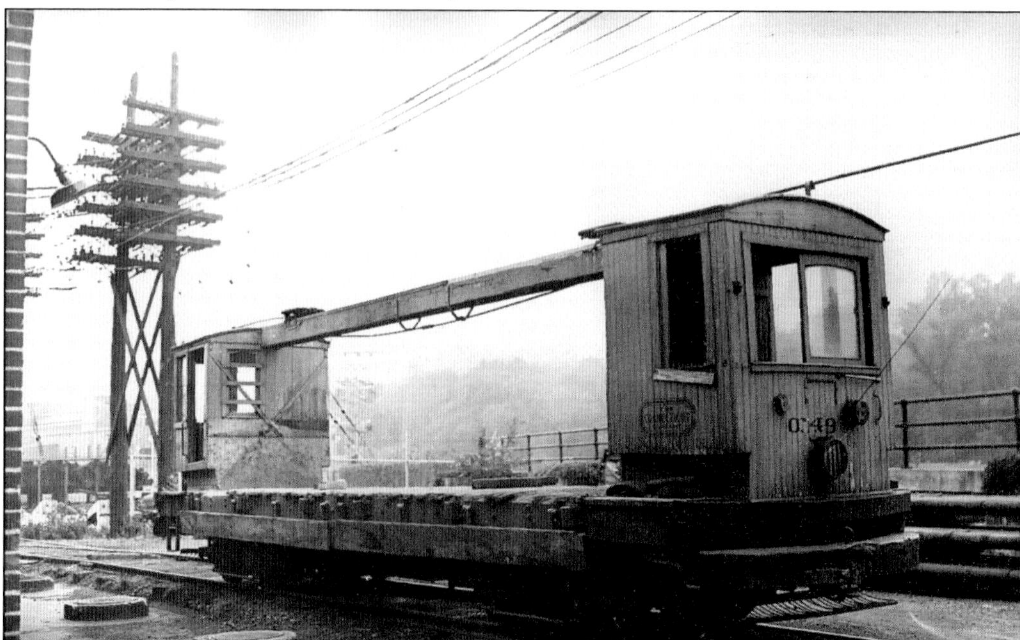

By 1935, flatcar No. 3, pictured at the top of the page, had been renumbered to Connecticut Company 0149. The cold New England winters had necessitated enclosing the cabs. The carpenters at the Waterbury car shop were capable of repairing or rebuilding almost any wood component of a streetcar.

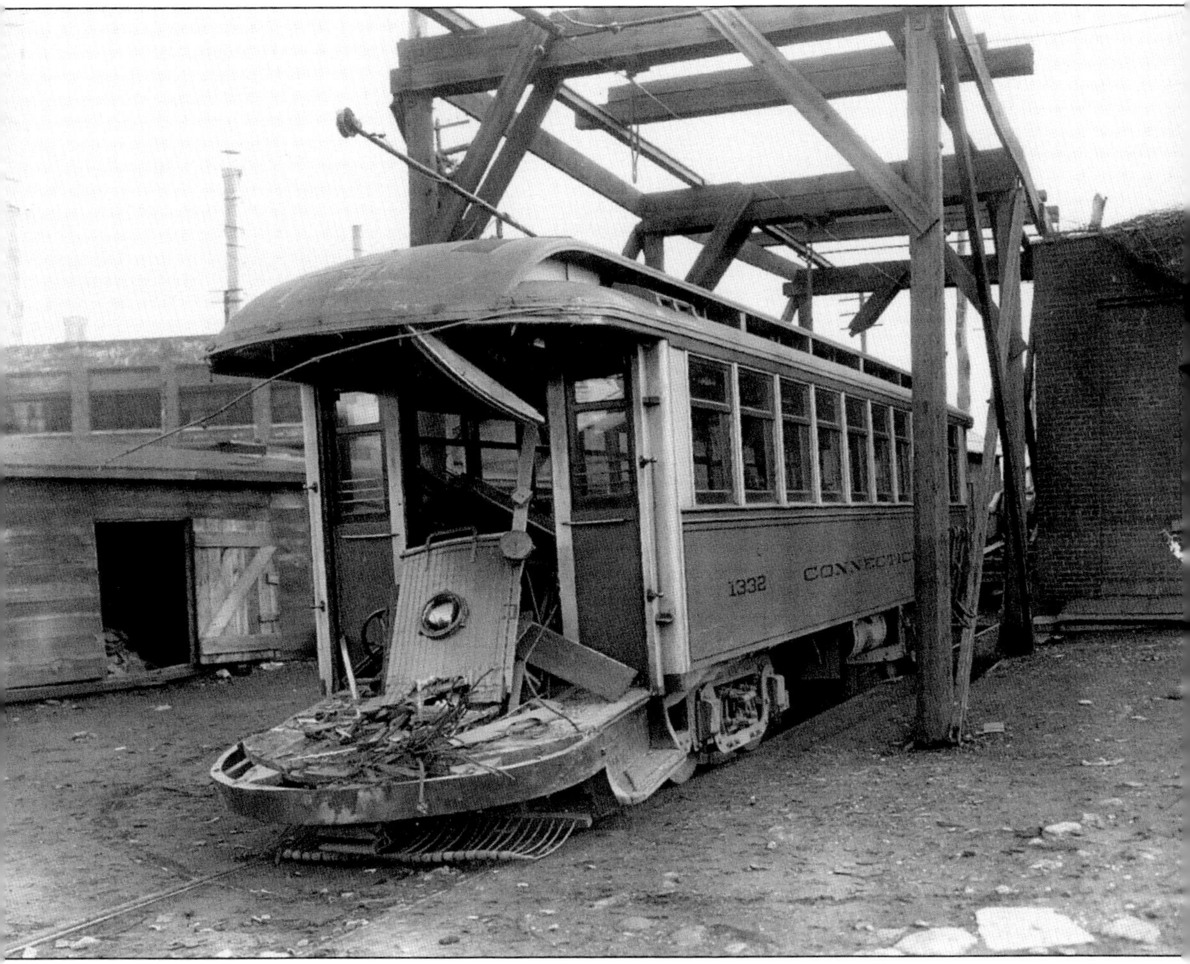

Just as with automobiles, trolley cars had accidents occasionally. Car 1332 is seen sitting in the Waterbury car yard after a collision with another car at Overlook Station on January 1, 1921. Six passengers were injured in the accident. The exact circumstances of this incident are not known today, but we can assume the motorman had quite a tale to tell after work that day. The shop crew in Waterbury could easily repair this car given the extensive facilities available to them. After it was repaired, this car returned to service and continued to run in Waterbury until the system shut down in 1937.

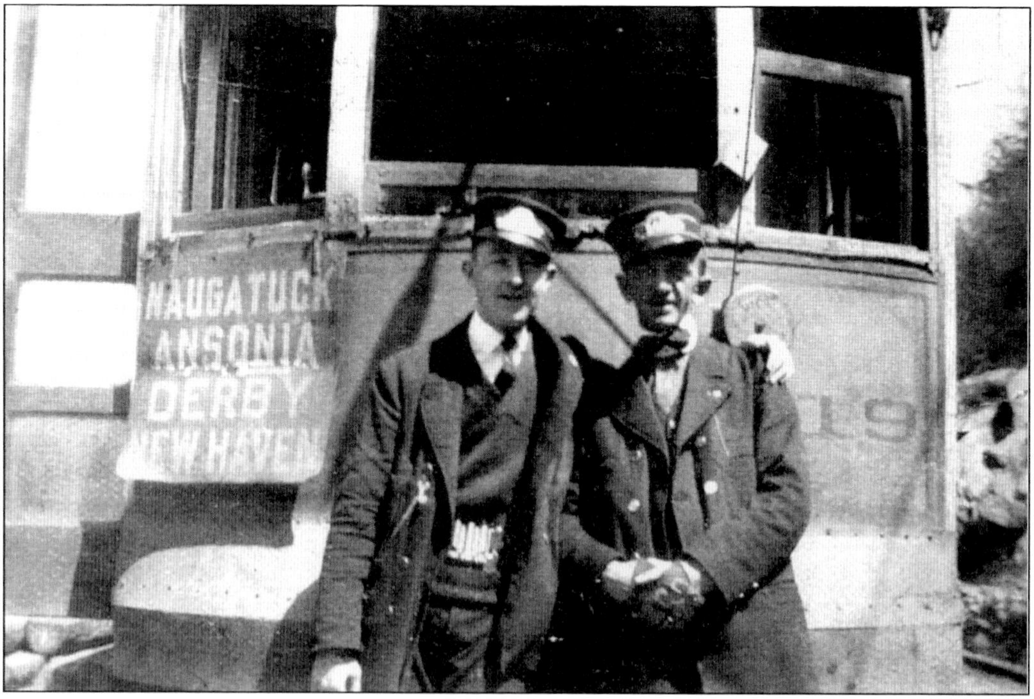

Employment on the street railway was a highly prized job after the First World War. It was vastly superior to doing manual labor. The handsome blue uniform with brass buttons gave the employees considerable pride in their job. The company demanded the highest standard of appearance and decorum from its employees. Street railway employees were prohibited from using foul language, smoking, or reading newspapers while on duty. Drinking to excess or patronizing a saloon while in uniform was grounds for immediate dismissal. The crew of car No. 1919 was certainly proud to have their photograph taken in full uniform in 1922.

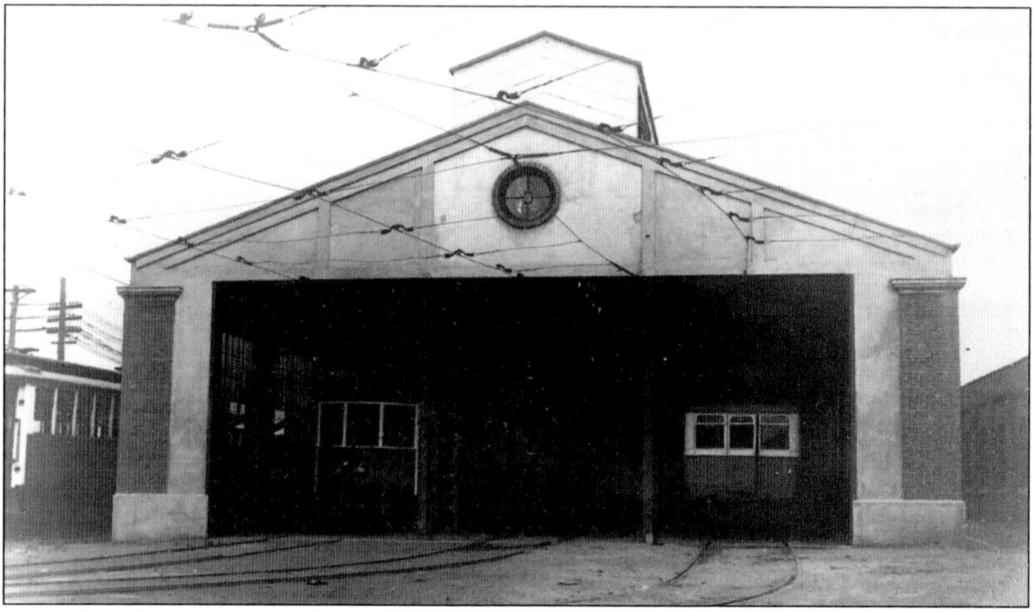

A closed trolley car and an early bus share one of the new Waterbury carbarns in this 1920s view.

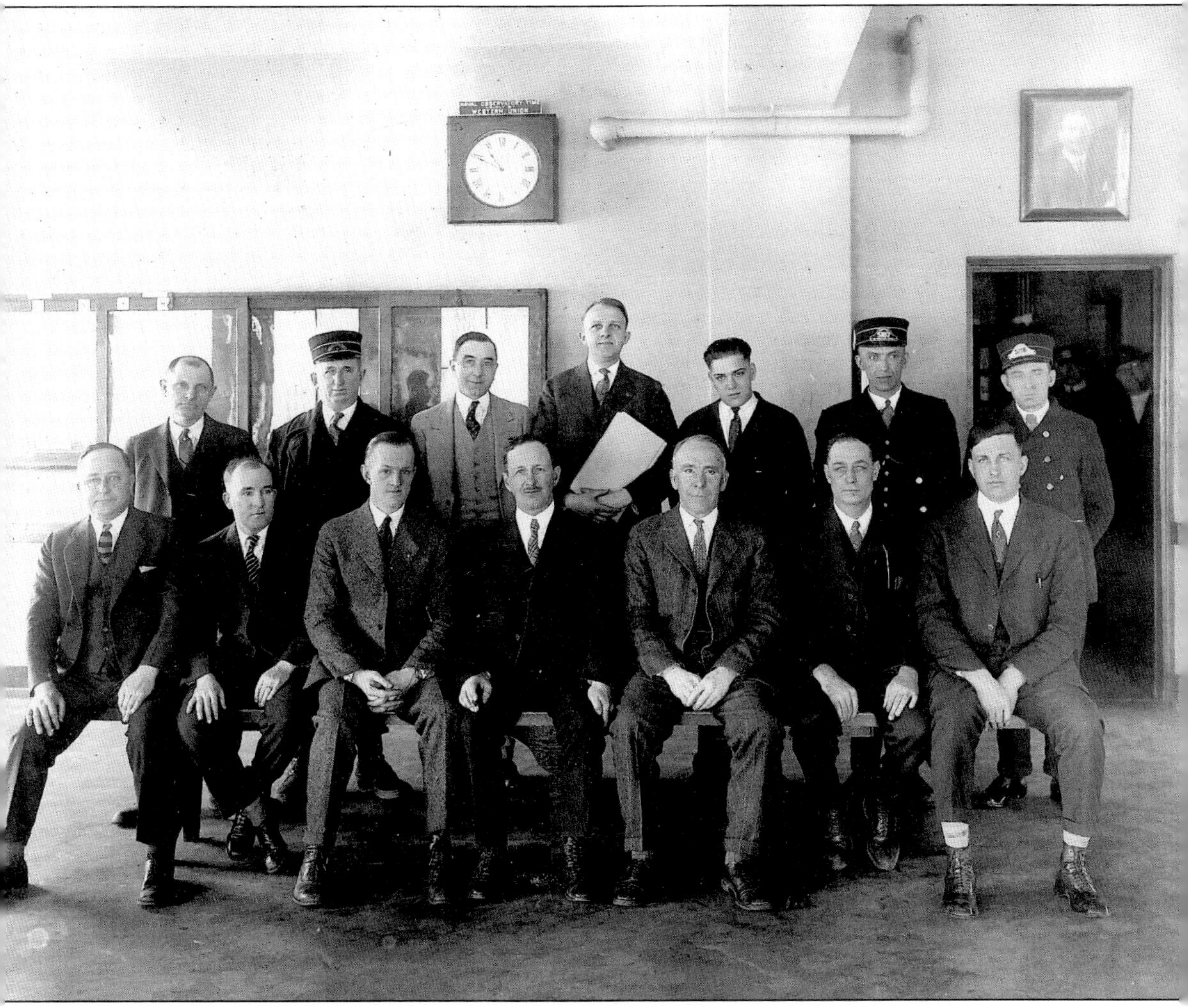

This picture shows the Waterbury division management and clerical staff in 1926. The gentleman in the photograph above the door is J. K. Punderford, vice president and general manager of the Connecticut Company. The gentleman seated third from the left is Waldo Plaisted, who later became superintendent of the Hartford division. The gentleman seated third from the right is C. H. Chapman, superintendent of the Waterbury division.

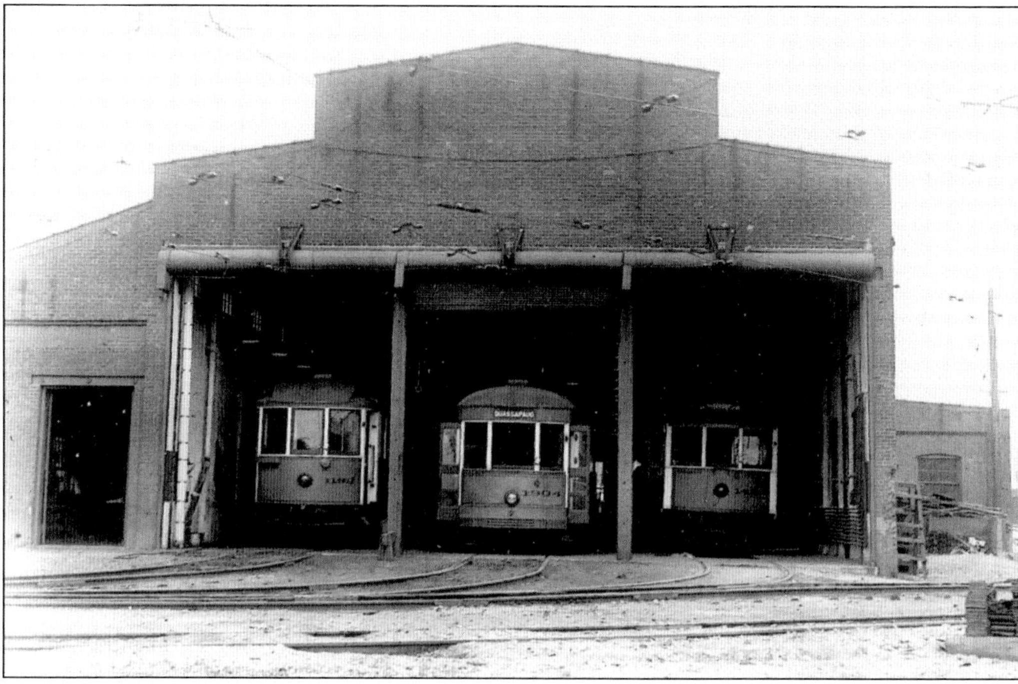

Cars 1182, 1904, and 1453 enjoy a rest in this 1920s view of one of the new carbarns in Waterbury. These three cars show the variety of cars typically seen in that era. Car 1182 is a wooden passenger car built in 1907. Car 1904 is a steel passenger car built in 1919. Car No. 1453 was built in 1911 as an open car and was converted into a closed car in 1920. Many of the open cars were eventually converted into either closed cars or work cars.

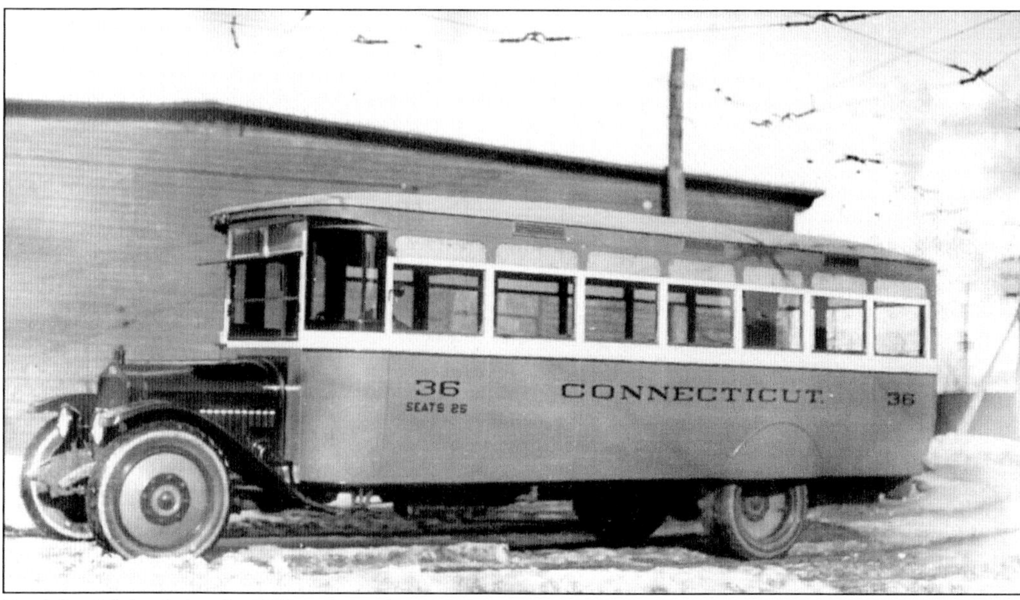

Bus No. 36, built by the White Truck Company in 1923, waits for a run on a snowy day. Because this early vehicle could only reach a top speed of around 15 miles an hour and was equipped with solid rubber tires, most likely tire chains would have to be attached before the bus would be released to cope with the snowy conditions on the Brass City's formidable hills.

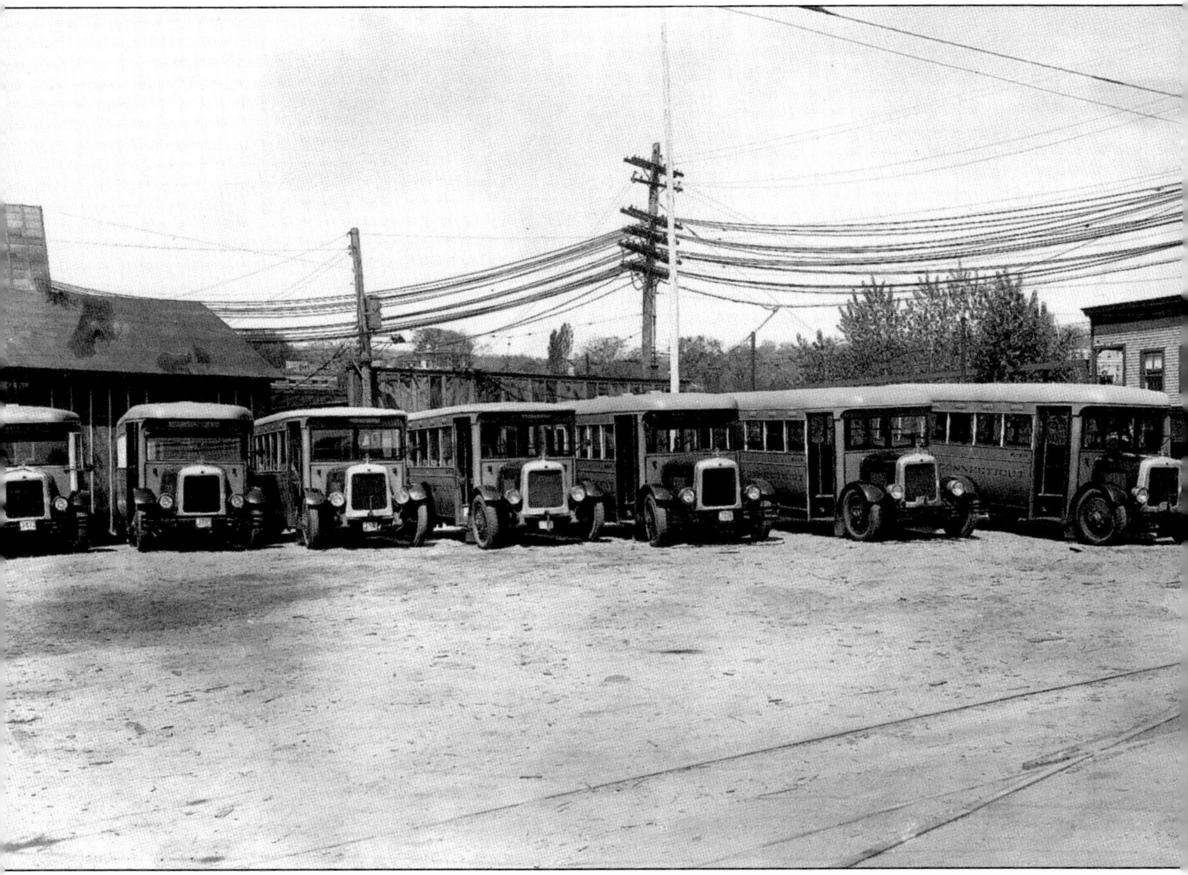

This mid-1920s lineup of Yellow Coaches shows three body-design variations. The typical bus of this style held a maximum of 30 passengers, as opposed to the 45 to 50 seated passengers and additional standing riders that the typical closed trolley car could carry. This photograph was taken at the old carbarn on West Main Street.

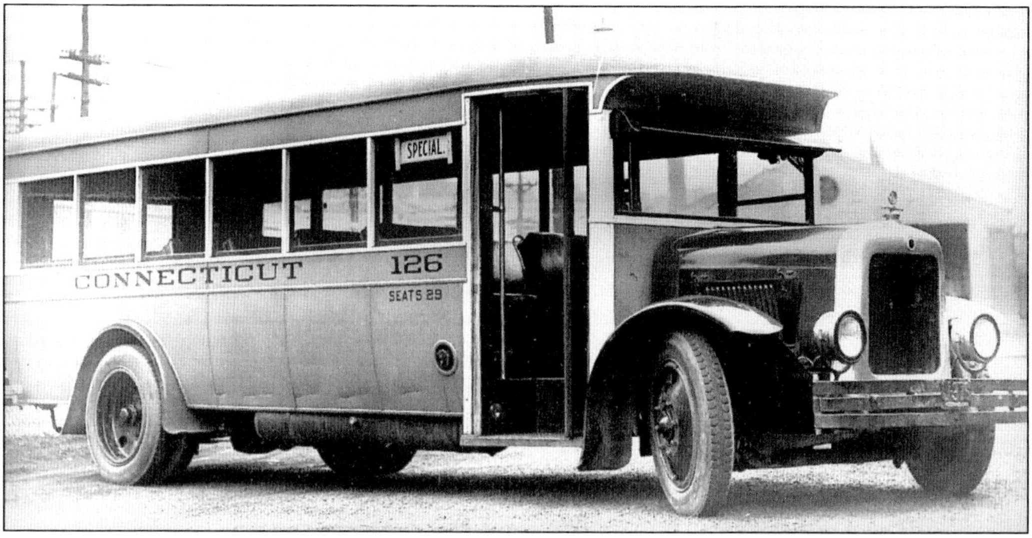

Bus No. 126, a 1926 Yellow Coach model Z-219, is about to head out on a special run. As is still true today, schools, churches, and other groups many times would charter a bus to go to an event that was not accessible by streetcar. Charters became a profitable business for the Connecticut Company.

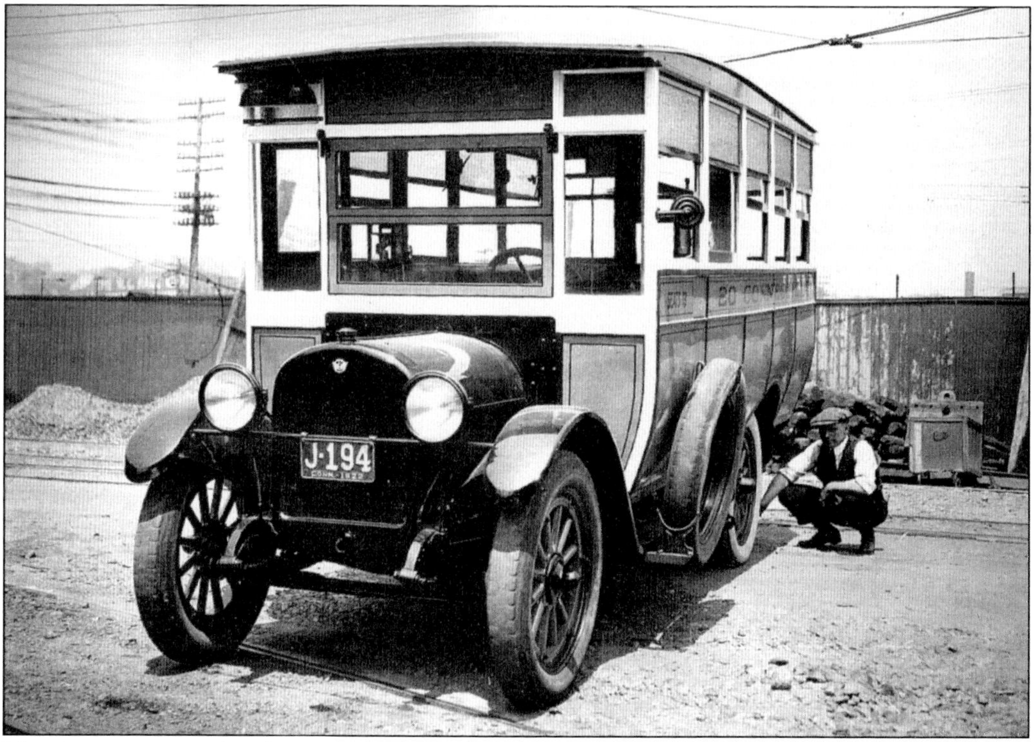

The driver is doing his "pre-trip inspection" on No. 20, a 1921 REO bus, before leaving the garage in 1922. The early buses were very primitive and undependable, yet people began to prefer buses because they were a more "modern" mode of transportation, even if the streetcars of the era were more comfortable and reliable. Buses were also more flexible, as they could go anywhere, while streetcars were tied to fixed routes.

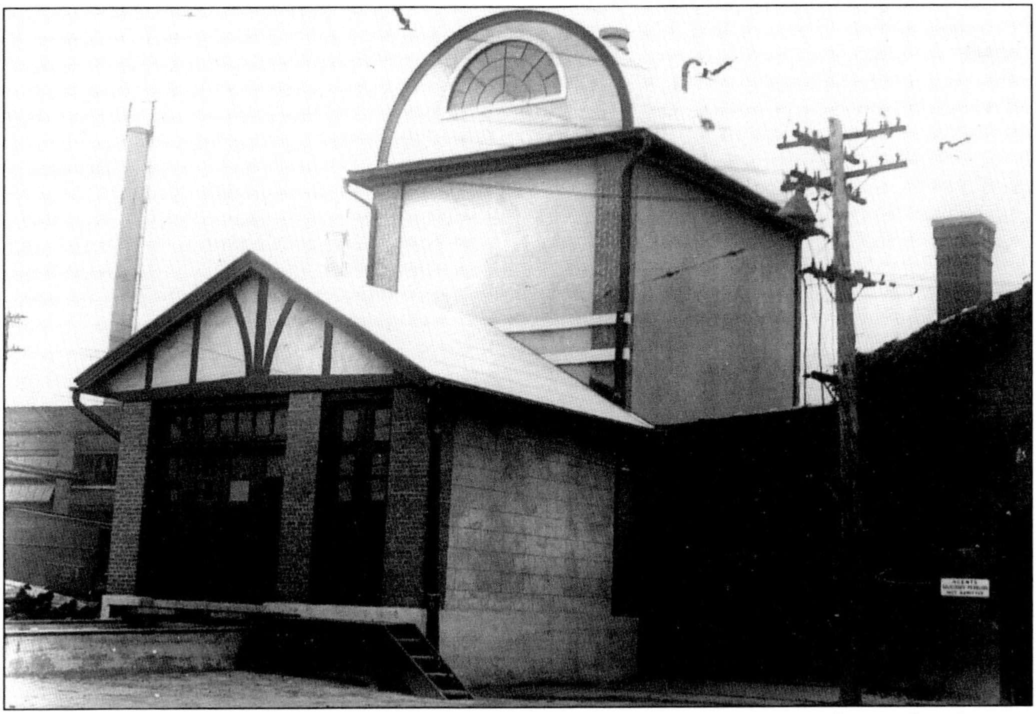

Even in a utilitarian structure, like this transformer building, many nice design details were included. One wonders if the white sign (at right) was successful in discouraging "agents, solicitors, and peddlers" from intruding on streetcar operations. This building supplied power to the streetcar system from hydroelectric power. First, the power was transmitted to this site from Bulls Bridge on the Housatonic River, 30 miles from Waterbury. Inside this building, the current was reduced to 11,000 volts, which was then fed to rotary converters that changed the 11,000 volts AC to 600 volts DC for use by the streetcars. In 1920 alone the Connecticut Company paid Connecticut Light and Power Company over $395,000 for electricity to run the Waterbury division.

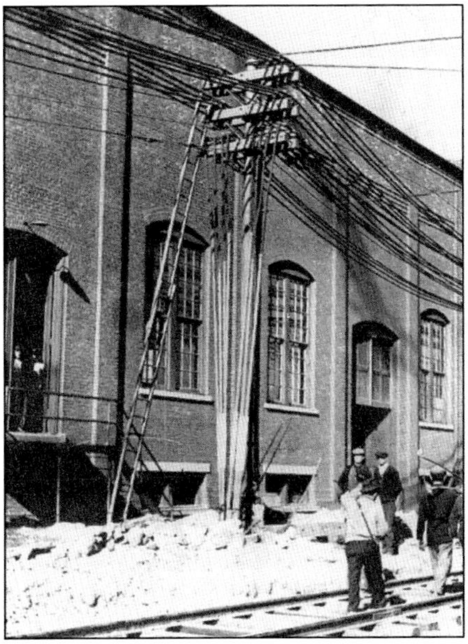

Once the power was sent through the transformer, shown above, it was sent through the rotary converter and then was sent through the maze of cable carrying 600 volts DC to the overhead wire on the Waterbury streetcar lines.

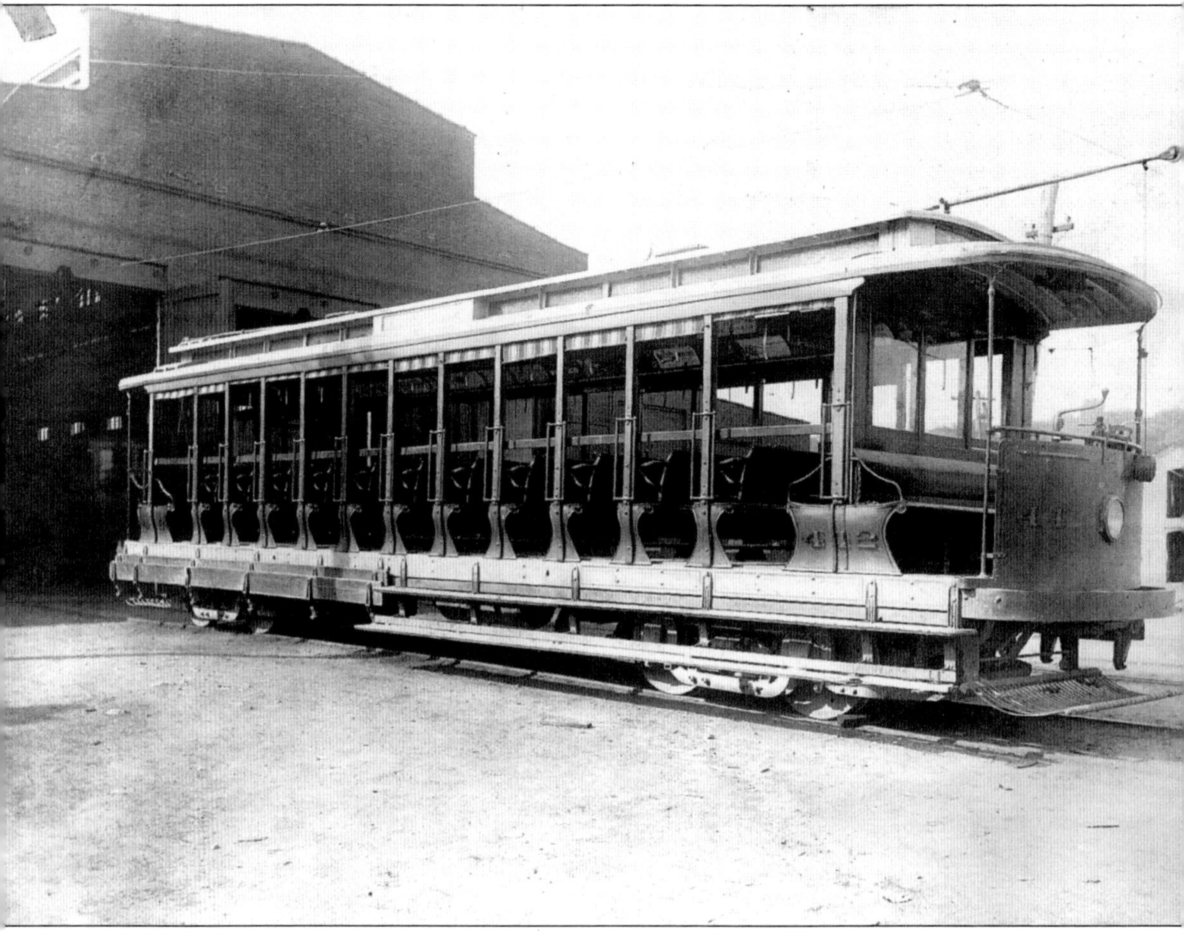

When hobble skirts (long skirts that are very narrow below knee) became popular in women's fashion starting in 1910, ladies began to have difficulty boarding the open streetcars because of the height of the single running board from the pavement. The Connecticut State Legislature passed a law requiring all streetcar companies to equip every car with an additional running board that was no more than 16 inches from the ground. Open car 442 is shown here with the double running boards that were mandated.

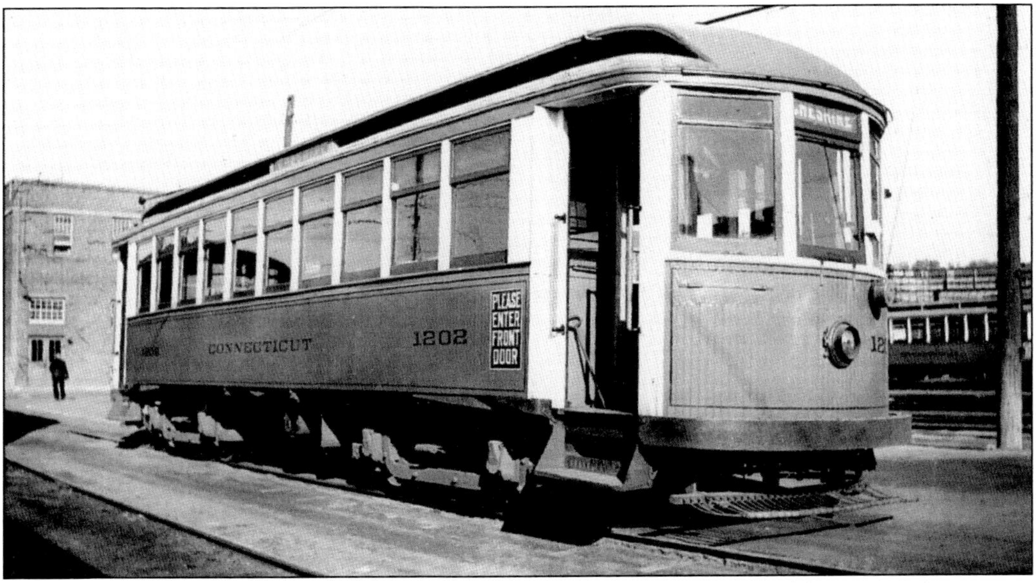

In an effort to curtail expenses, many street railway companies transitioned from two-man to one-man crews. This photograph of car 1202 shows the "Please enter front door" sign that streetcars were equipped with in order to make this transition to a single-man operation. Car No. 1202 was normally assigned to the "shuttle" car that ran between Milldale and Cheshire.

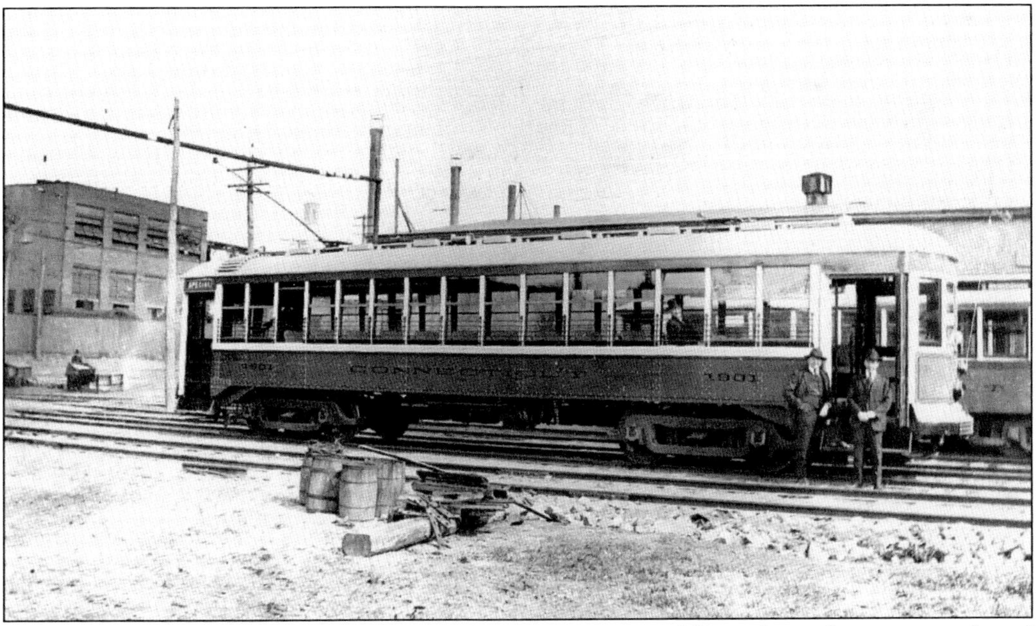

Virtually brand-new in this 1919 photograph, car 1901 is one of 50 steel cars that were purchased from J. G. Brill Company in 1919. Fourteen of these cars operated on the Waterbury division suburban runs. This car was transferred to the New Haven division in the 1920s, and it ran until all streetcar service was discontinued in New Haven in 1948.

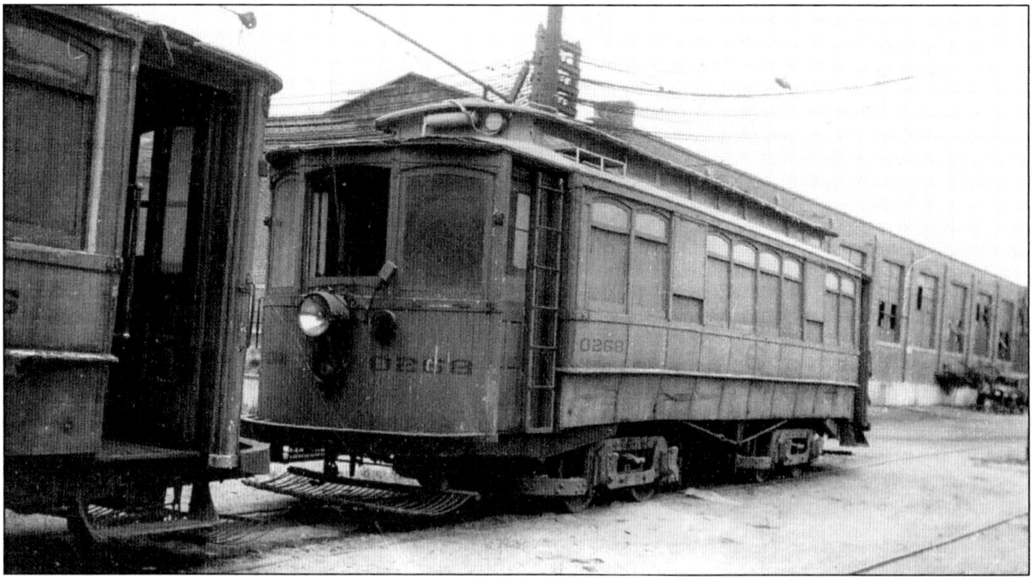

Connecticut Railway and Lighting Company car No. 22, built in 1901, was converted into work car No. 0268 in 1919. It became a sand car in 1919 and ran until Waterbury discontinued streetcars. Many older passenger cars got a second lease on life as work cars after they became obsolete and were no longer usable for passenger service.

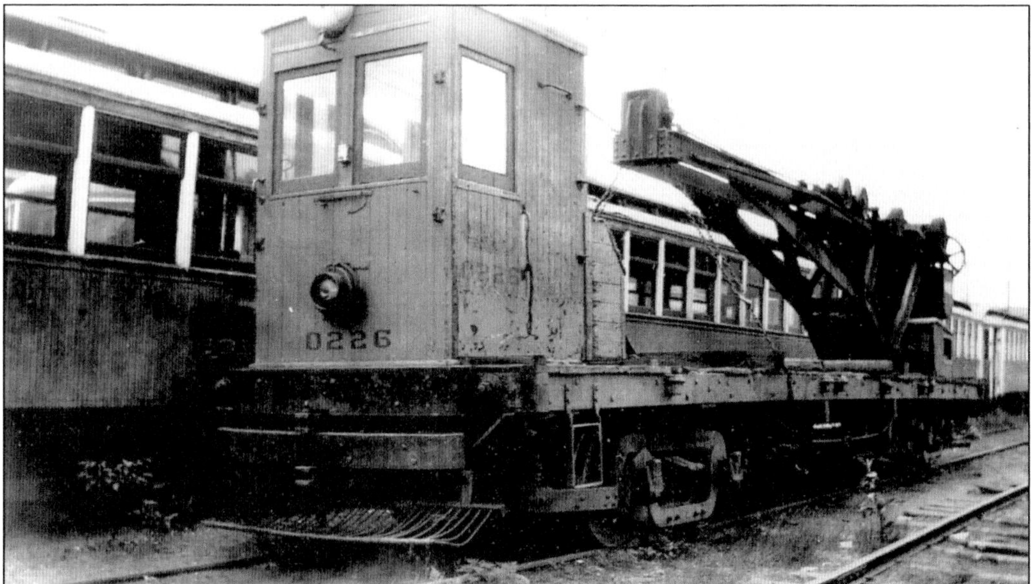

The Wason Manufacturing Company in Springfield, Massachusetts, built cars like this double-truck crane car manufactured in 1911. These cars were built as work cars at the factory and were not conversions like No. 0268 in the previous photograph. After Waterbury discontinued streetcar service, this car was sold to Third Avenue Railways in New York City, where it operated until being scrapped by New York City Transit in 1948.

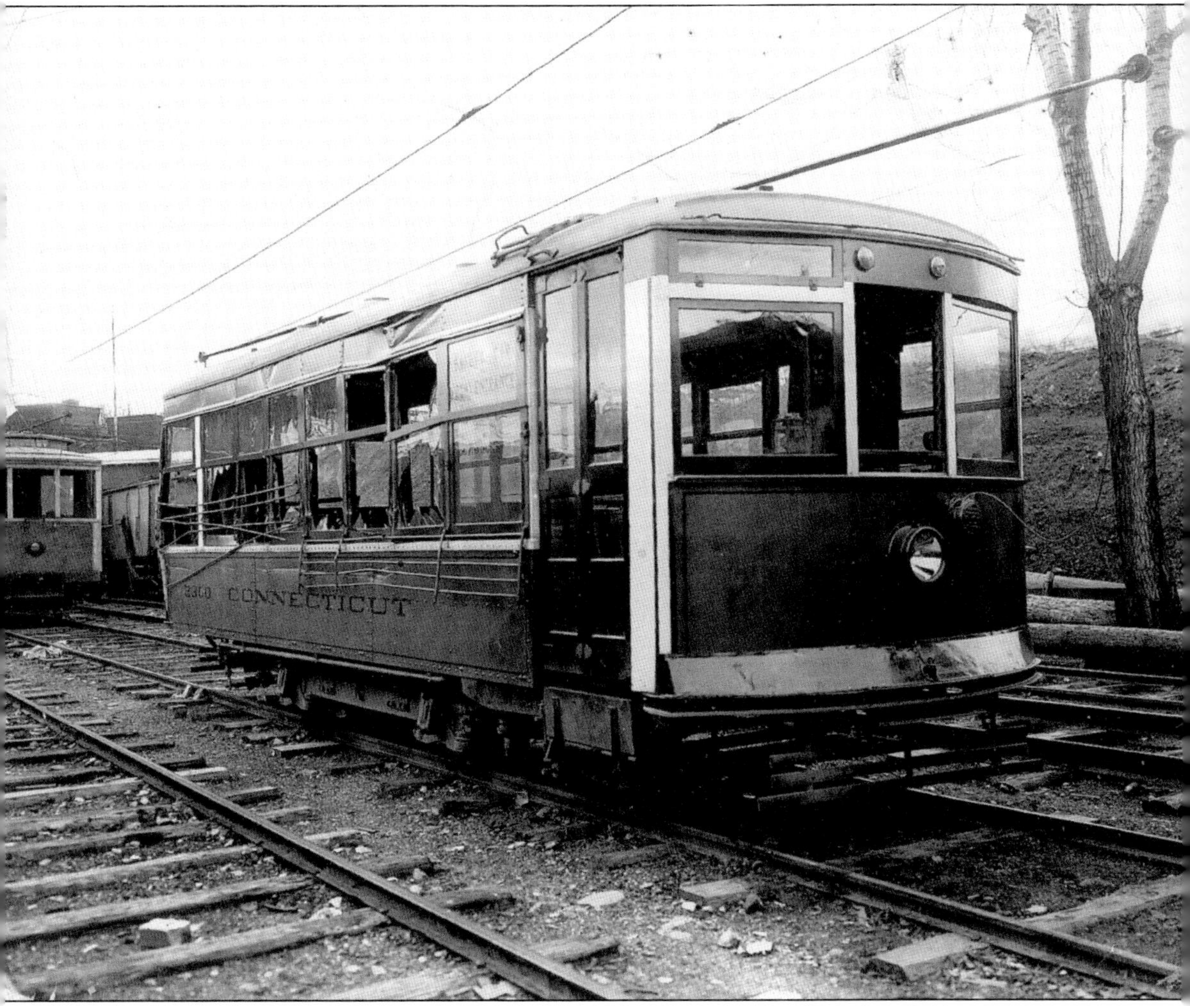

A truck owned by the Economy Grocery Company in Waterbury collided with No. 2300 on Bank Street on December 6, 1920. Records show that $225 was collected for the damage. This was relatively minor damage for the Waterbury car shop crew to repair, and the car was most likely back on the line in a matter of days. These cars were a radical departure from previous streetcar construction. The new models were built with a stressed-skin body like an airplane, and were very lightweight. The new cars weighed only about 13,000 pounds, while the conventional streetcars (like the one parked behind No. 2300 in this view) weighed as much as 40,000 pounds.

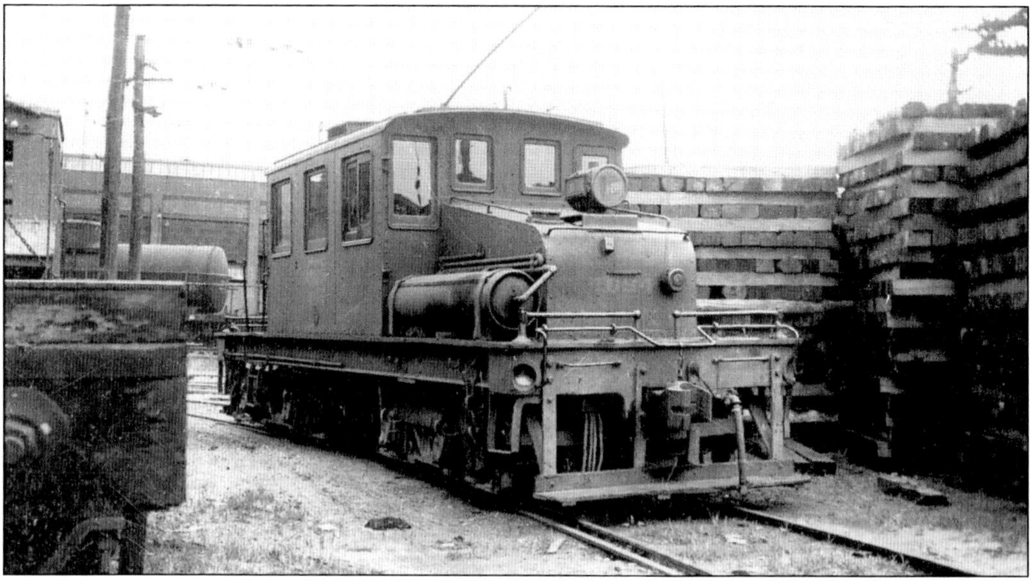

The Connecticut Company had an extensive freight operation in Waterbury. Two 45-ton electric locomotives, built by Baldwin Westinghouse in 1912, were used to haul steam road cars to service Chase Brass facilities and other customers in the city. These locomotives were able to negotiate the tight corners on Waterbury's streets and drew 600 volts DC power from the overhead wire just like the streetcars. Car No. 1054, shown here, was disposed of in 1937 when all streetcar service in Waterbury ended. During World War II it served the military at an ammunition depot in New Jersey, and finally ended up in Maryland on the Hagerstown & Frederick Railway. The car was scrapped in 1955.

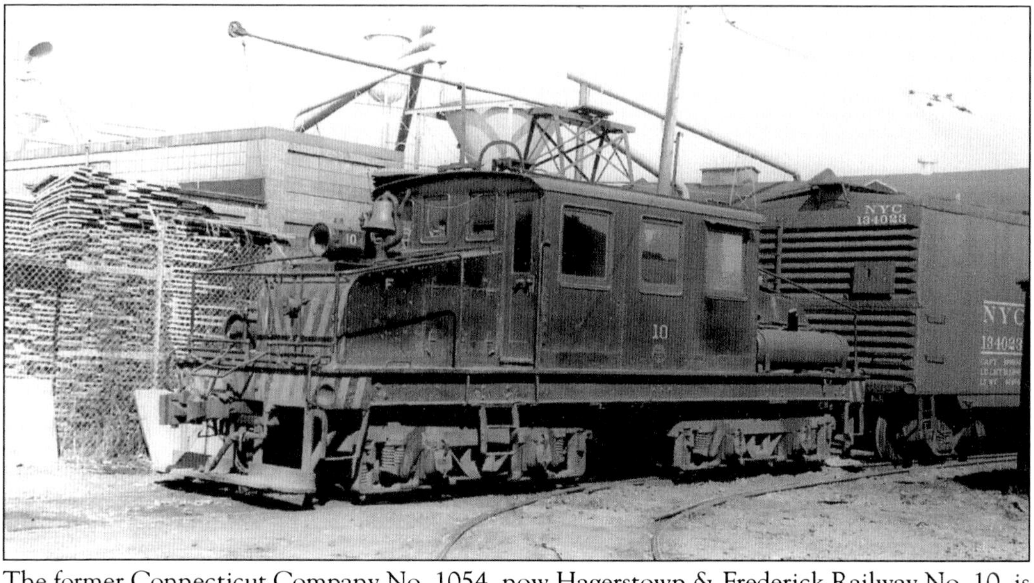

The former Connecticut Company No. 1054, now Hagerstown & Frederick Railway No. 10, is pictured in Hagerstown, Maryland, in 1955. Unfortunately the car was scrapped soon after this photograph was taken. (F. S. Bennett Collection.)

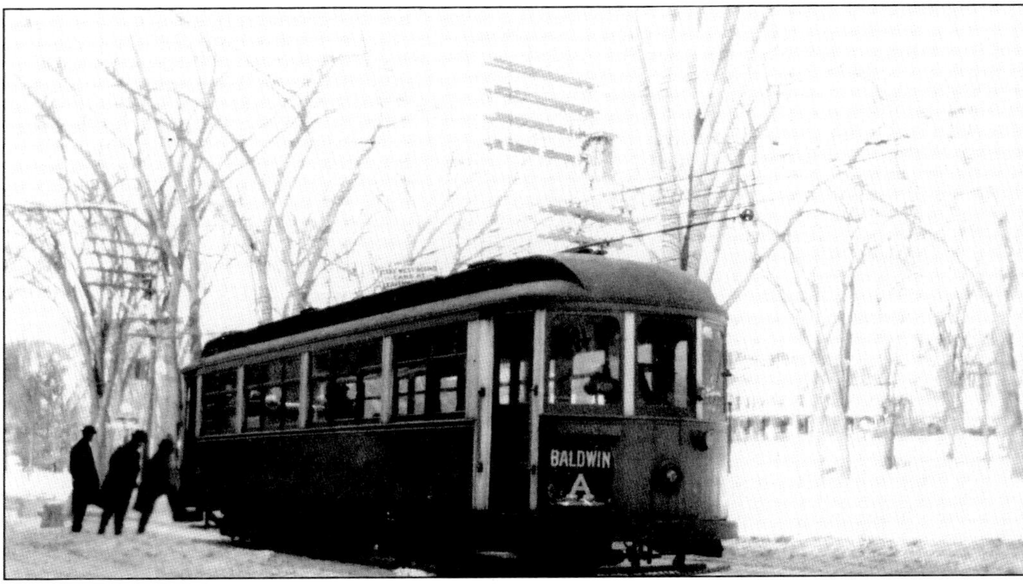

Undaunted by the snow, the trolley cars still ran. Connecticut Company wooden car 768 is shown loading passengers on a snowy day in 1922. The route of this car will take it over East Main Street to Franklin Street, where it will then head south on the Baldwin Street line to Hopeville.

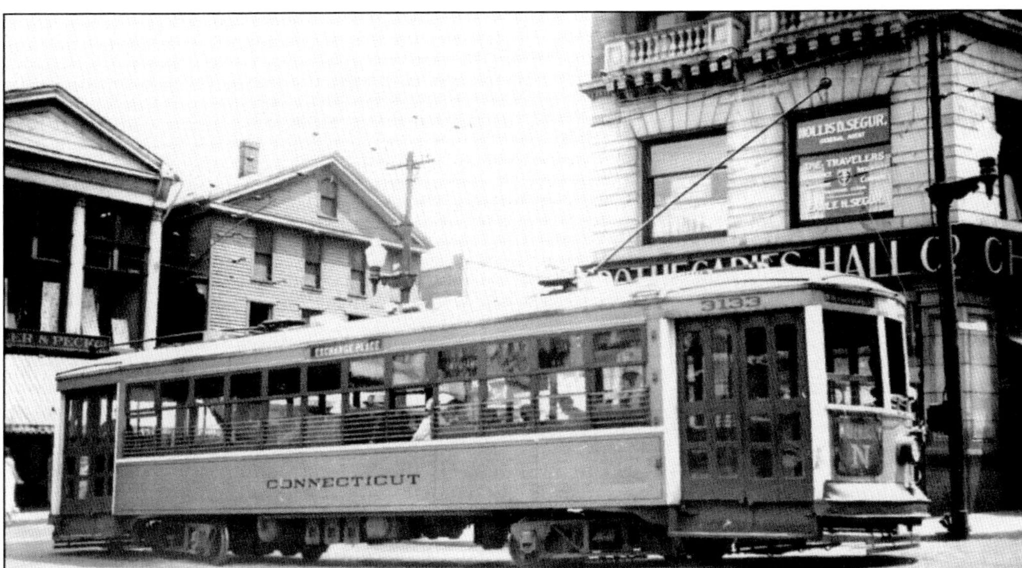

Connecticut Company 3133, a 1923 Osgood-Bradley Car Company product, squeals through the tight curve on its way back down South Main Street to Naugatuck. The background buildings look the same in 2005, but Apothecaries Hall Company and the Miller & Peck department store are now defunct. The Hollis D. Segur Company is still doing business, although no longer at this location.

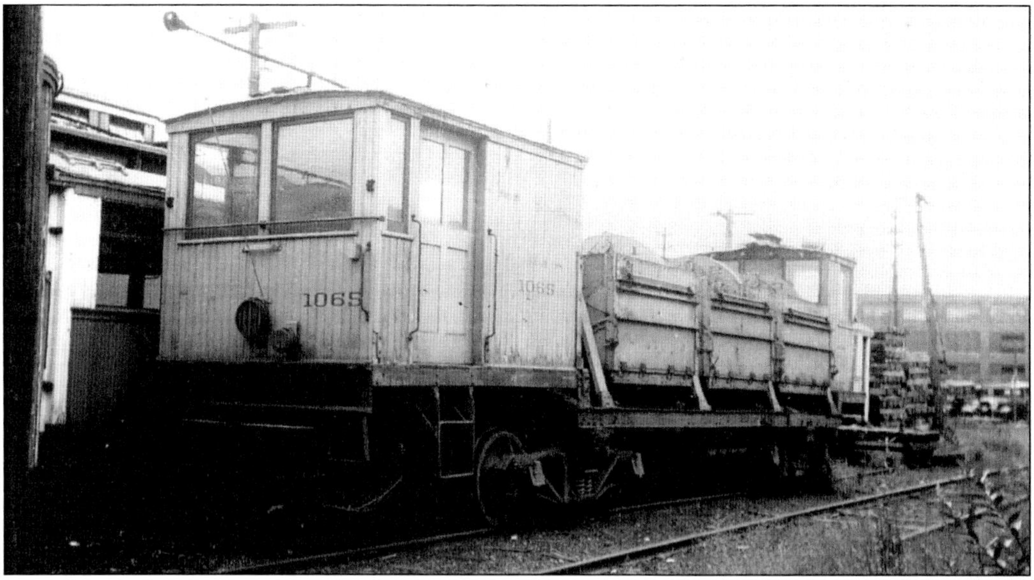

The Connecticut Company did a considerable business hauling aggregate stone for local quarries for use on construction jobs near the streetcar routes. Twenty-four of these dump cars were delivered in 1913 and 1914 for use around the Connecticut Company system. The 1000-series cars were revenue cars as opposed to work cars, which had a "0" as the first digit in the car number.

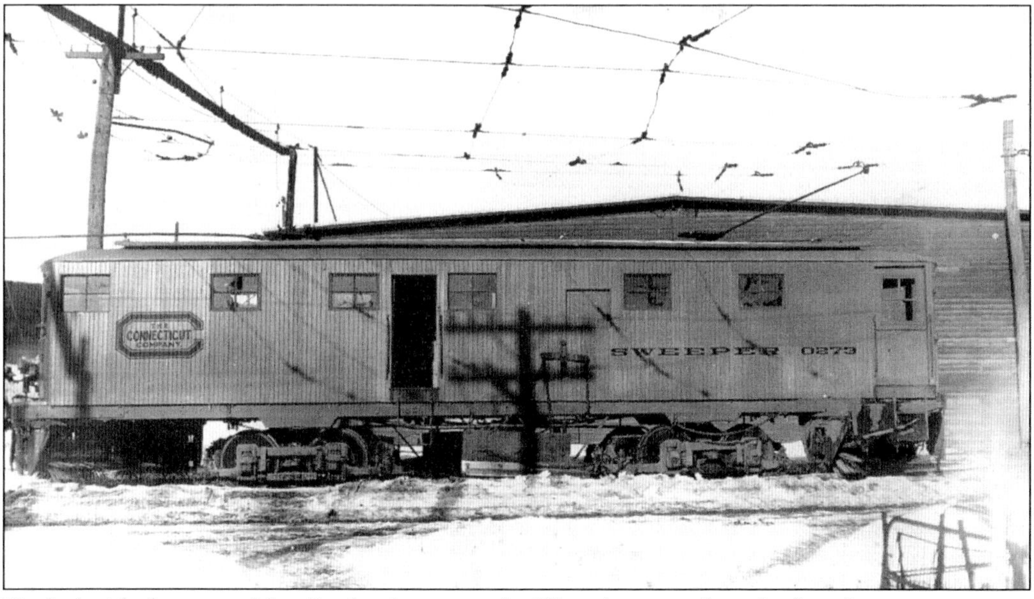

To deal with the snowy New England winters, the Waterbury car shops built eight snow sweepers like No. 0273 pictured here. This car started life as open car No. 376 before it was converted to a snow sweeper in the 1920s.

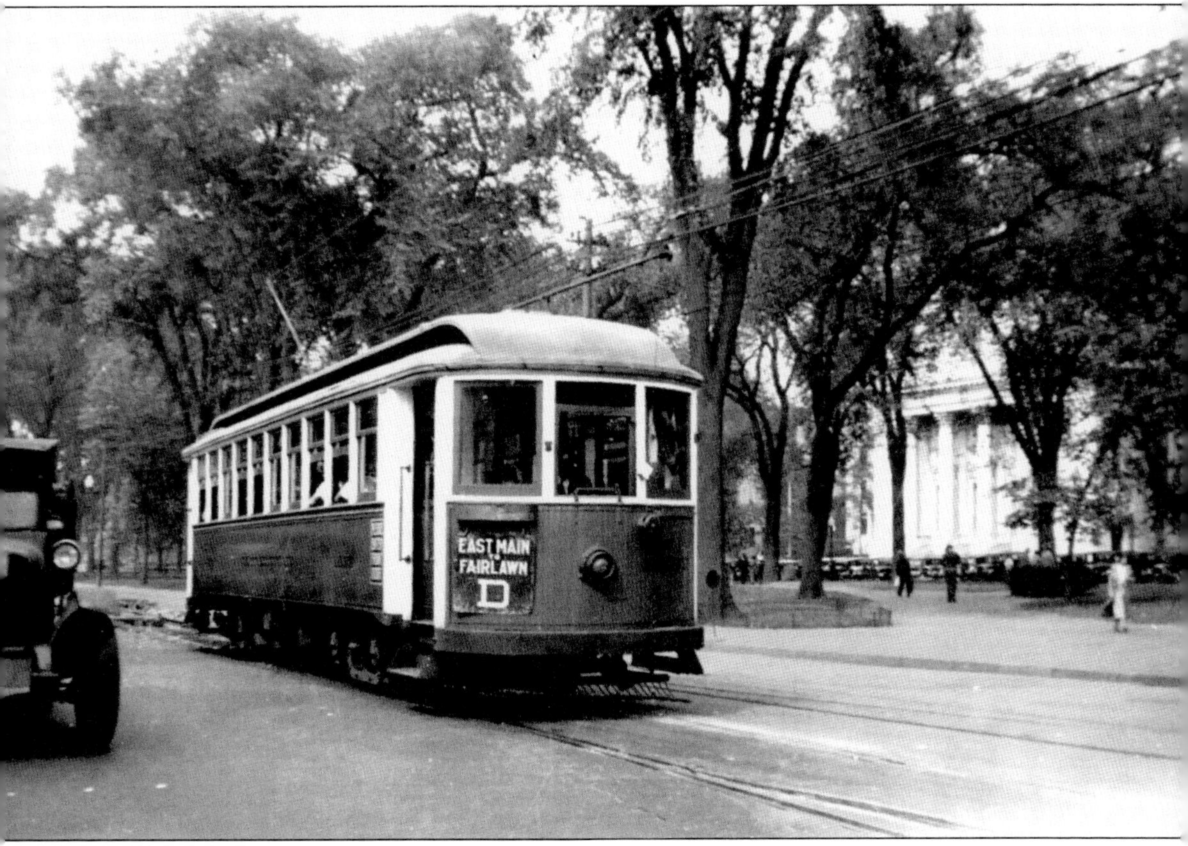

Connecticut Company No. 1537 heads outbound to East Main Street and the Fairlawn section, passing the recently completed Roman-style Immaculate Conception Catholic Church, visible through the trees shading the green on the right.

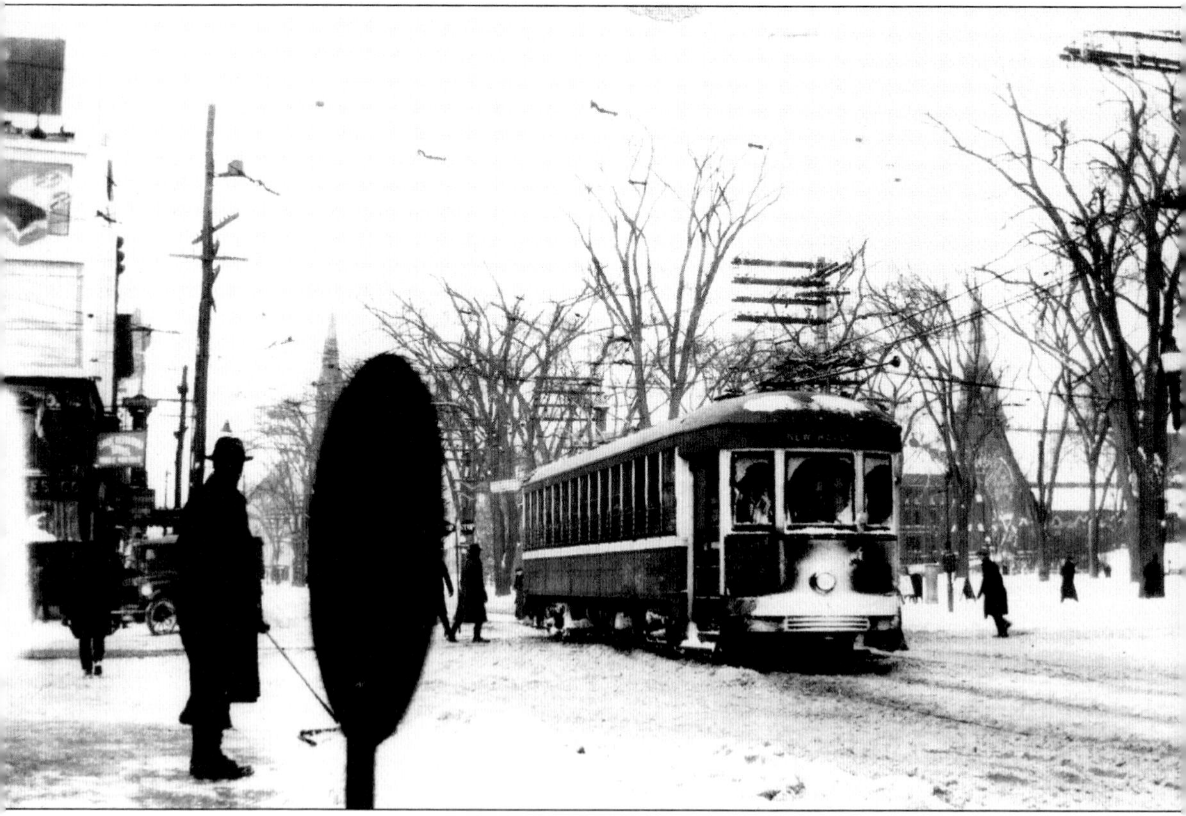

A New Haven–bound car departs the Waterbury Green in this 1922 winter scene. Passengers were able to travel between Waterbury and New Haven via either Cheshire Junction or Derby. (F. S. Bennett Collection.)

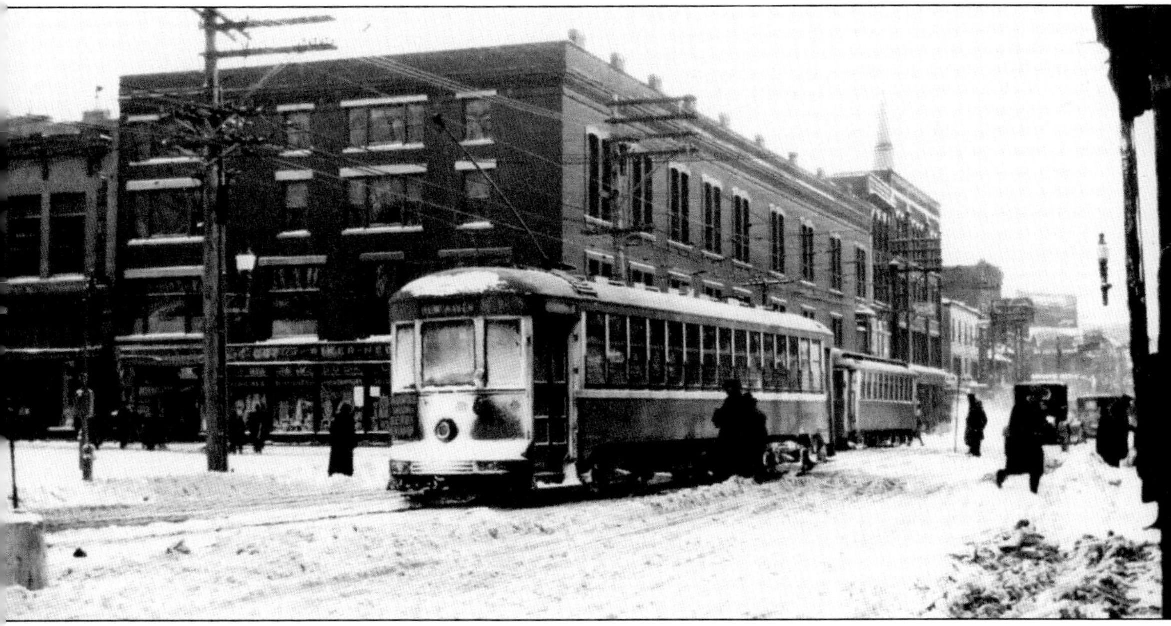

Lots of snow on the ground did not stop the streetcars in this 1920s view of downtown Waterbury. The church steeple seen in the background belonged to the original Immaculate Conception Church. That church was soon replaced by the magnificent new edifice on the green that is shown on page 41. (F. S. Bennett Collection.)

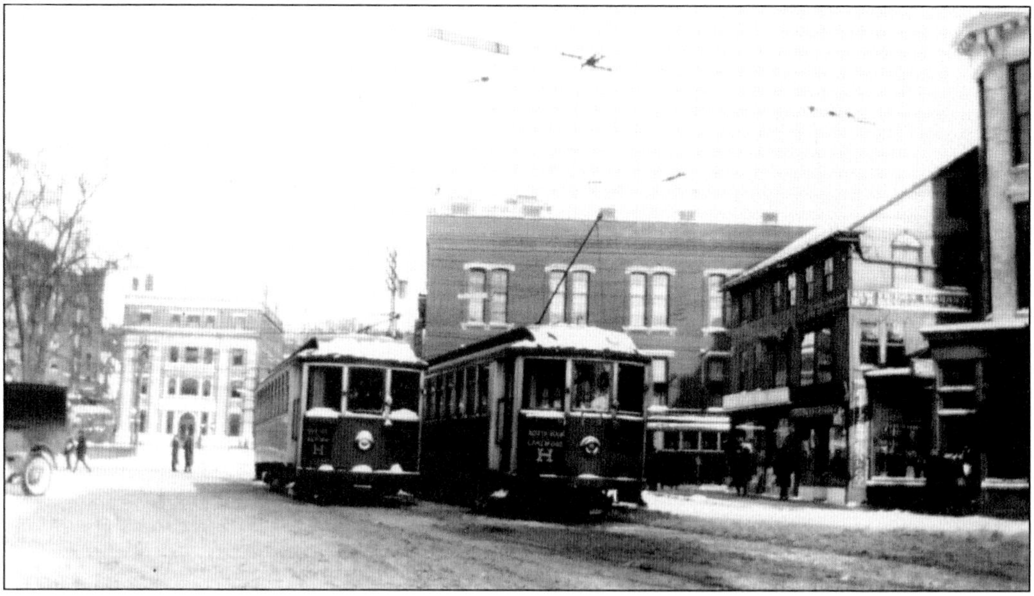

Look on page 11, and you will see this same street scene as it appeared in the 1880s. Note the changes that have occurred over the intervening years. This picture was taken in 1922. (F. S. Bennett Collection.)

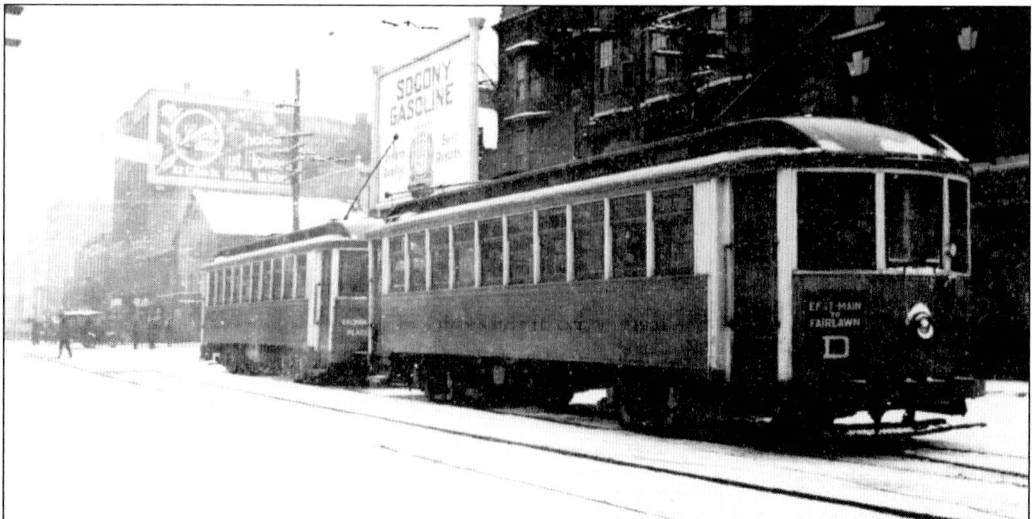

See winter in Waterbury in this 1922 view of West Main Street at Exchange Place. The extensive street railway network in Waterbury helped make possible the growth of the suburban communities in the Naugatuck Valley.

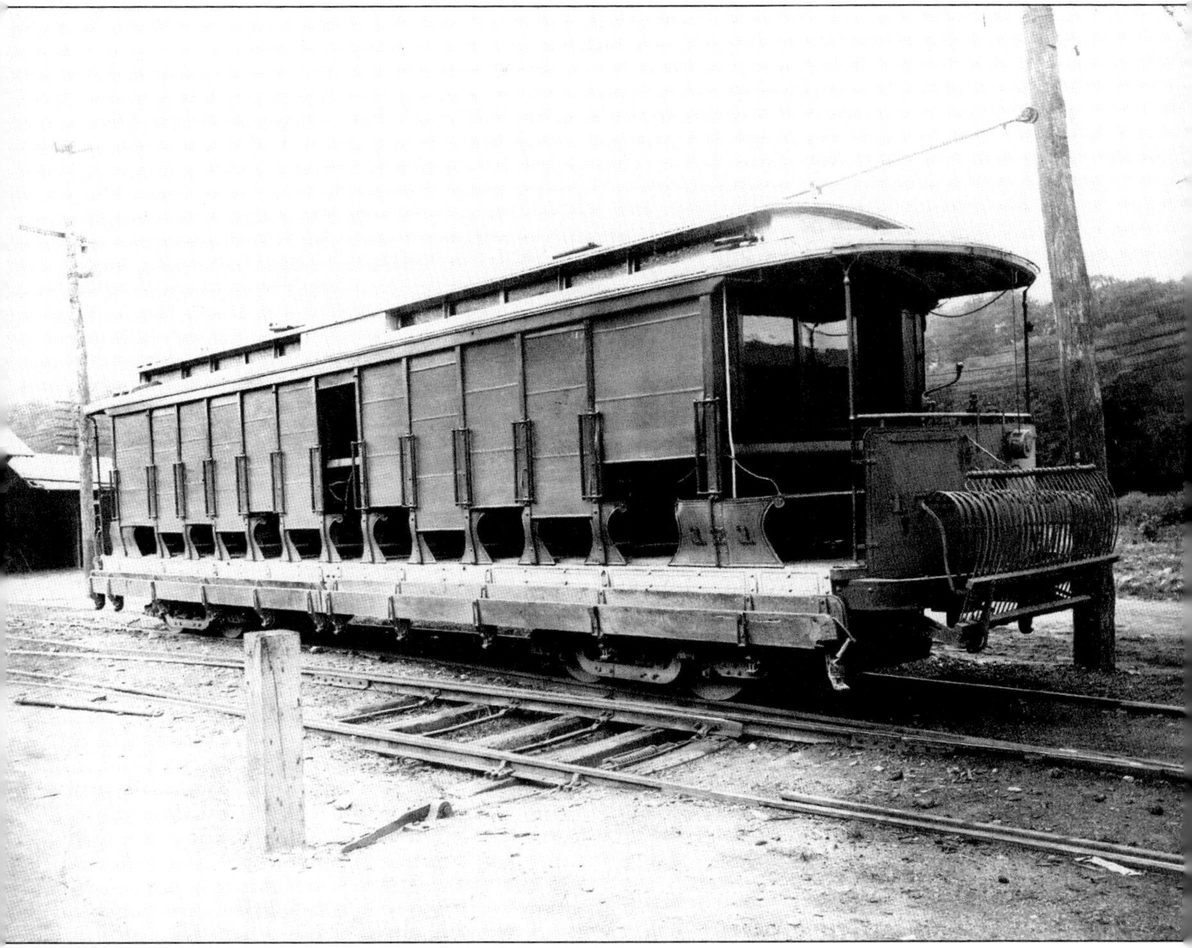

This image of Connecticut Company open car 171 provides a good view of the canvas sides that could be lowered in the event of an unexpected shower while the car was out on the line. Open cars were normally only operated from May 1 through the end of October; they sat out the winter in a nice warm carbarn. This car was renumbered 1470 in 1915. In 1936 it was transferred to the New Haven division, where it operated until it was scrapped in 1948 after the New Haven lines were converted to bus service. This picture was taken in 1914 at the West Main streetcar yard.

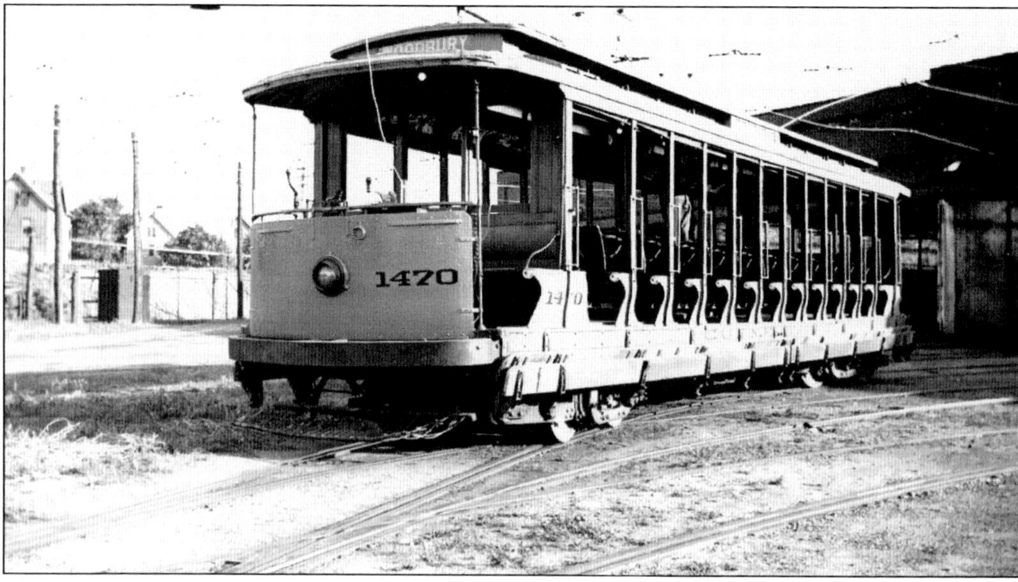

Here is open car 1470, originally numbered 171, as it looked in 1938, when it was the last Waterbury open car left in service. In 1936 a number of Waterbury open cars were transferred to New Haven—for use on Yale Bowl Specials—and were renumbered. This car ran in New Haven until 1947, the last year open cars were used, after which time it was scrapped.

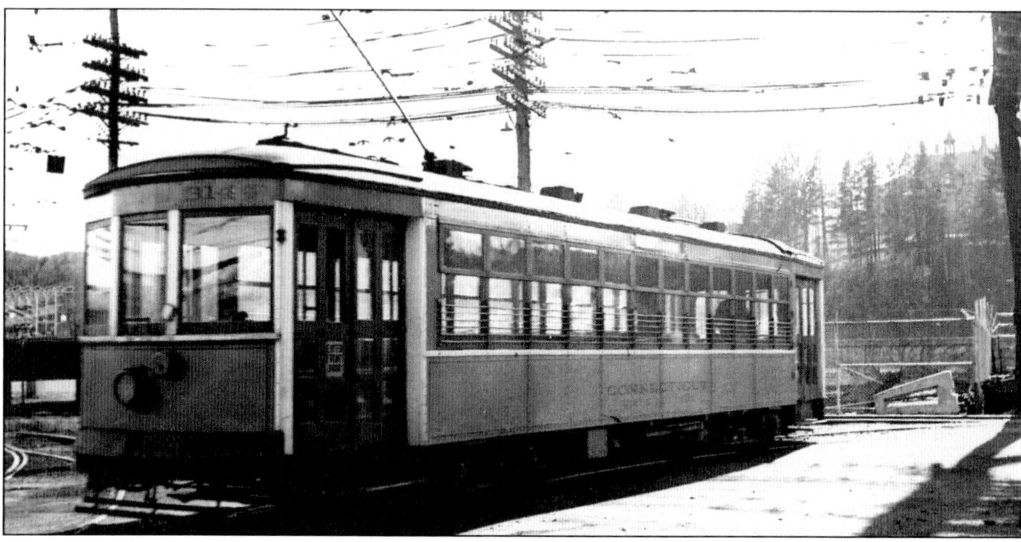

The early 1930s saw the Waterbury city streetcar system still going strong. Many cars, like this one, ran along the routes, allowing residents access to businesses and industries along the line. Automobile competition was not yet too serious, and although the Depression was in full swing, most people could still afford the 10¢ fare.

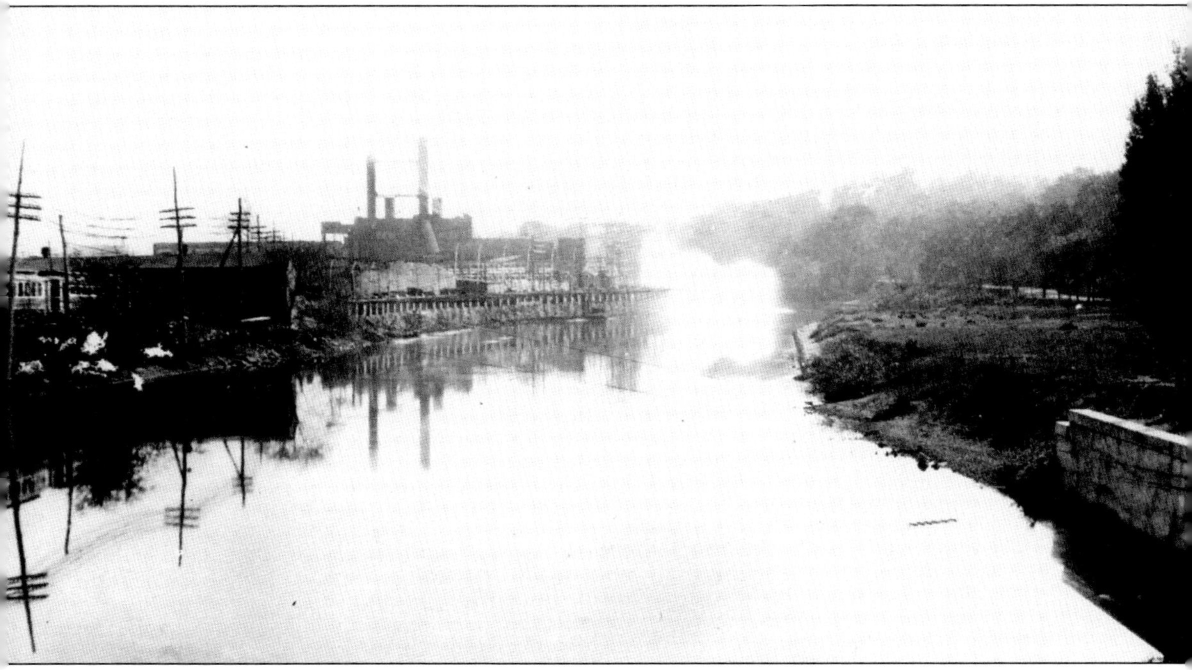

This panoramic view of the Naugatuck River, as seen from the West Main Street Bridge in 1918, shows the carbarn on the left side of the river. In New England, many cities and factories grew up around the rivers for the obvious access to transportation and power that the rivers provided.

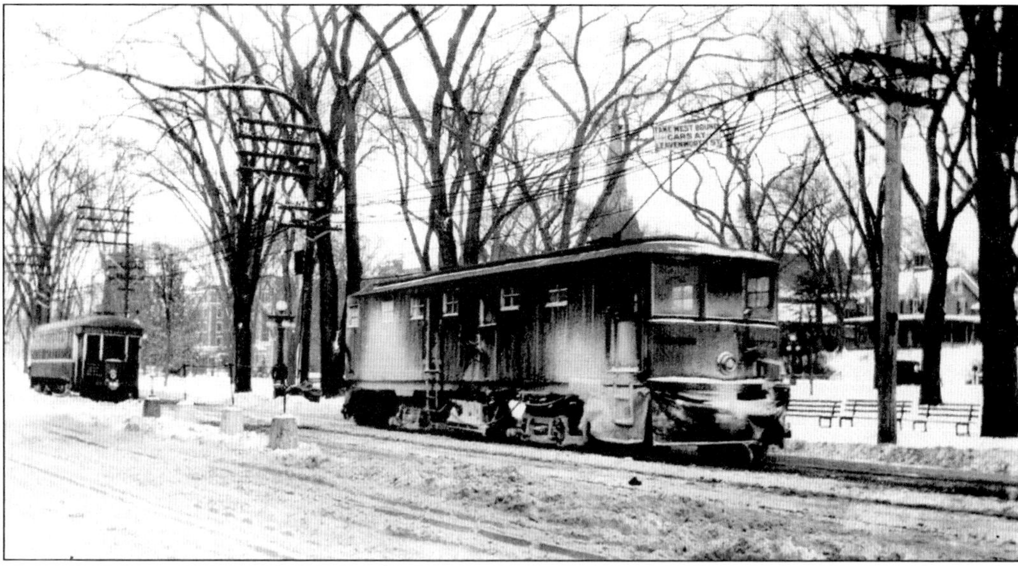

Winter operations were always troublesome on the Waterbury lines, thanks to the famous New England winters. Snowplows and sweepers were kept busy at such times, and more than once crews worked 24 hours or more without relief to keep the city lines open. (F. S. Bennett Collection.)

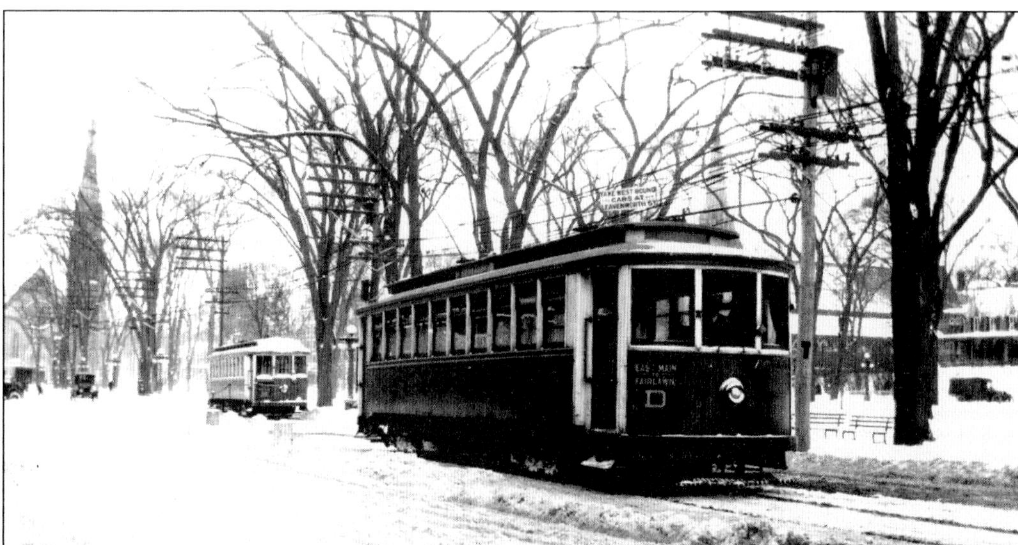

Streetcars were able to operate in the worst of weather conditions and could run in deep snow, while the early buses could not. This made the streetcars perfect for transportation in Waterbury, as this1922 scene on the green indicates.

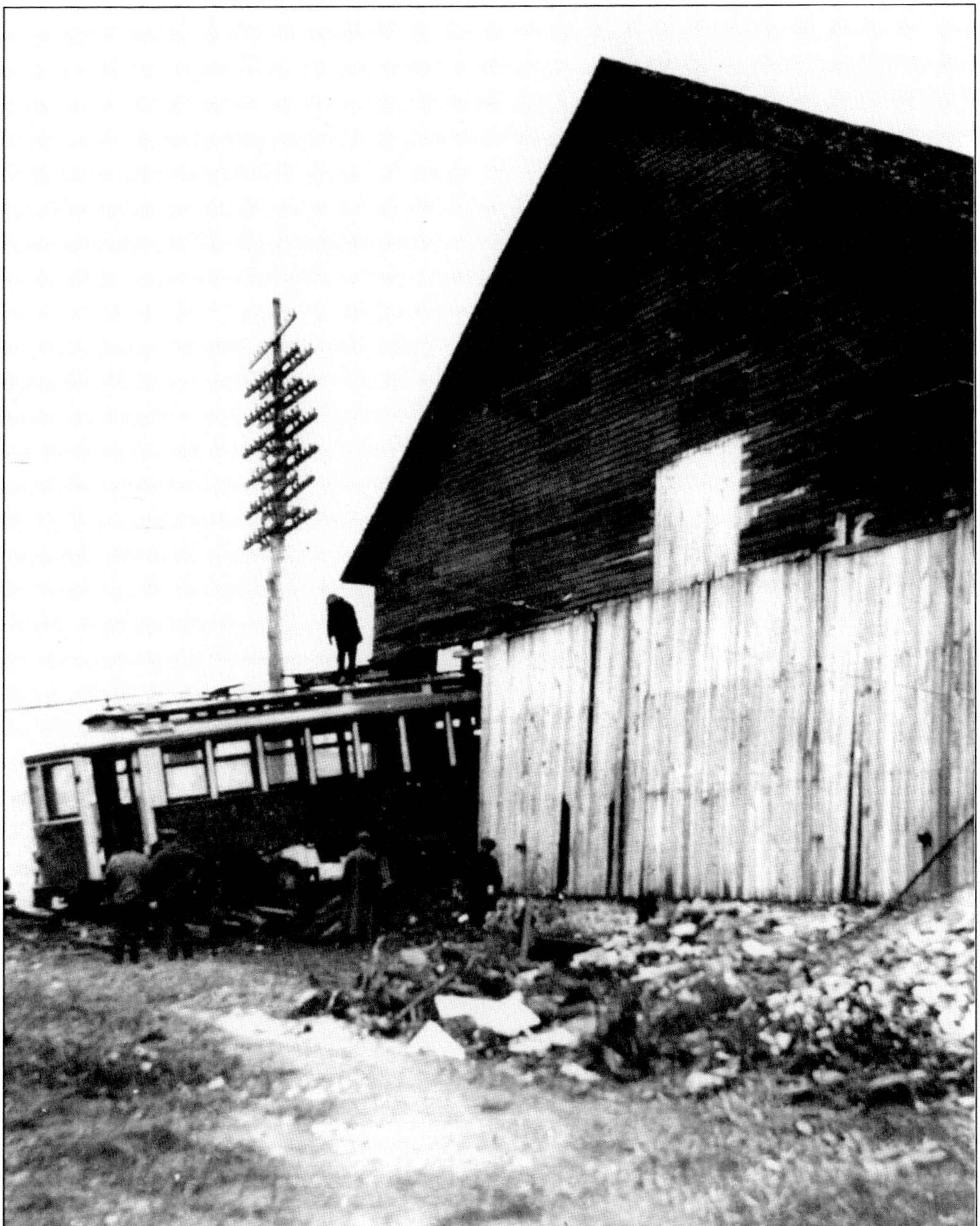

The details of this incident have been lost to history; the car has come out of the back of the old Waterbury Traction Company barn. Perhaps the brakes failed or the operator was not paying attention. In the early years of the streetcar industry, the turnover of the operators and conductors who worked on the cars was high. About half of them resigned, and the others were discharged for drunkenness, incompetence, insubordination, and failure to follow orders. Note the obvious repairs to the back of the barn; apparently, it was not uncommon for cars to run through the back wall of the building. Because of accidents like this, many safety mechanisms have been incorporated into our modern rail systems.

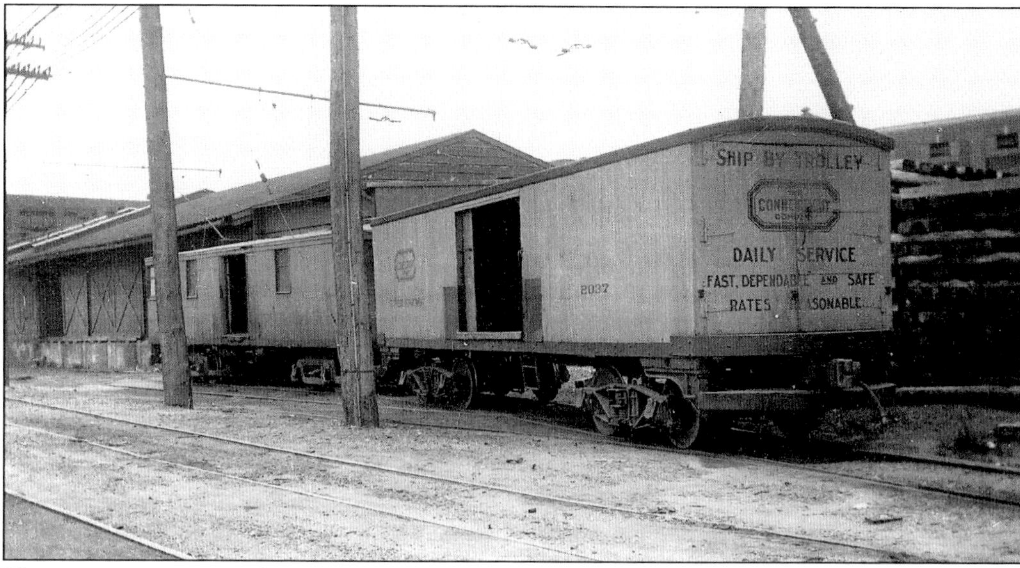

The extensive street railway system in Connecticut made the Connecticut Company's freight service ideal for shipments to local retailers. For the first time, a store or business could call in an order to a vendor in the morning and receive the shipment in the afternoon. Wholesalers were the primary customers in cities like Waterbury. Food, dry goods, pipes, and electrical and hardware products were all shipped in substantial volume on the streetcar system. Freight car 2037 is shown here at the Waterbury freight house in 1935. By that time almost all the package freight had been lost to trucks.

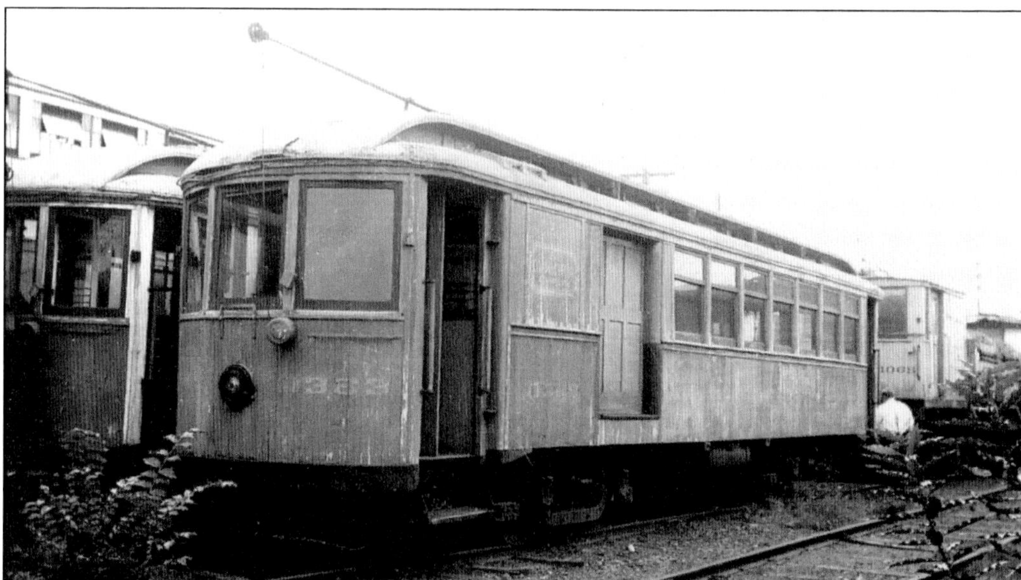

On some of the less populated lines, there was a need for both passenger and freight service; however, there was not enough business to dedicate a car for each, so cars were built that combined these two uses. This combination car was used on the Woodbury line to haul passengers as well as pouched mail and newspapers. In 1931 it was converted into a work car.

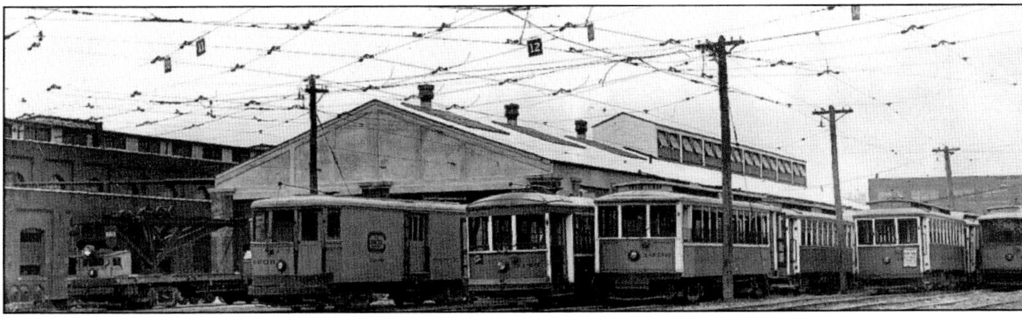

By 1930 the Connecticut Company had made the business decision to motorize all its streetcar lines in Connecticut, and as a result discontinued all heavy car repairs. If a car broke down, another would be pulled out of the carbarn to take its place. With the closing of a number of Waterbury lines in the early 1930s, the division had more than enough cars to cover all the runs. If the repairs were not too expensive, they would be completed and the car would be put back into service. If the job involved major repairs, the car would be permanently removed from service and put in dead storage or, in some cases, scrapped.

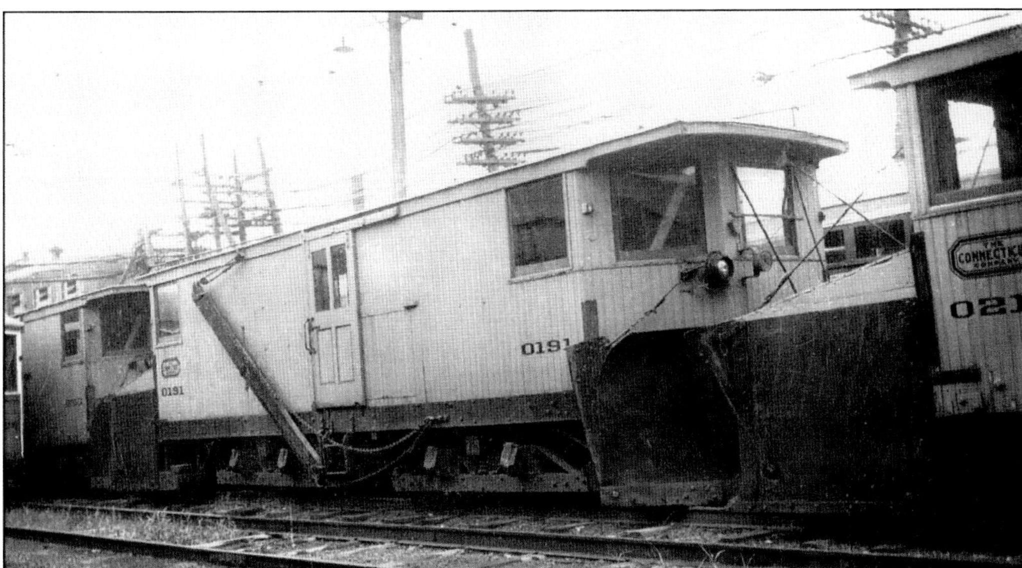

Since a typical Connecticut winter means snow, and lots of it, the Waterbury fleet of snowplows has been serviced and is waiting for winter to arrive in this August 1935 view at the carbarn. Over the years, the Connecticut Company acquired or built a fleet of snow-fighting equipment that included plows, sweepers, and sand cars. Plows were normally used on the suburban lines, where the snow could be pushed to the side of the road, and the sweepers were used in the city, where space was limited.

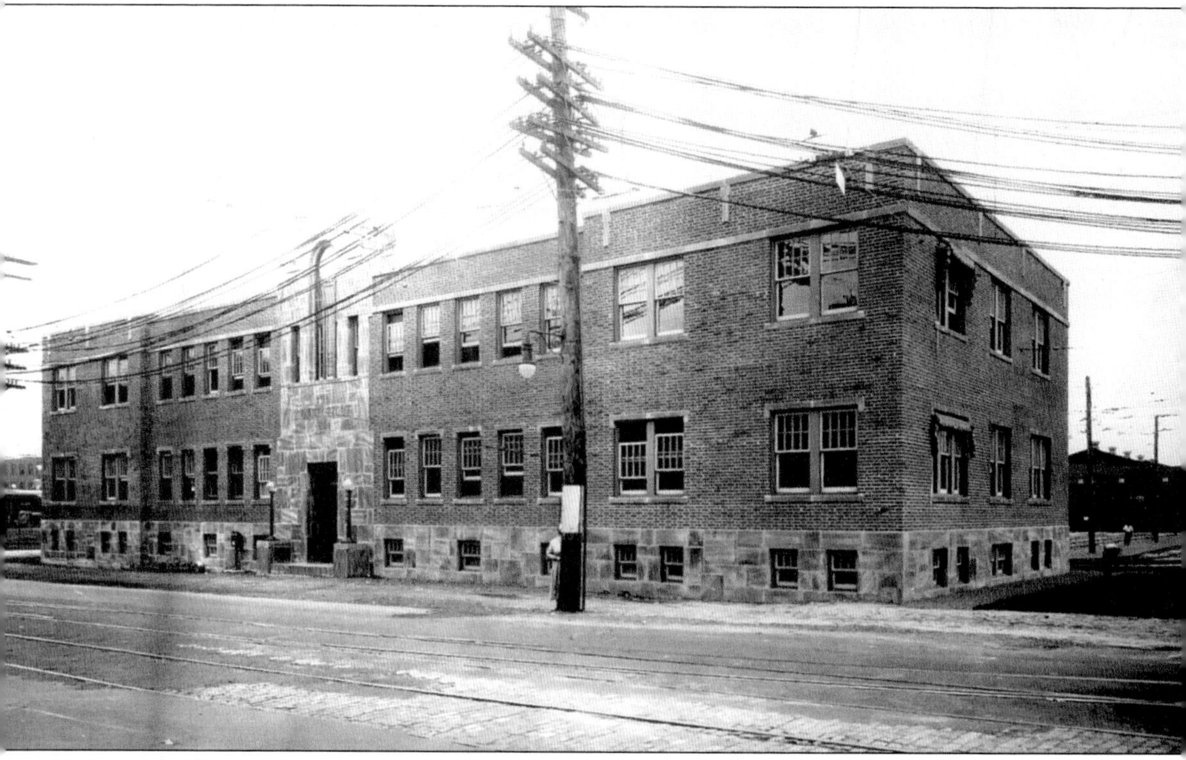

At the height of trolley usage, division offices, such as this Waterbury office on West Main Street, were built to house all the personnel needed to keep the system running. This building remained unchanged—except for the company name—into the 1970s, when it was razed. Note the awnings on the corner windows to provide relief from the sun setting over West Side Hill, out of sight to the right.

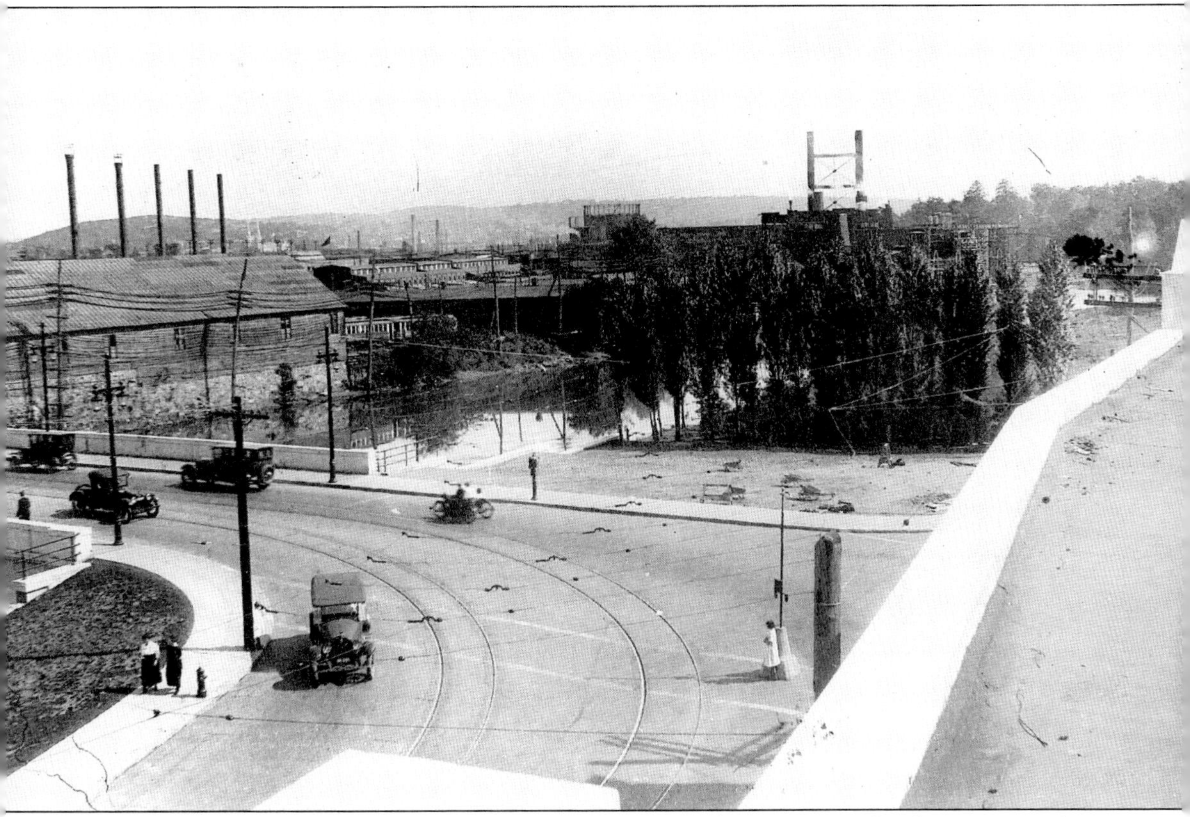

This view of the West Main Street Bridge, over the Naugatuck River, provides the viewer with an example of how the trolley cars and early automobiles shared the roadways.

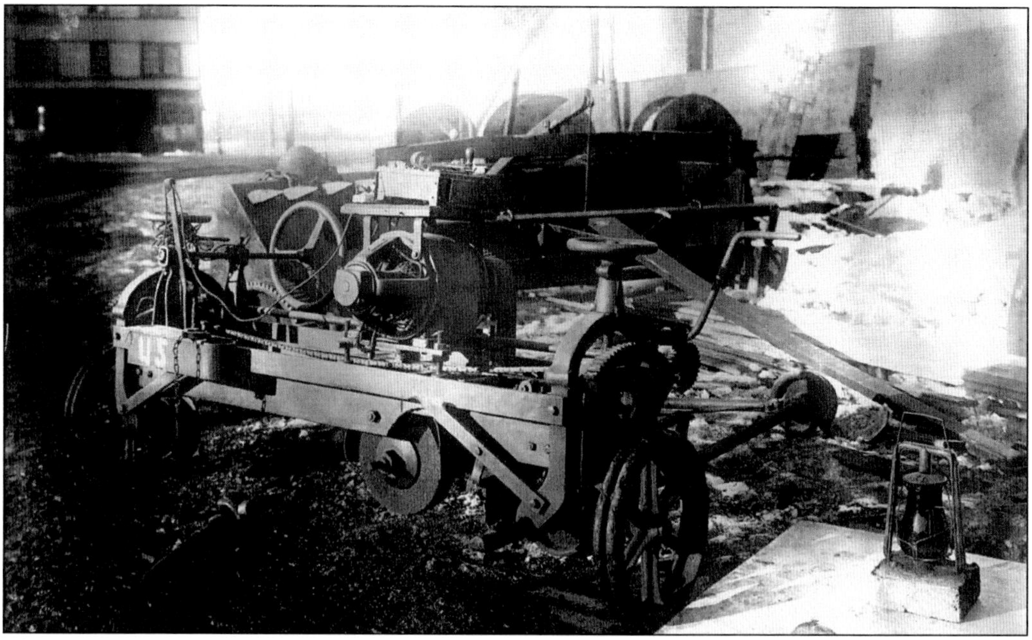

This interesting piece of machinery is a portable rail grinder, which was used to smooth rough spots when rails were replaced. Rail grinding was an essential component of right-of-way maintenance. The Connecticut Company also had rail-grinder cars; these were usually older passenger cars that were converted into work cars.

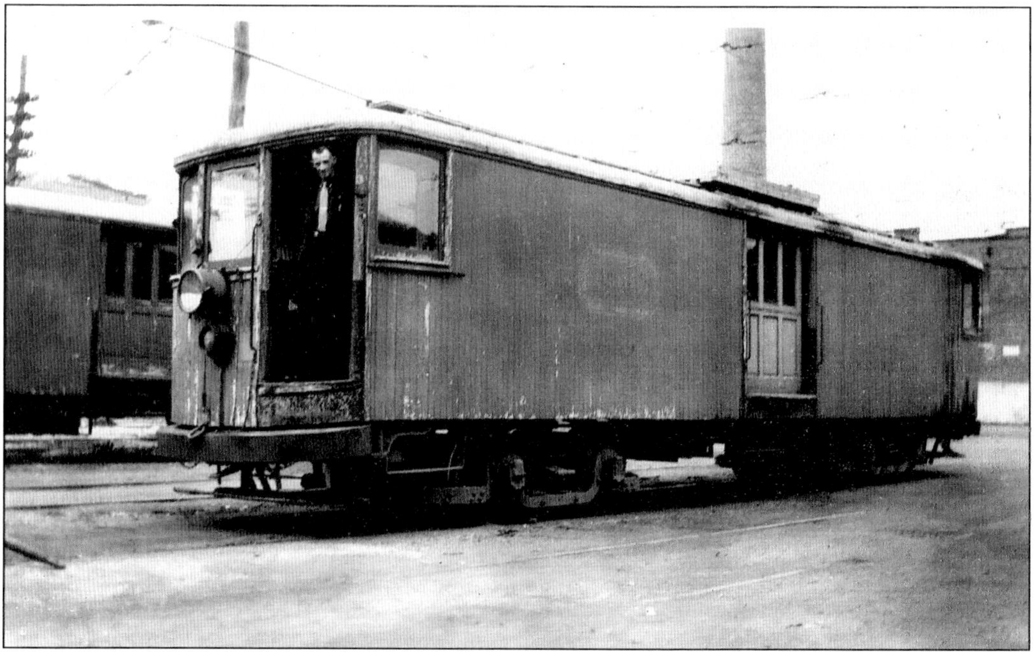

The Connecticut Company built many of its own work cars, like No. 0205 shown here. Although it looks like an express car, this was actually used to carry tools for track projects and for re-railing cars.

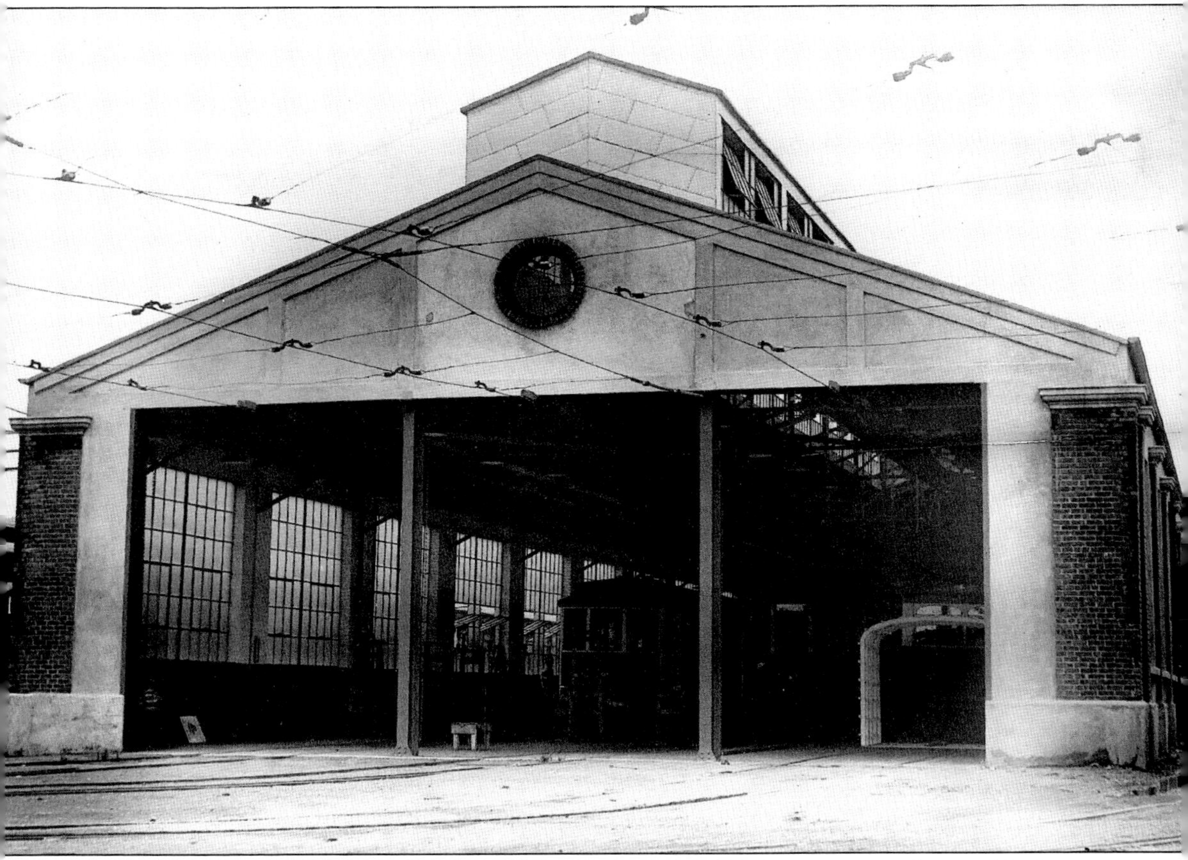

The Waterbury carpenter shop is shown in this 1920 view. All the cars manufactured before 1917 were made of wood, and when repairs were needed, they were performed by company craftsmen who could work on the wooden cars. Cars purchased after 1917 were all-steel construction and different skills were required to repair them. The Connecticut Company also built many of its express and work cars in its own shops, equipping the cars with trucks and electrical equipment purchased from manufacturers such as General Electric, Westinghouse, and Taylor.

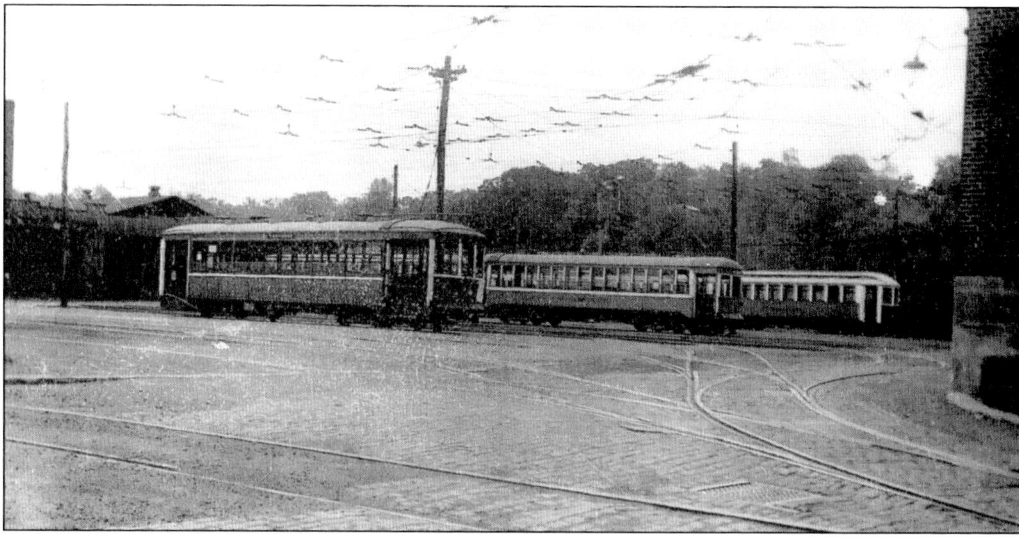

As with motor vehicle traffic today, there was a morning and afternoon "rush hour" during the week in many cities. Waterbury was no different, which meant many cars operated only four or five hours during a day, running in the morning and evening, Monday through Friday. During the remainder of the day you could find the cars "laying over," as is shown in this picture of the Waterbury car yard in 1935.

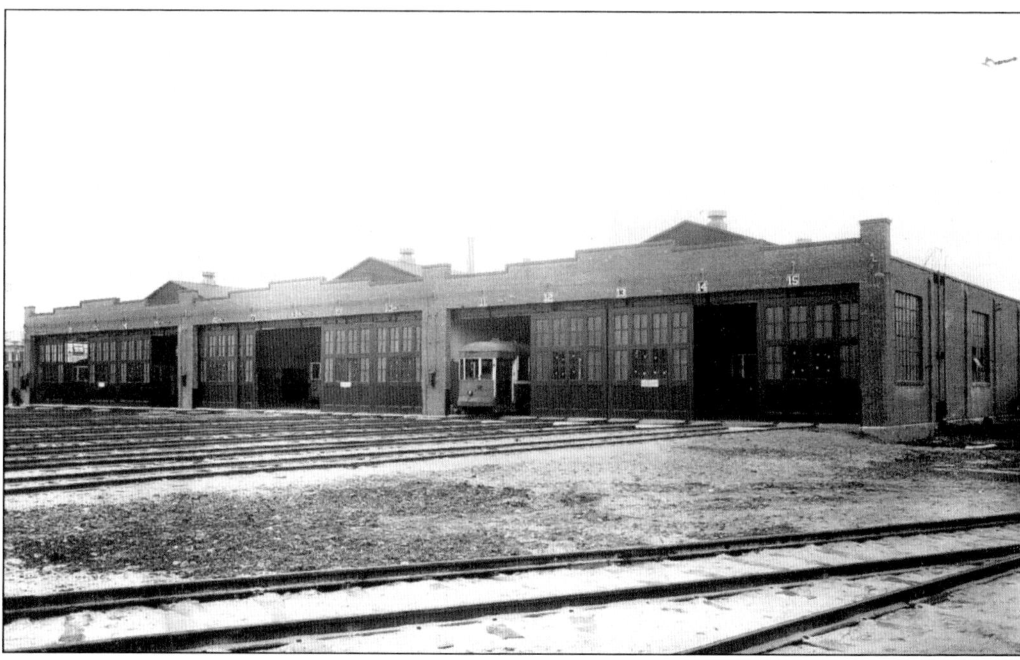

A new carbarn was built for the Waterbury division in the 1920s. The structure had 15 bays and could hold more than 100 streetcars inside. This building was torn down in the 1970s, as were many of the other buildings connected with the streetcar line.

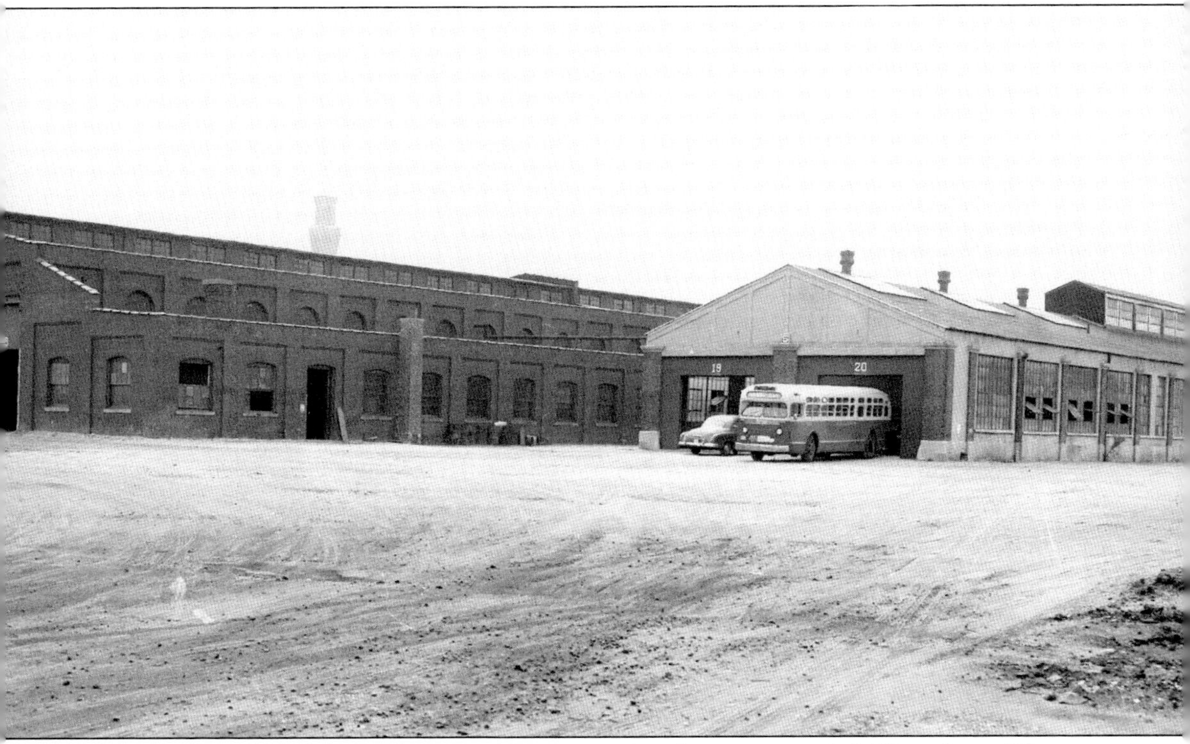

Here is a 1950s view of the carbarn area 20 years after the streetcars left Waterbury. These buildings were torn down in 1974. There is a 1920s view of this site at the bottom of the facing page. (F. S. Bennett Collection.)

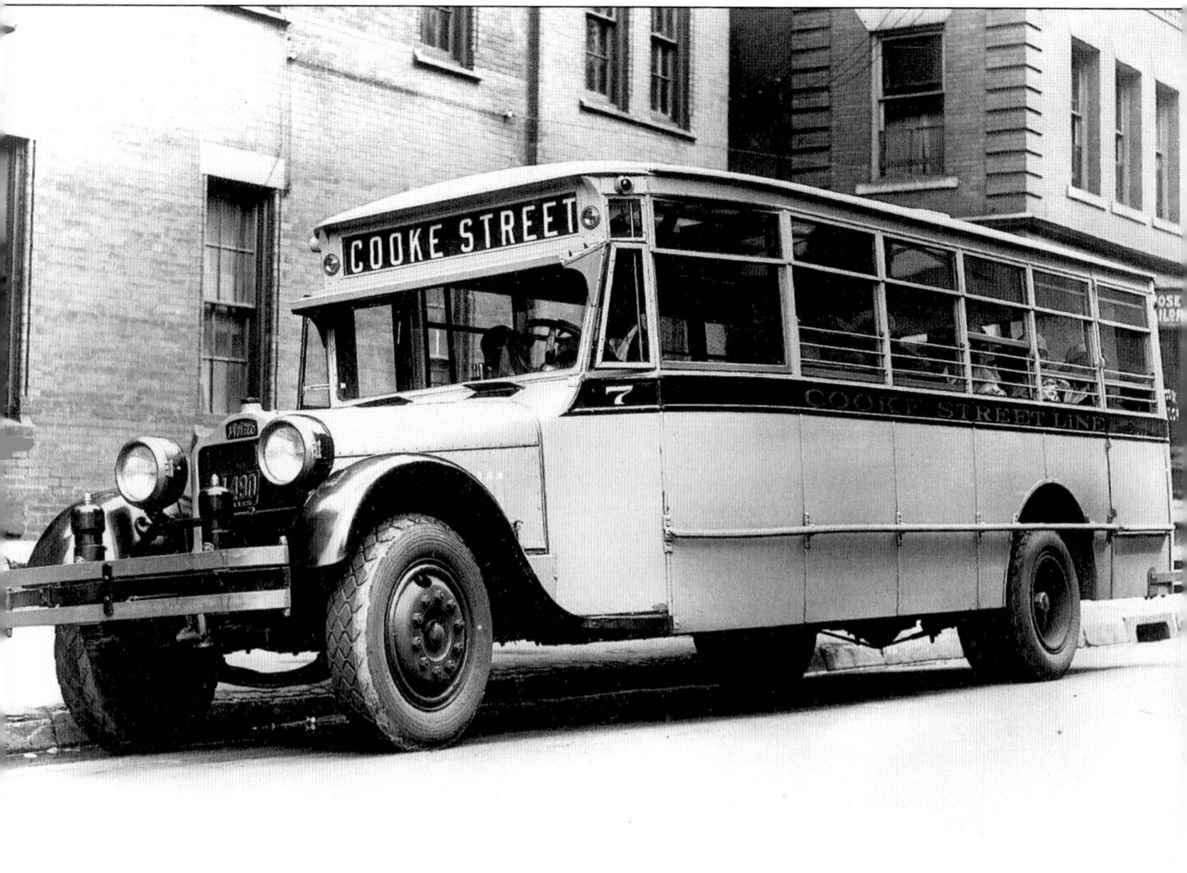

Cooke Street Lines' White bus No. 7 heads from Exchange Place to its namesake destination, Cooke Street, on a warm day in 1926. Cooke Street Lines was the local passenger bus service. In just seven years the company would extend its operations into the East End of the city and begin running over the routes of the Waterbury & Milldale Tramway, which ceased operations in 1933.

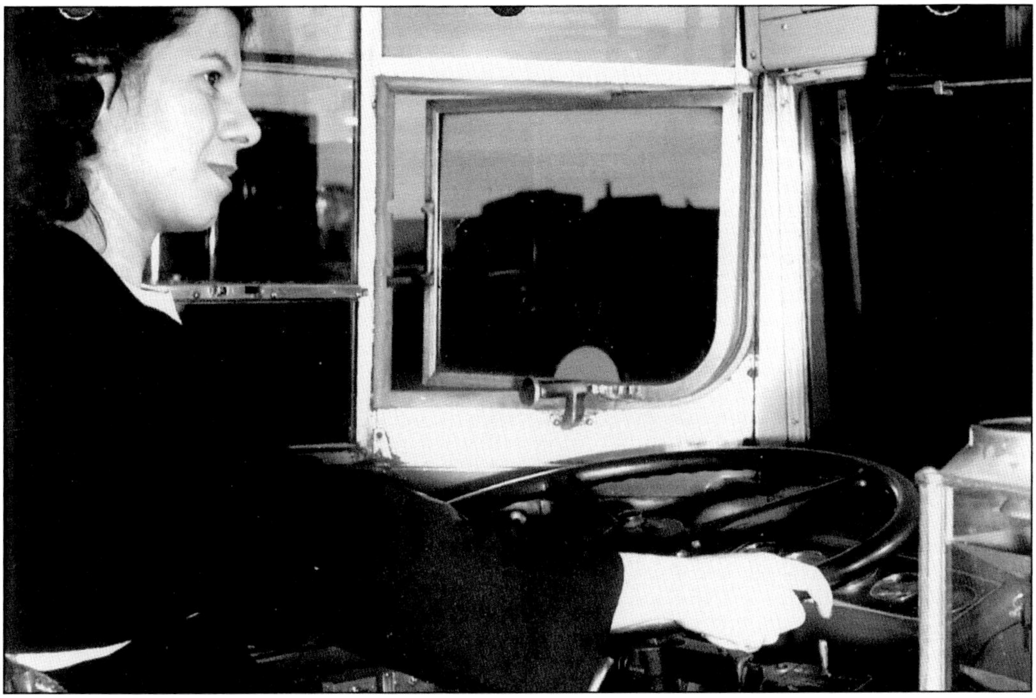

During the manpower shortages of World War II, Connecticut Railway and Lighting hired women to do many of the jobs normally held by men. Among those female employees was this confident driver, who is about to take her ACF (American Car & Foundry) bus out on a run. Labor shortages were also prevalent during World War I, and some streetcar companies strongly considered hiring "conductorettes" and motor ladies at that time. While women were hired for such jobs in many other cities, this never happened in Waterbury.

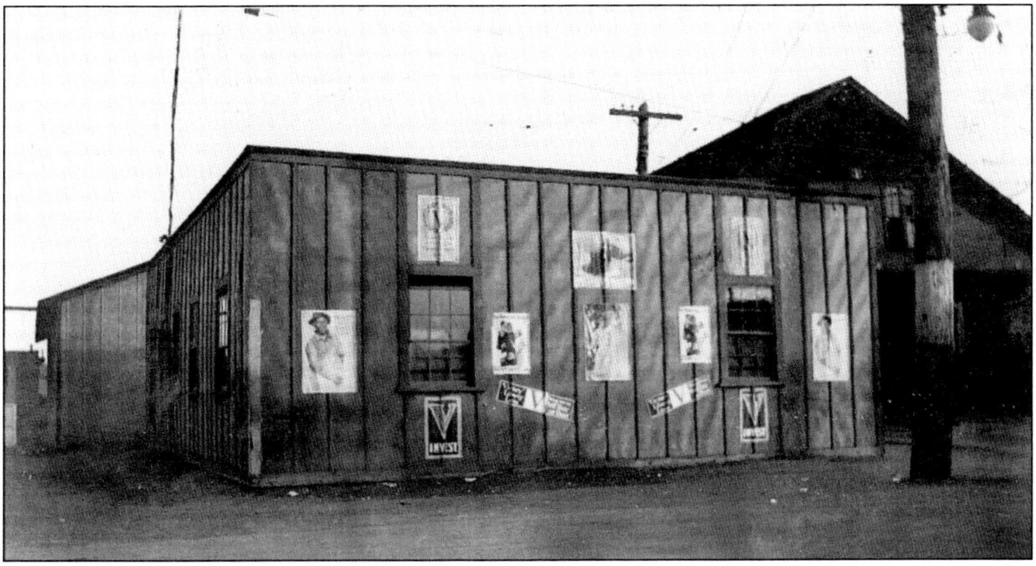

The display of patriotic posters on this West Main Street building in January 1918 provides evidence of America's involvement in the European war, which raged on for another 11 months after this photograph was taken.

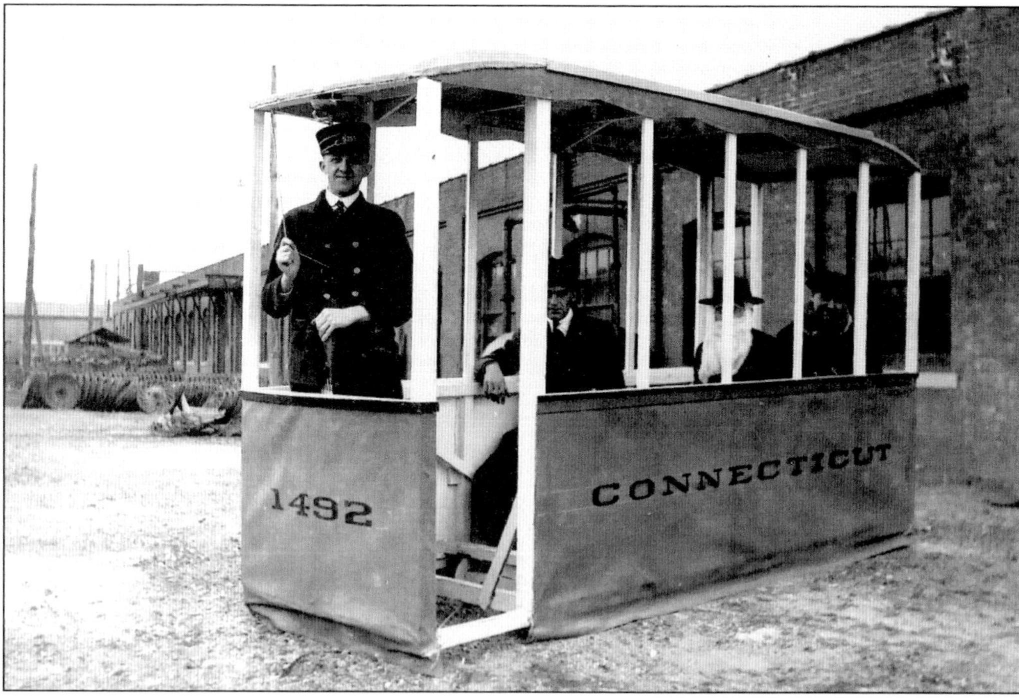

Here is a photograph of what appears to be some type of stage prop. The building in the background is the Waterbury carbarn, so it is possible that the carpenter shop built this for a local theater production. The only notation on the back of the picture is the date, 1918.

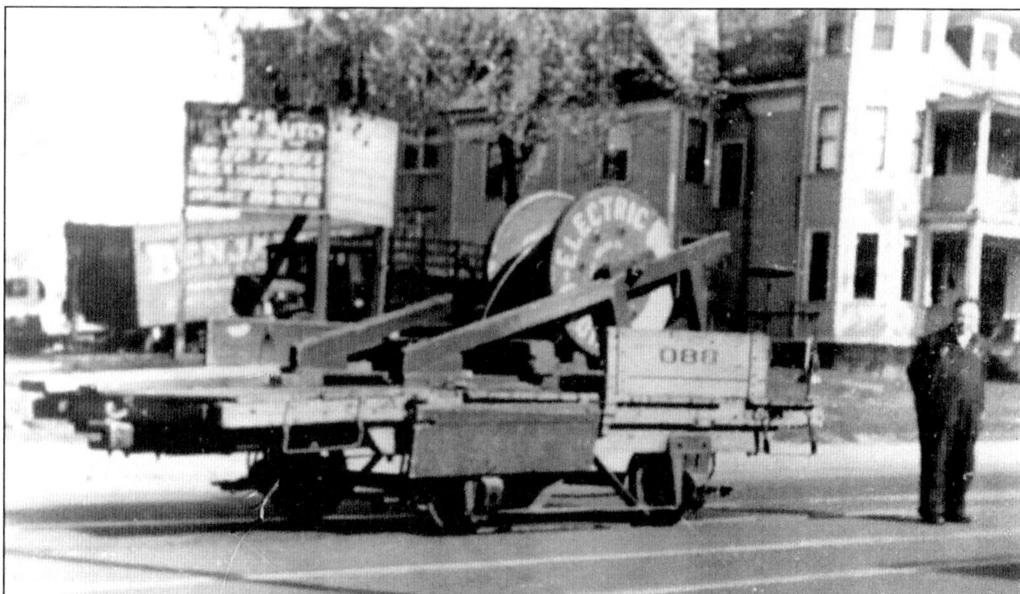

This little single-truck flat car is being used by the line crew to replace some wire in downtown Waterbury. Car No. 088 was built by the Hartford shops in 1898 and was not scrapped until 1941 in Hartford. In order to maintain the ever-increasing amount of trackage it owned, the Connecticut Company had more than 350 different pieces of work equipment positioned all over the state.

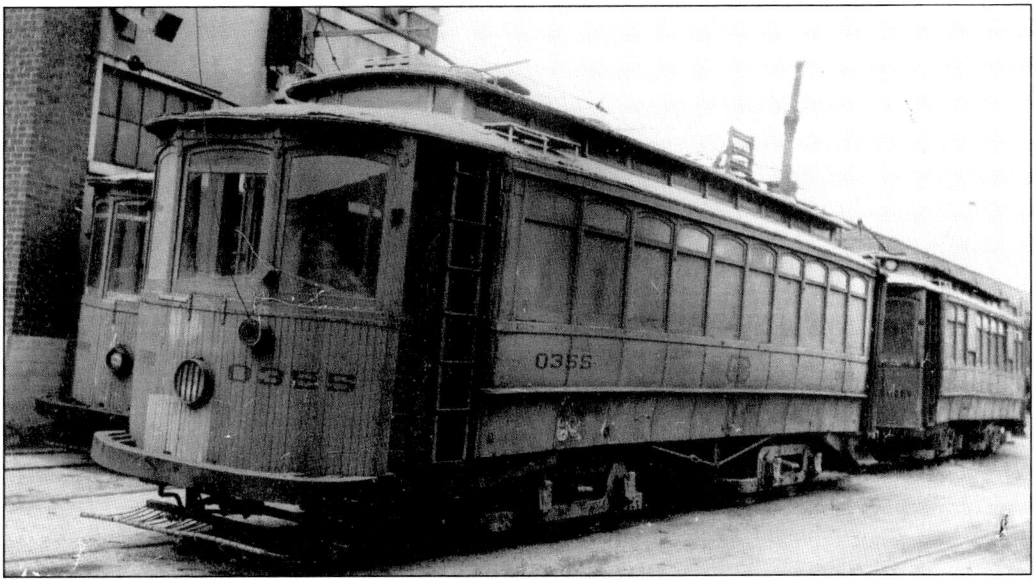

Just like the snowplows, the sand cars sat idle during the warmer months. Here we see three Waterbury cars sitting at the West Main Street carbarn in August 1935. Sand cars were used to spread sand and salt on the roadway and rails during inclement weather. In converting these former passenger cars, all of the seats were removed and replaced with bins to hold the sand and salt. As the cars ran along the street, track workers inside the cars would shovel the material into chutes, which served to spread the material on the pavement below.

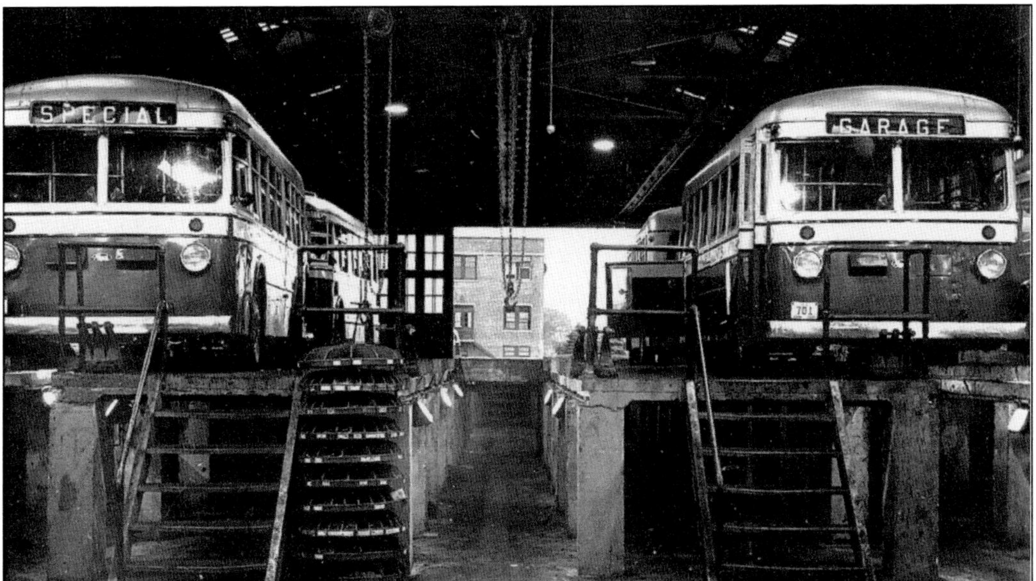

Following the conversion of the lines from streetcar to bus, there was little need for the Waterbury carbarn to store cars. So the barn was converted into a bus repair facility, as shown here. The pits remain from the streetcar days, with a few modifications to accommodate the buses. Here we see two of the fleet of 1936 Mack buses that Connecticut Railway and Lighting purchased to replace the Waterbury streetcar fleet. Look on page 24 to see this same building with streetcars inside.

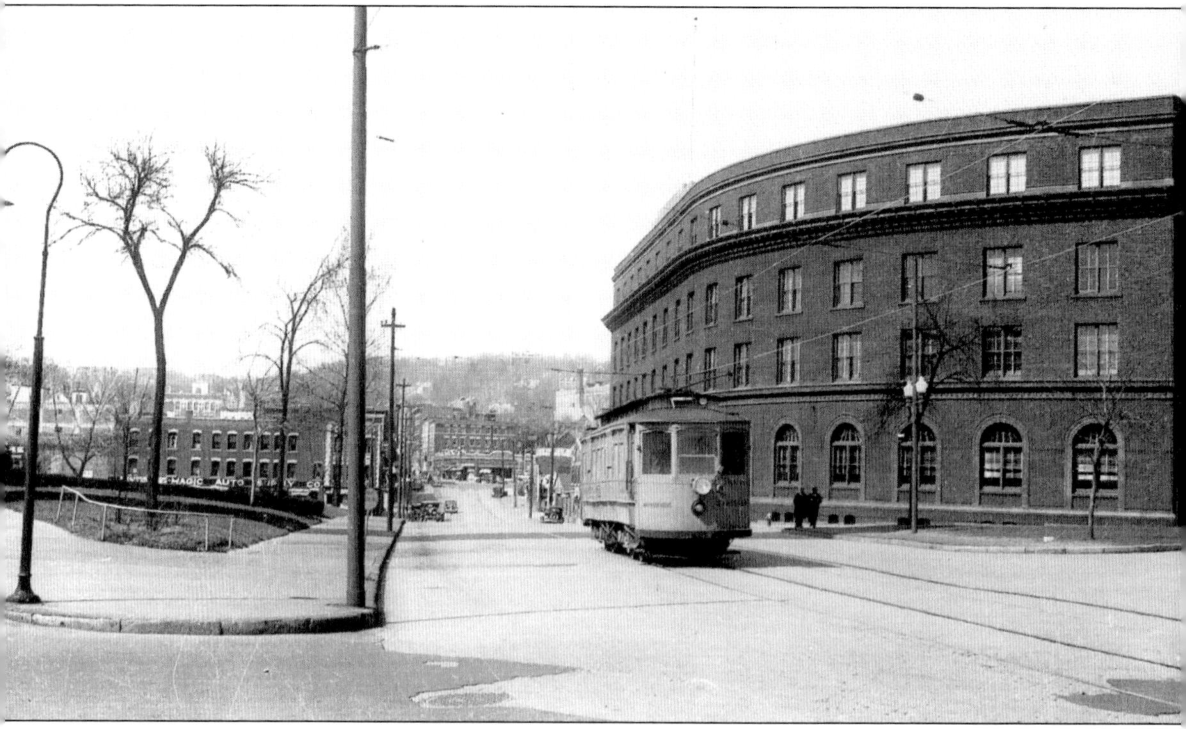

Waterbury is also known as the "Brass City," because of the brass companies located there. Anaconda Brass was one of Waterbury's principal industries, and the company employed many people. The streetcar system provided transportation to and from work for many of these employees. The brick structure on the right is the Anaconda Brass Building, pictured in April 1937. Sand car 0268 is shown running on Meadow Street, heading south. The New Haven Railroad station is on the left.

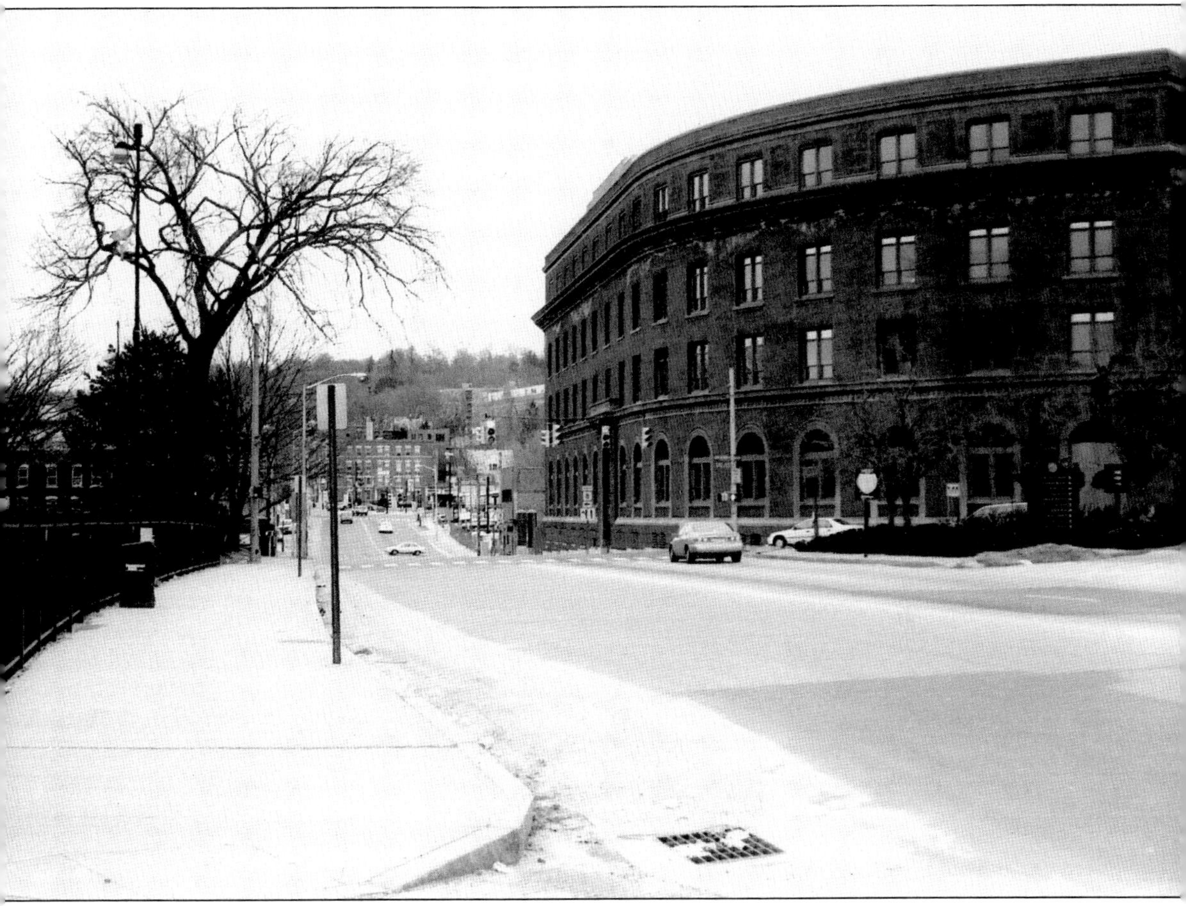

This 2005 view of the same location on Meadow Street shows that much in the area remains much the same. The former Anaconda Brass Building, constructed in 1913, is now the Superior Court House in Waterbury.

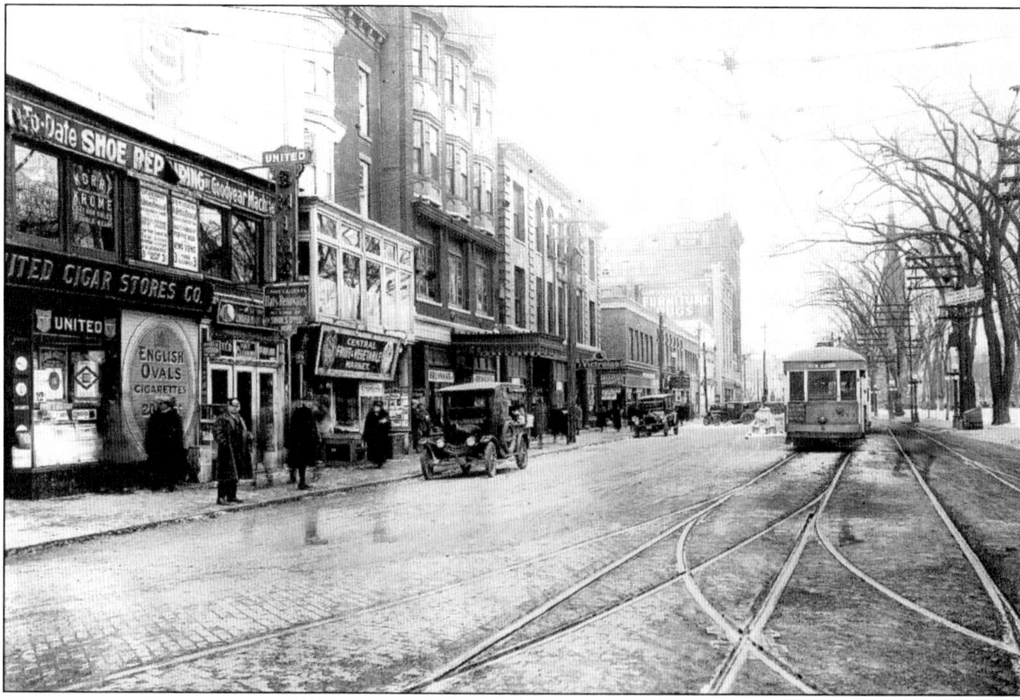

Connecticut Company car 1911 is seen here on the green in 1922. It will soon leave for Cheshire Junction on its run to New Haven. Car 1911 was later transferred to New Haven. This is one of the few cars that was not scrapped, but rather was obtained by interested parties for preservation. It is now on display at the Shore Line Trolley Museum in East Haven, Connecticut.

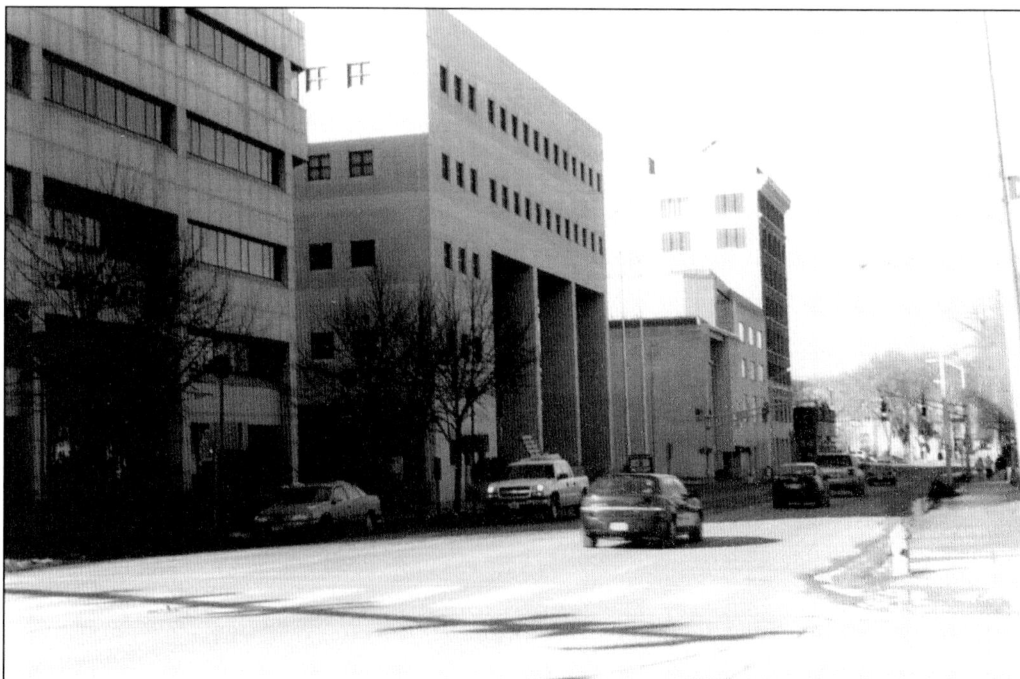

Here is a view of the Waterbury Green in 2005.

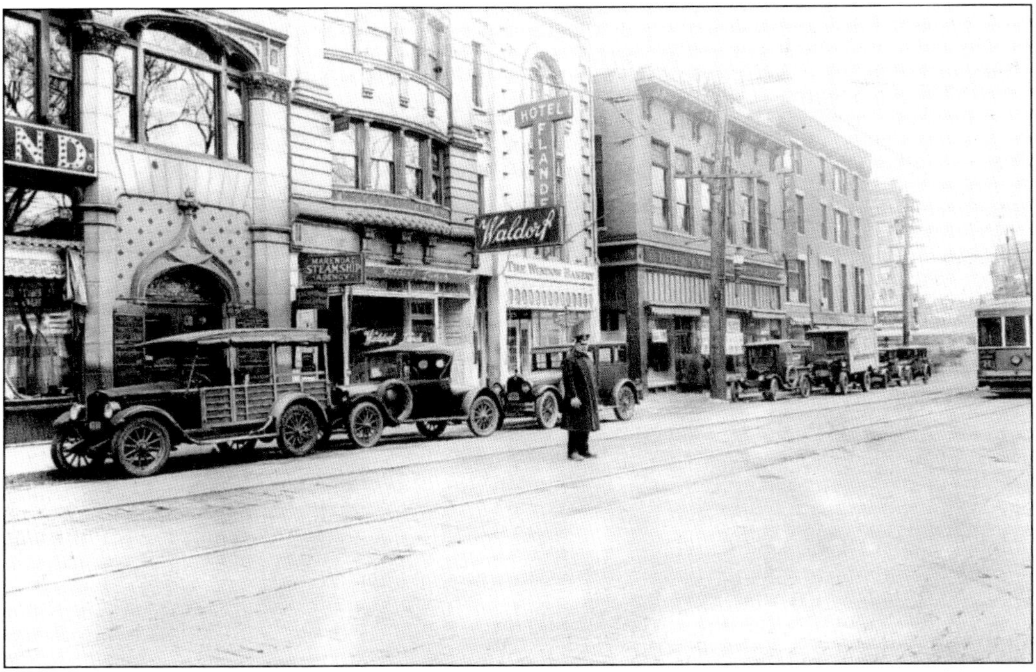

North Main Street in Waterbury sports both trolley cars and automobiles along its cobblestone pavement in this 1922 view, looking south toward Exchange Place. Among the North Main Street establishments pictured here are Waldorf Lunch (third building from left), the Window Bakery (white building near center), and the Mohegan Market (second building from right).

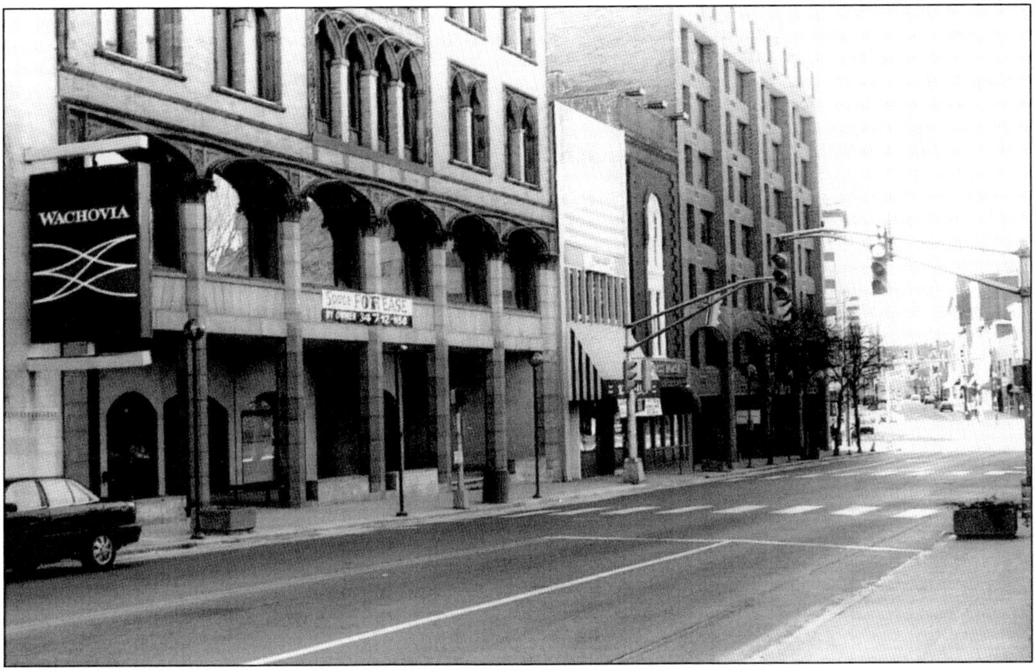

In this 2005 view of North Main Street you notice that while much has stayed the same, much has changed as well. The Mohegan Market is gone, but the former Window Bakery building is still there, although it is now home to a cocktail lounge.

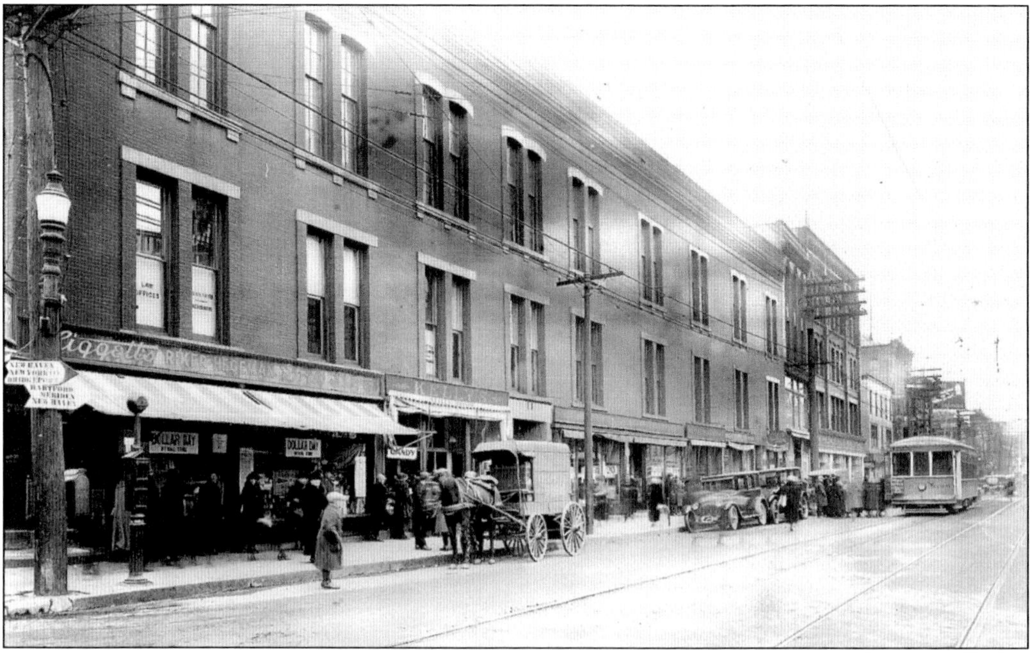

In 1922 it was not uncommon to stand at Exchange Place and look down East Main Street and see the old and the new merge—a horse-drawn delivery wagon, streetcars, and automobiles. With the increase in automobile traffic, direction signs (like those on the pole to the left) began appearing. The familiar red fire alarm boxes, also seen here, were 1890s technology, like the streetcars. The alarm boxes remained part of the Waterbury scene much longer than the streetcars; the boxes disappeared from Waterbury streets in the early 1960s. Below is a 2005 photograph of the same area.

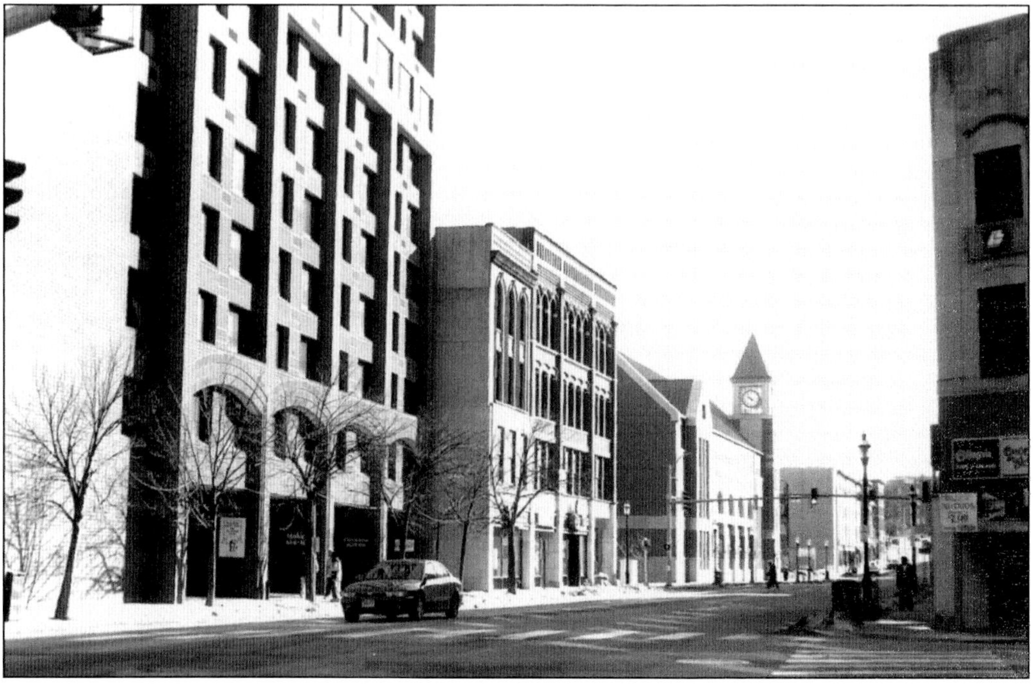

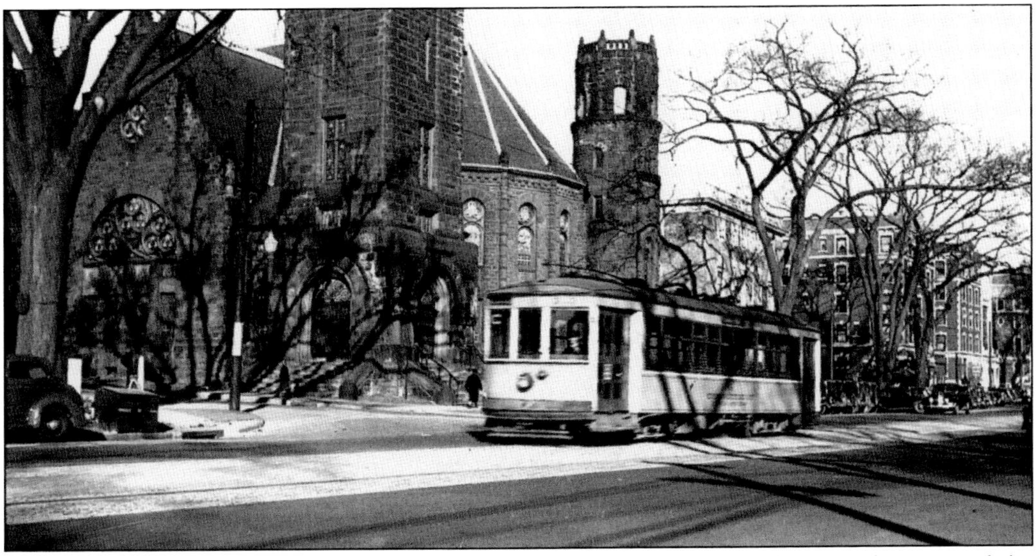

In this view from March 1937, you can see the transformation of the trolley car, the automobile, and the roadways in Waterbury. No longer were the roads made of cobblestone, and the more boxy style of the early automobile had given way to a more aerodynamic, rounded design. Connecticut Railway and Lighting Company car 3134 is shown here passing the Second Congregational Church on West Main Street, outbound from the center.

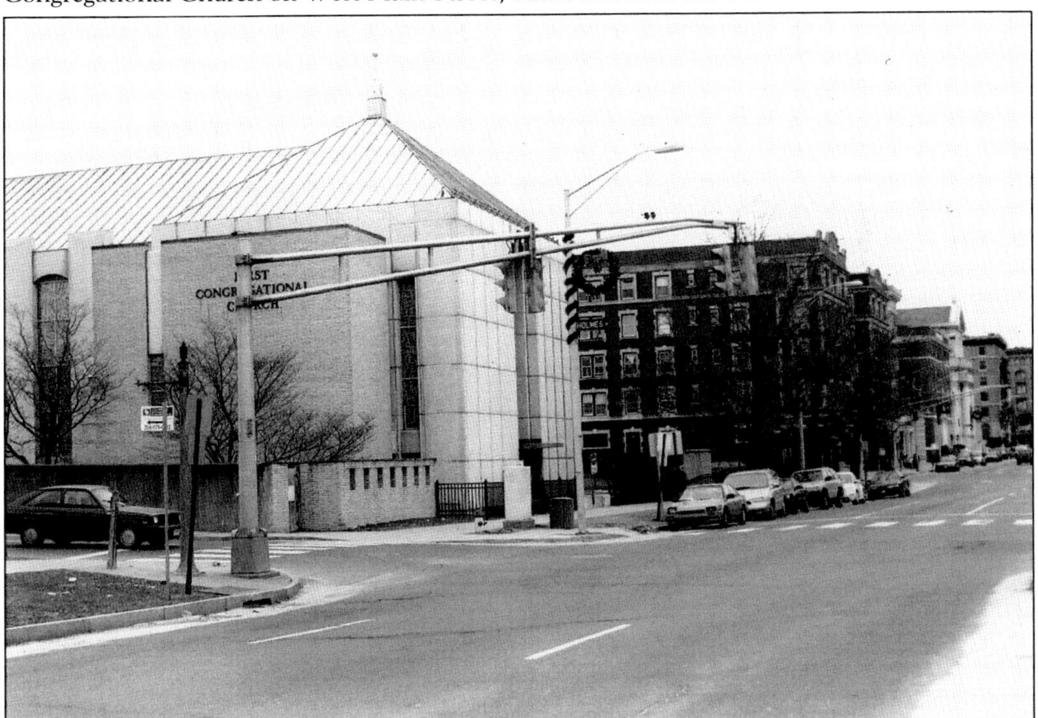

Unfortunately, the Second Congregational Church building was destroyed by a fire in 1960, so its congregation merged with the First Congregational Church. A new First Congregational Church building was erected in 1965 on the former site of the Second Congregational Church and the Waterbury Club.

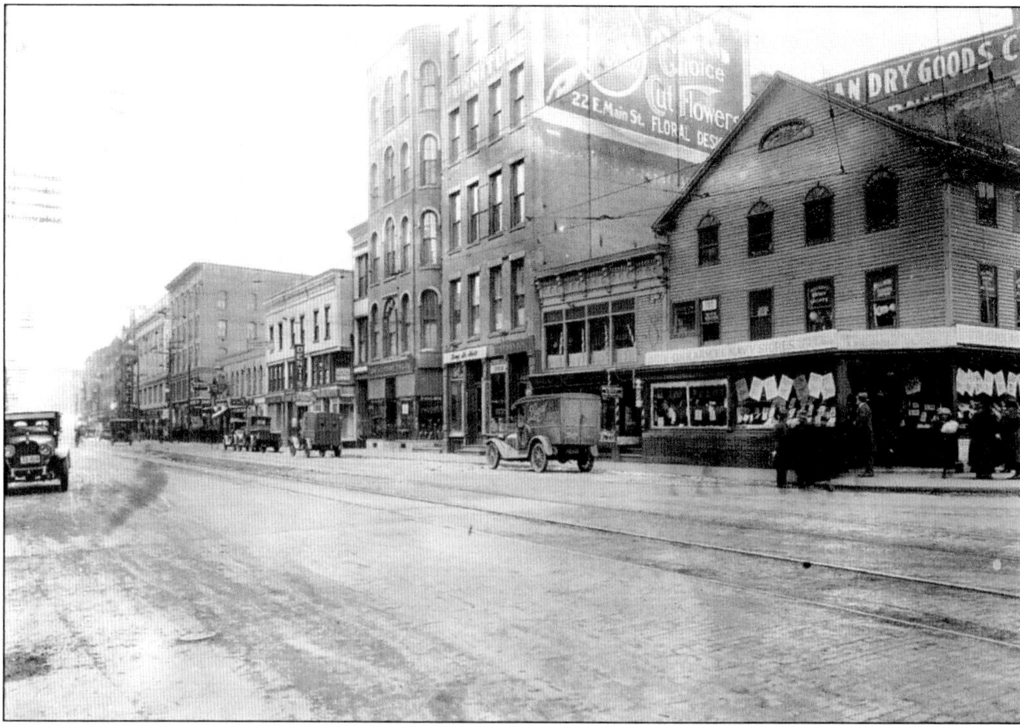

This view of East Main Street from Exchange Place once again shows the cobblestone streets, which accommodated both streetcar and automobile traffic. Since the time of this photograph, the corner building has been removed, and the Brown Building now stands at the site. Further up the street is the Palace Hotel.

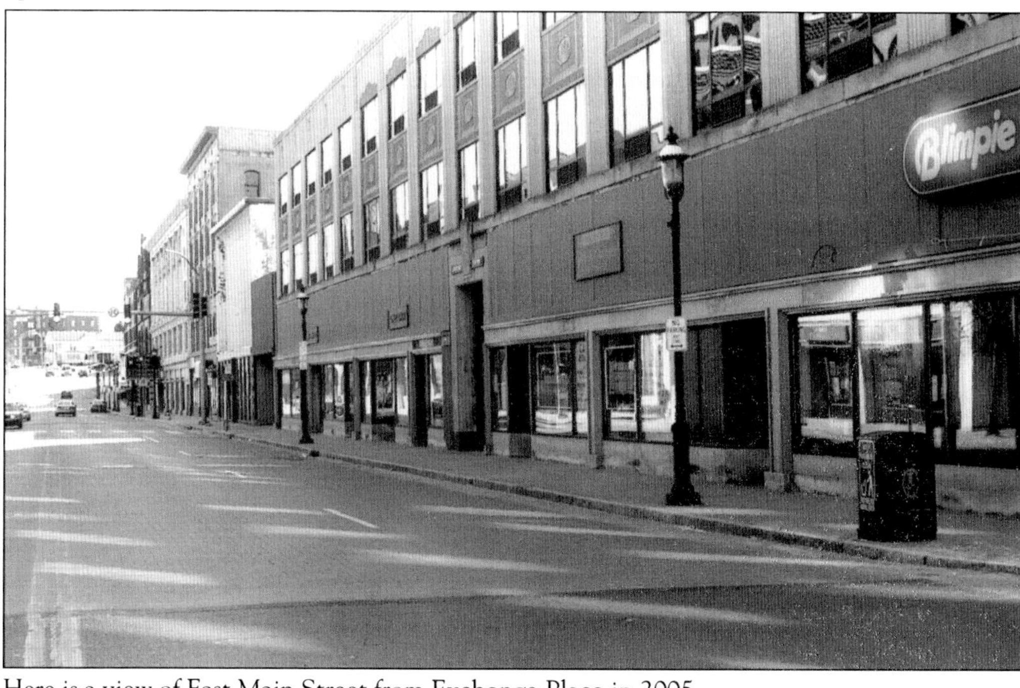

Here is a view of East Main Street from Exchange Place in 2005.

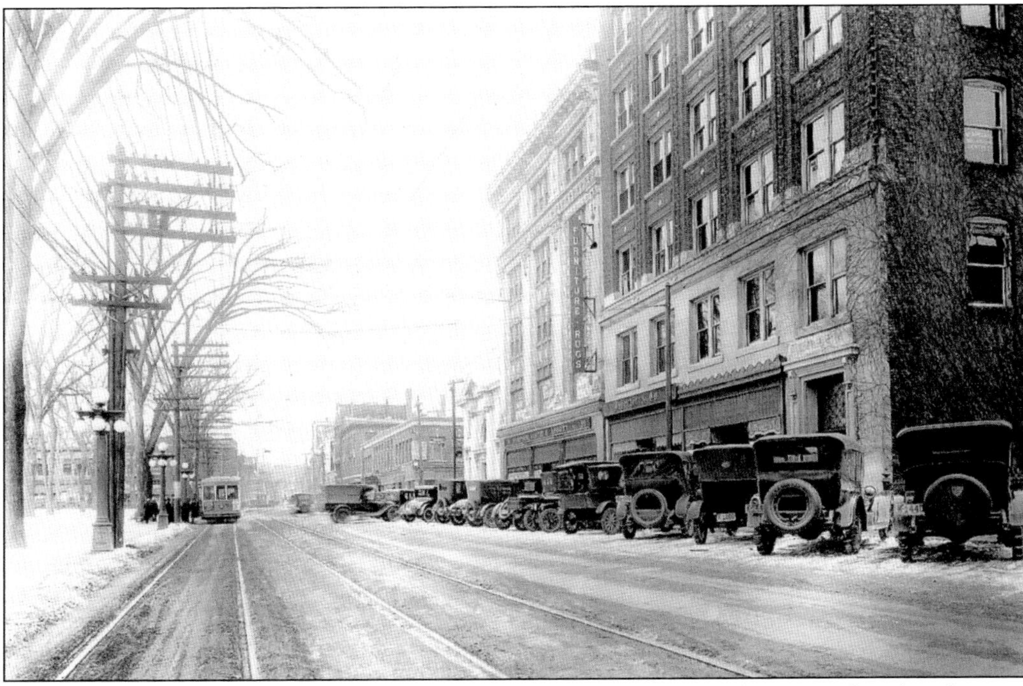

Snow remains on the roadways in this shot of West Main Street, looking east, but that does not hamper hearty New Englanders. The trolley cars are still running, and most of the cars have chains on their tires for better traction.

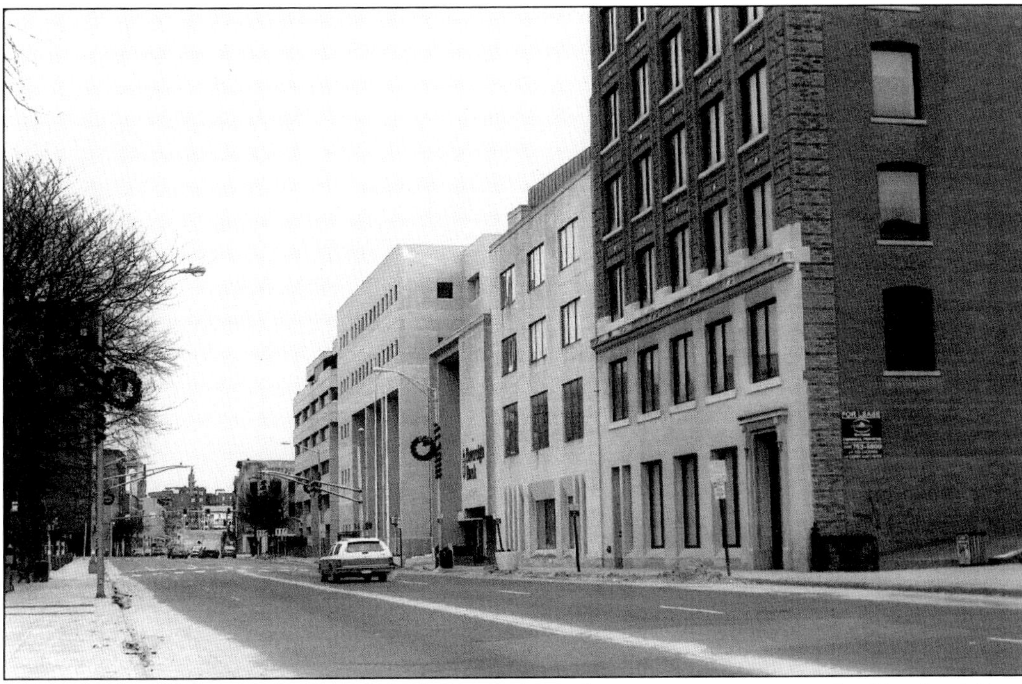

West Main Street in 2005 is much different from the previous view, as the Rowland State Government Center now occupies part of the site, and the facades of the remaining buildings have been altered.

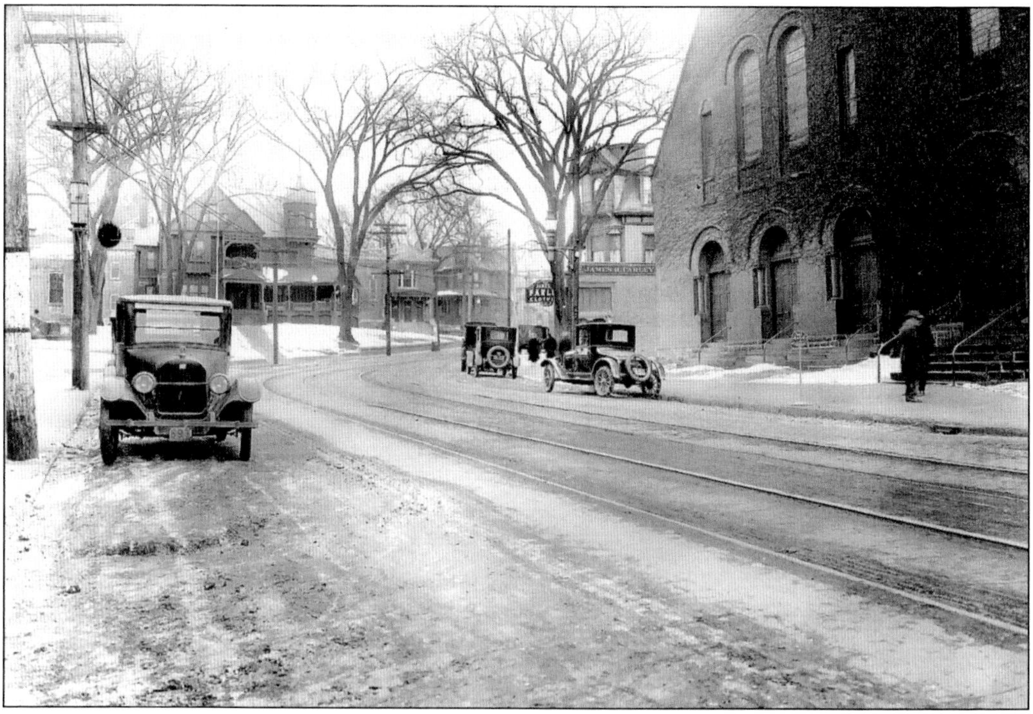

This 1922 view of North Main Street, just above the green, shows the First Methodist Church on the right. The early-model automobiles on the street are a harbinger of the hard times to come for the streetcar lines in the United States.

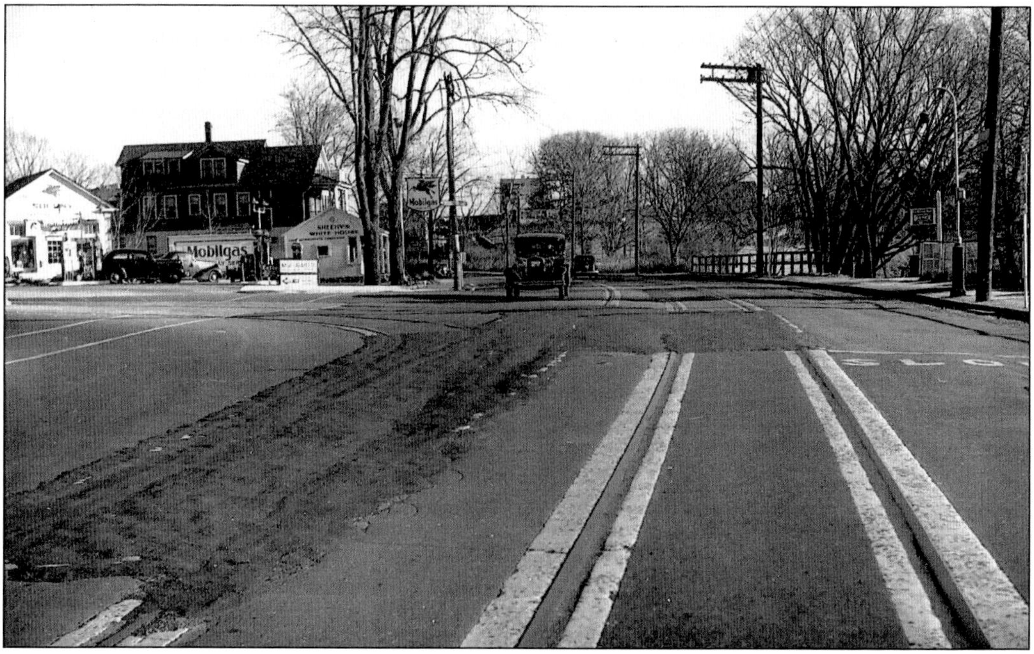

This 1938 view of East Main Street and Meriden Road shows the demise of the streetcar system, as the tracks in the streets have been paved over. The line to the left is the former Waterbury & Milldale route to Milldale; straight ahead is the line to Cheshire.

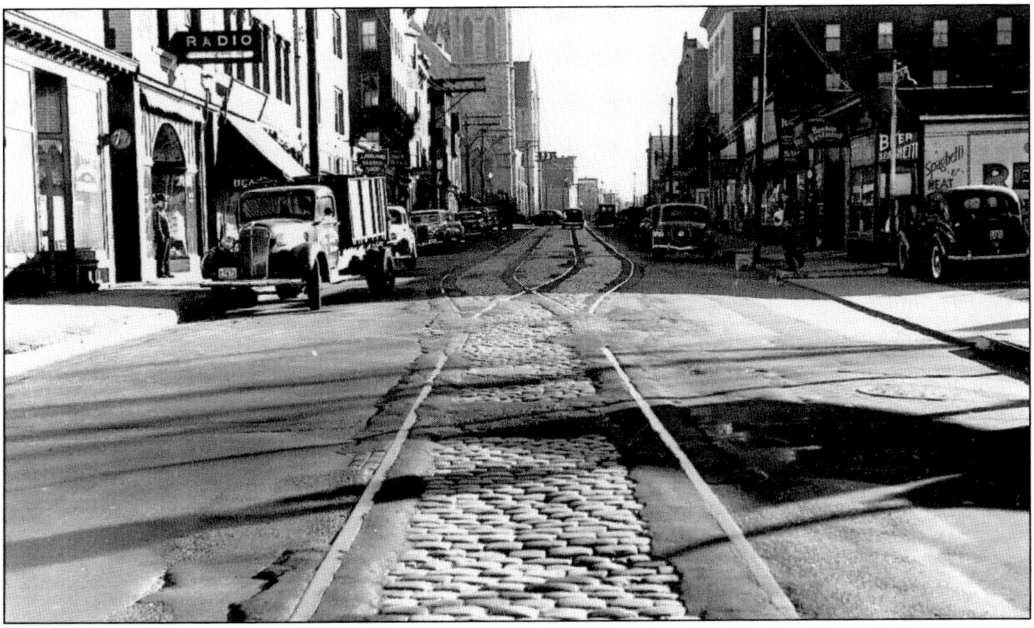

As was the case in many cities in the early 1900s, new immigrants to the United States stayed with friends and relatives who already lived in this country, and various ethnic communities were created as a result. The area around South Main Street and East Clay Street, near St. Ann's Church, was the French section of Waterbury. This 1937 view of South Main Street shows the "history" of the street, from cobblestones and trolley cars to automobiles and motor coaches.

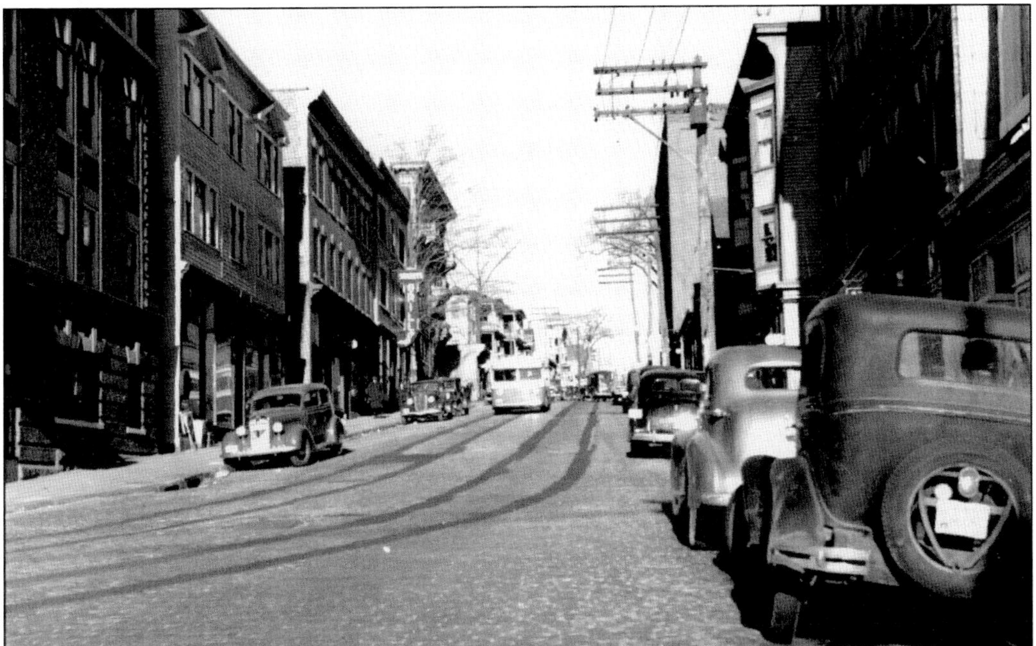

Here is a view of North Main Street, looking north above North Square, in 1938. Although the bus looks like it is traveling on the trolley tracks, they have actually been paved over, and the overhead wire, which supplied power to the trolley cars, is no longer in place.

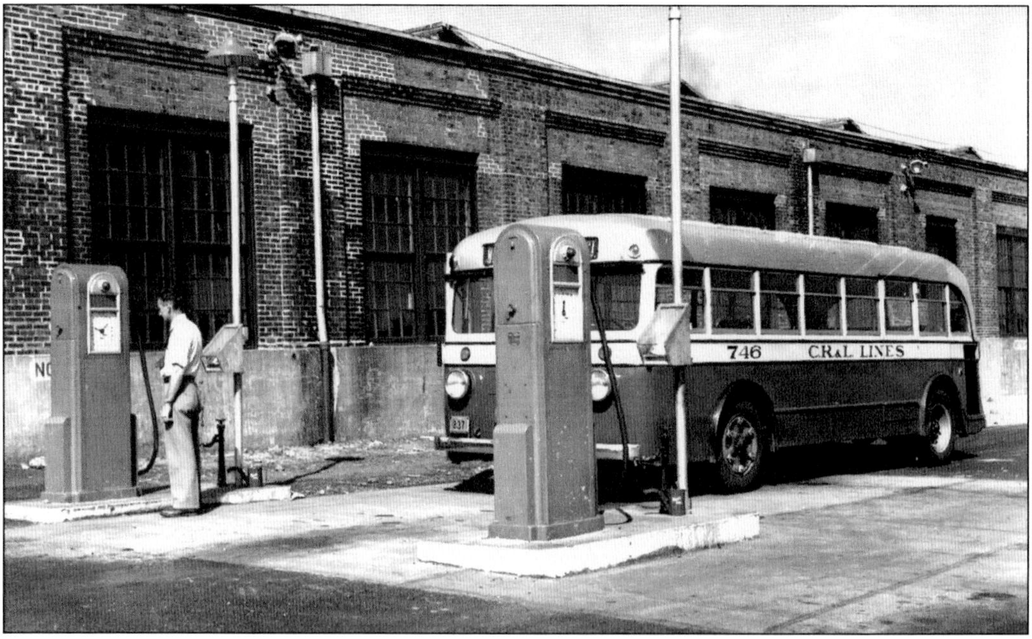

The changeover from trolley car service to bus service also necessitated a change in fuel source. While the trolley car used electricity supplied by the overhead wire for its power, and could run all day without stopping for fuel, the buses used gasoline, which meant stopping to fill up two or more times a day. The bus company had fuel islands, like this one, installed at the former carbarns to provide gasoline for the buses.

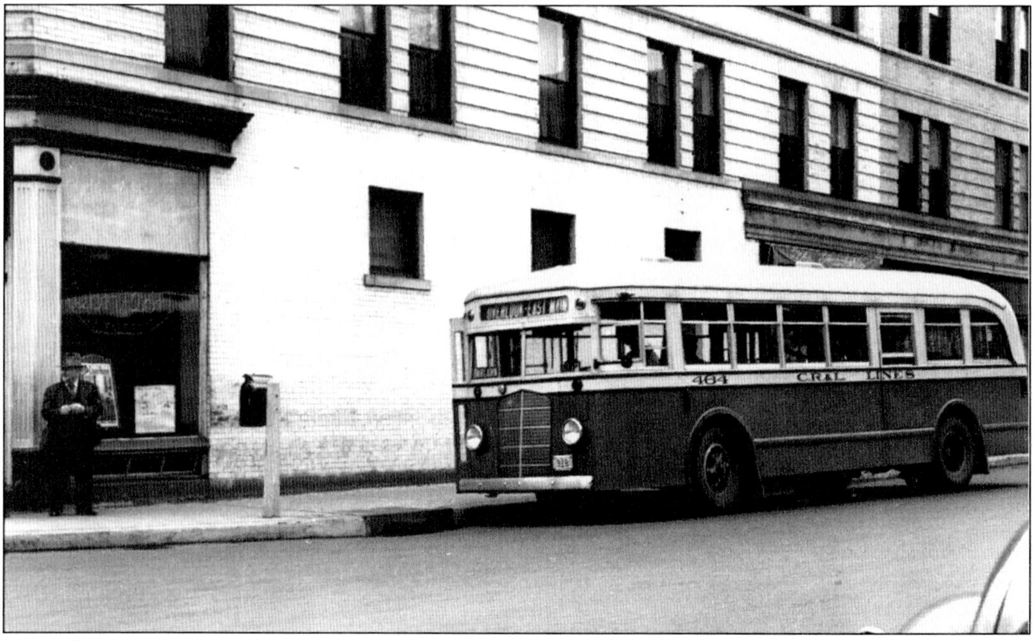

This 1936 ACF motor coach, one of the buses purchased to replace the streetcars in Waterbury, exemplifies the progression from the style and size of the early motor coaches toward the more modern buses of today. The Hotel Waterbury is in the background, at the corner of West Main and Willow Streets, in this 1939 view.

Three

WATERBURY SUBURBAN LINES

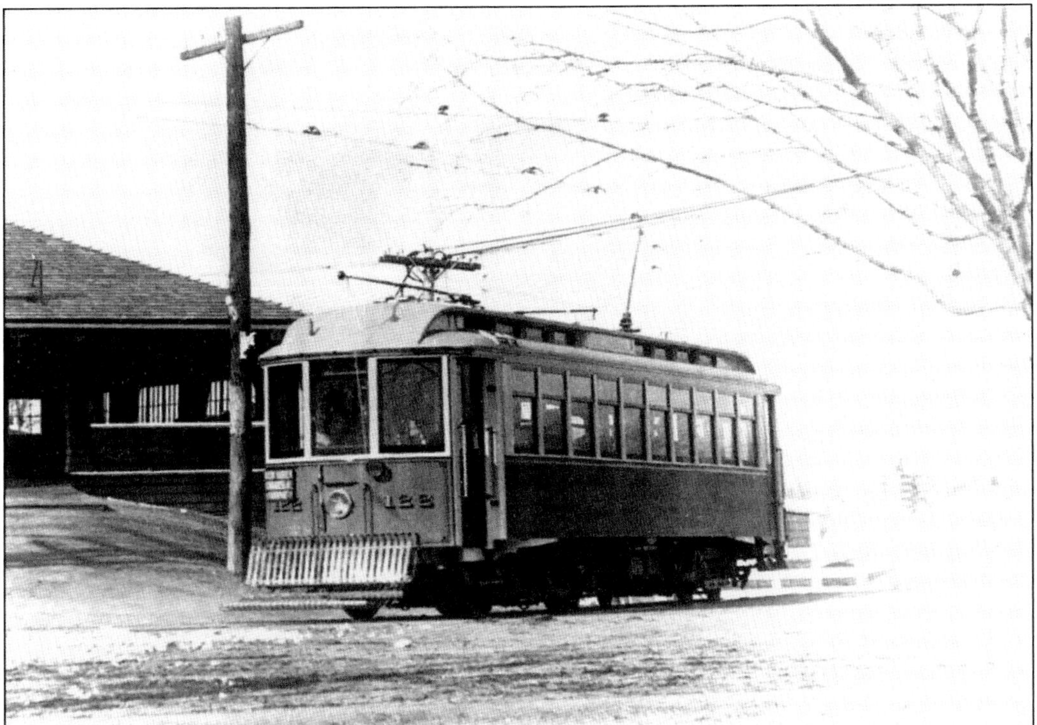

Cheshire Junction is the scene of this 1914 photograph. Car 122 is en route to New Haven, rounding the curve from the Waterbury line onto the line from Milldale to New Haven. This was a major transfer point for passengers traveling by streetcar from Waterbury to New Britain and New Haven.

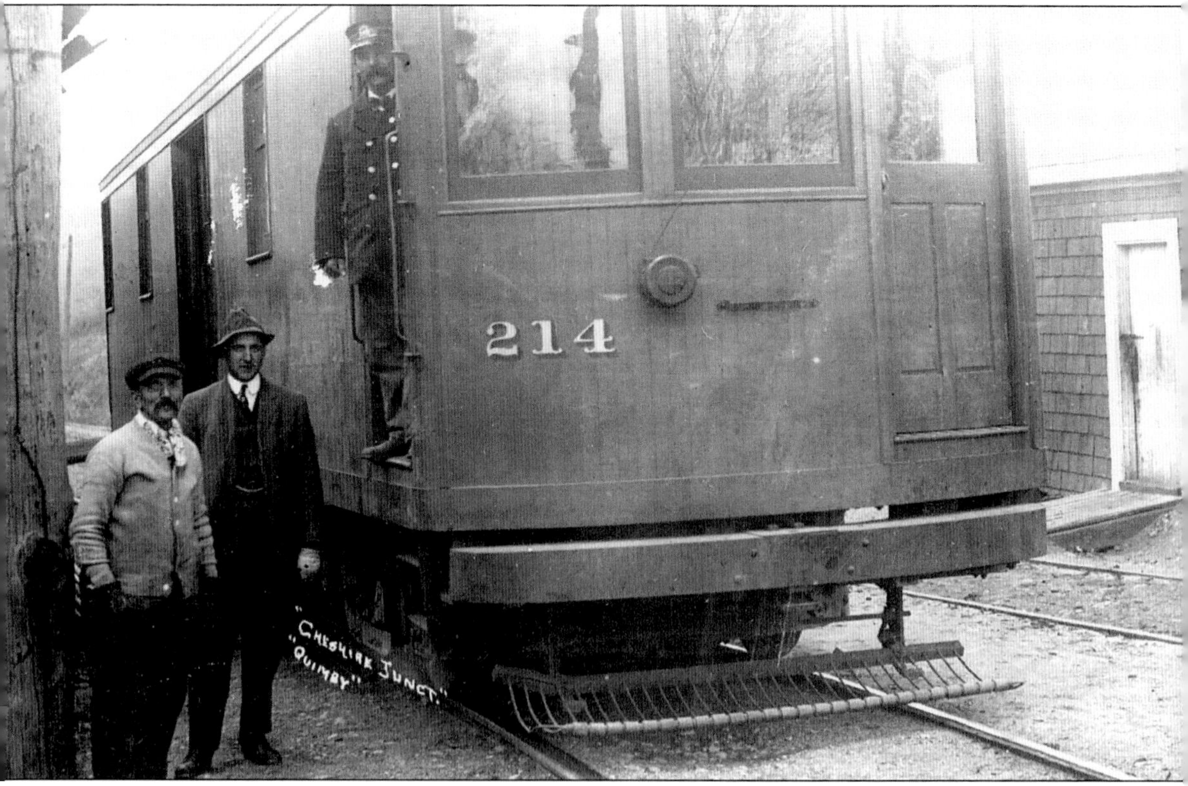

Here is a 1912 view of express car 214 at Cheshire Junction, where the line from Waterbury met the north–south line that ran from New Britain to New Haven. Express packages and less-than-carload (LCL) freight were handled in box motors like 214, while closed-pouch mail and newspapers were normally carried on the platform of passenger cars. In 1909 the company reported that the express business had doubled since 1907; milk, meat, and metal products were the primary freight that was handled, including more than 200 cans of milk a day transported from Woodbury to Waterbury and New Haven.

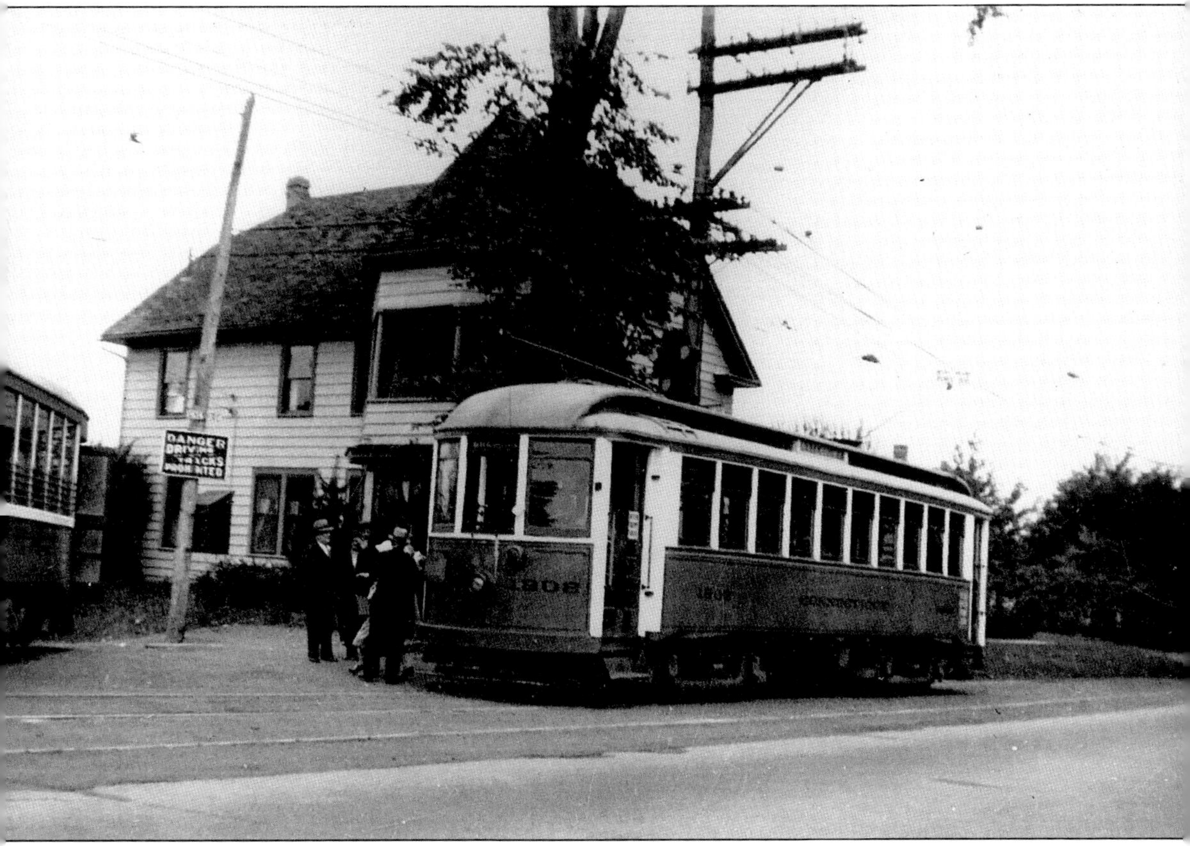

Here is a picture of Cheshire Junction taken in 1932. The line from Waterbury only had streetcar service until August 1934; motor coach operation began the next day. The line from New Britain had already been converted to motor coach in 1931.

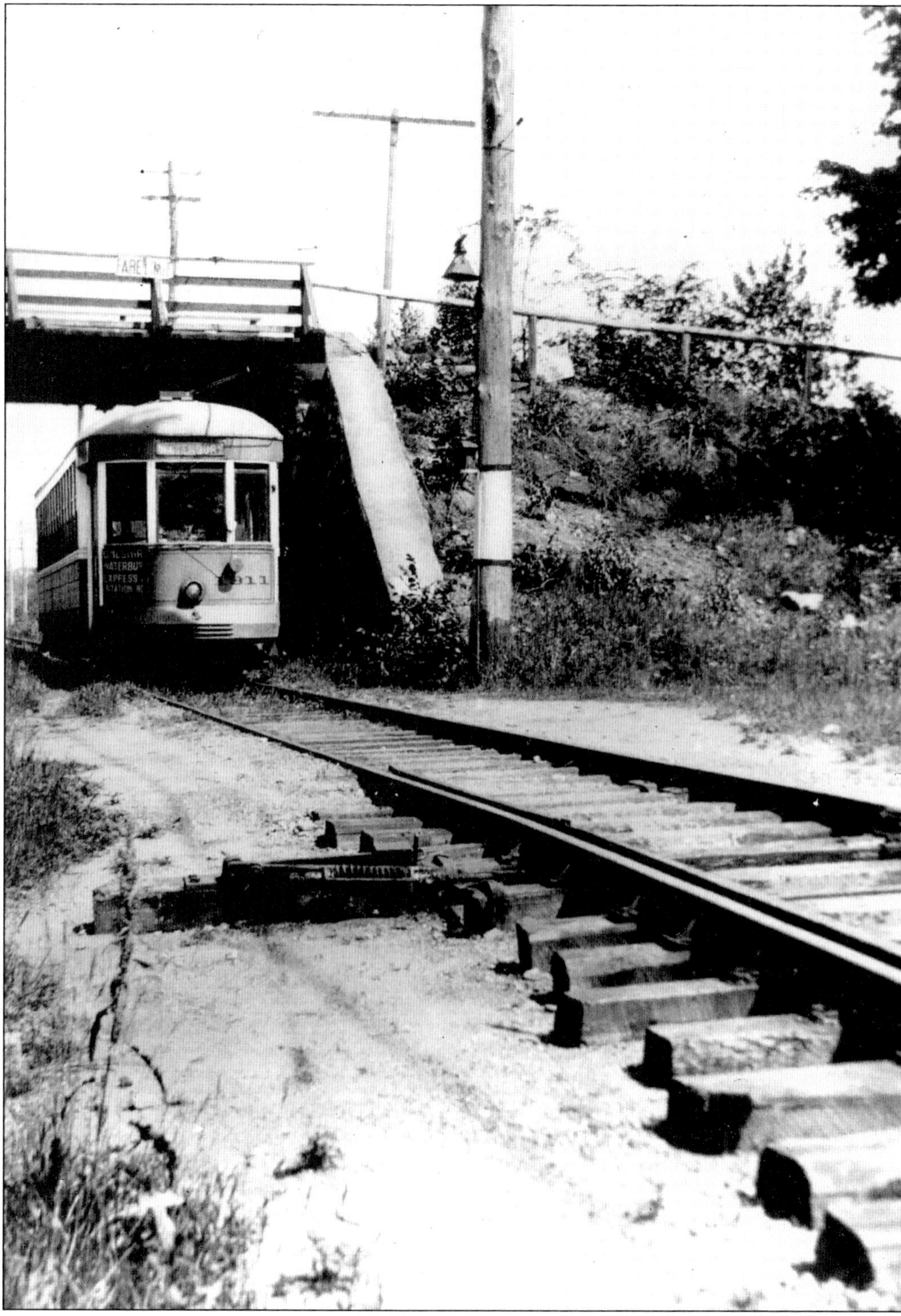

Here is Waterbury-bound car 1911 on the Cheshire line in 1934, the last year of streetcar operation here.

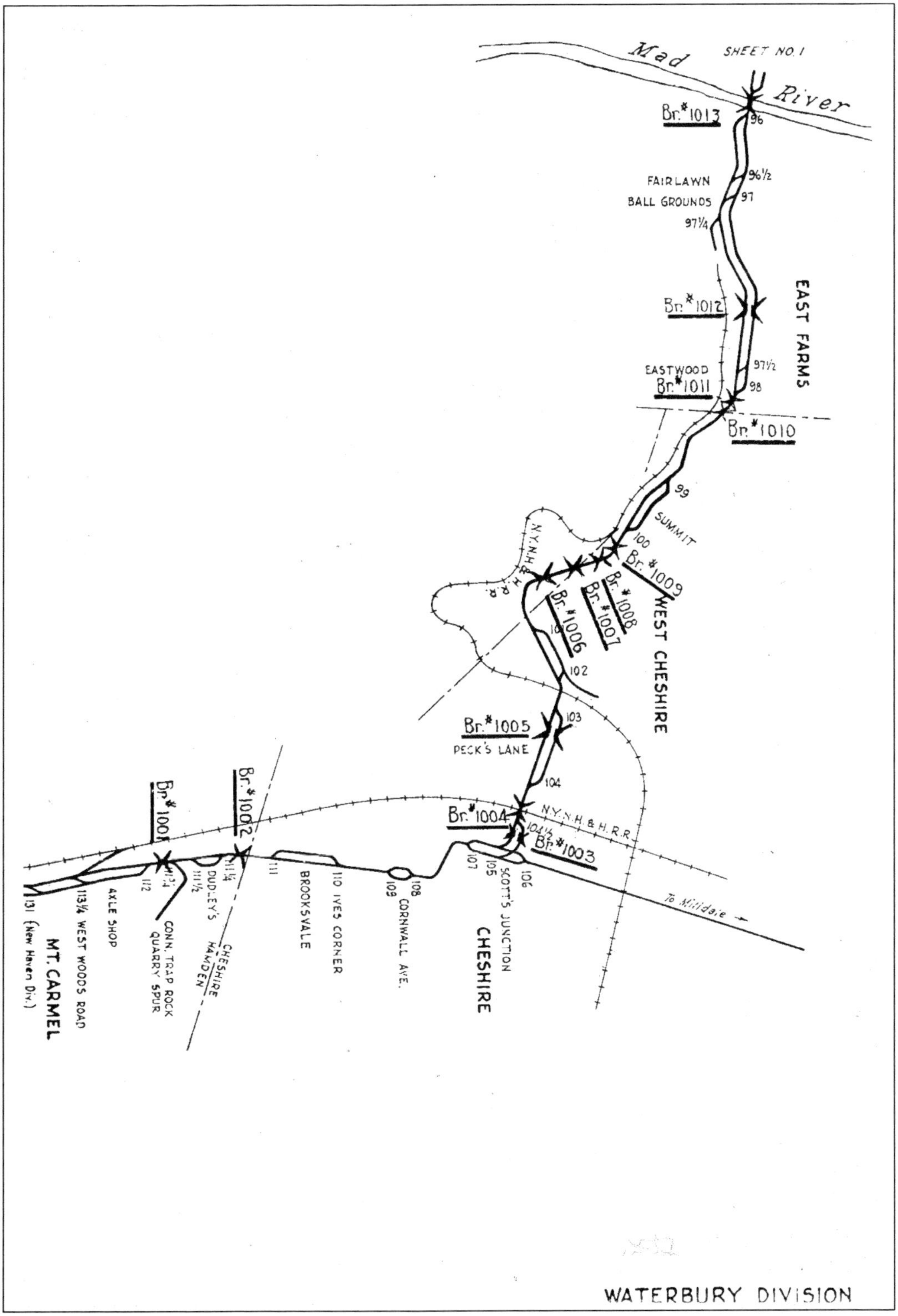

A 1920 map of the Cheshire line is pictured here.

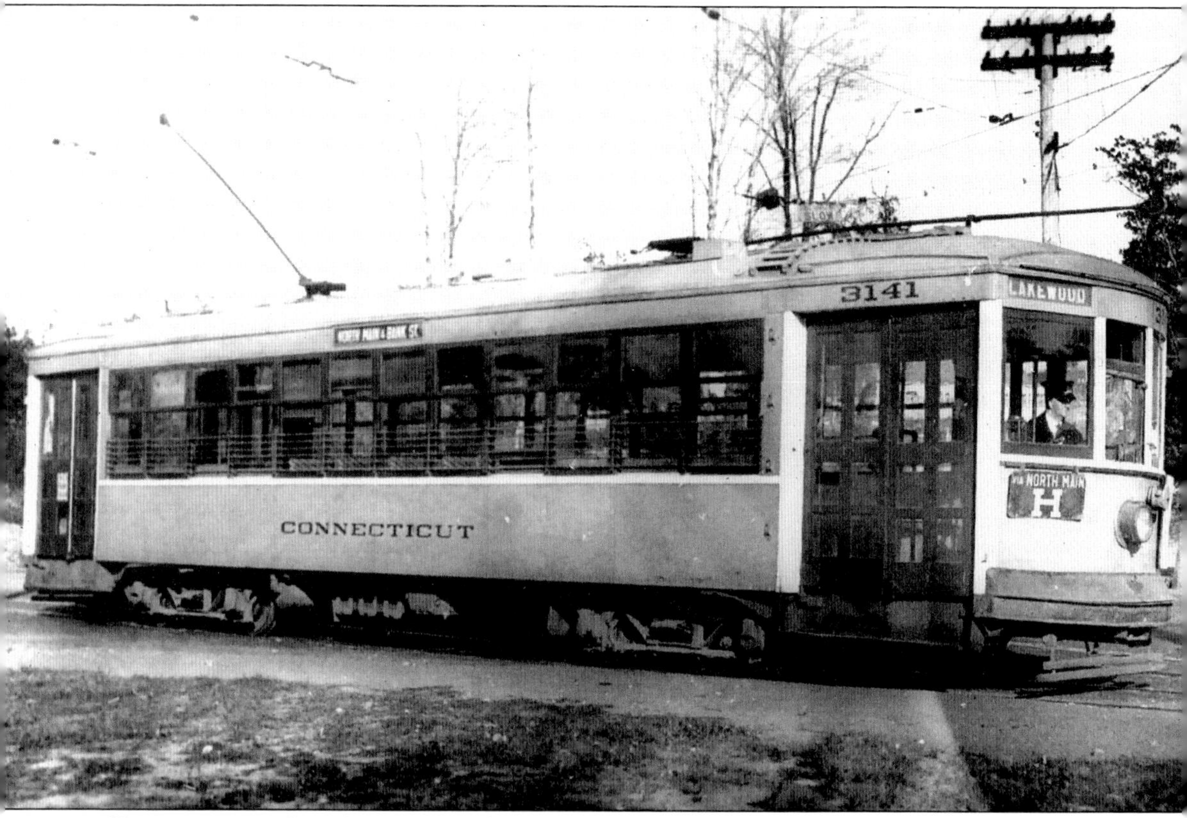

Here is a view of car 3141 on North Main Street at Lakewood Road. The 3100s were all-steel cars purchased from Osgood Bradley Company in 1923. When the remaining Waterbury lines were converted to motor coach in 1937, twenty-three of the 3100s, including No. 3141, were sold to Third Avenue Railways in New York. Third Avenue scrapped the bodies and used the motors and controls to build new center-entrance cars for use on the Broadway line.

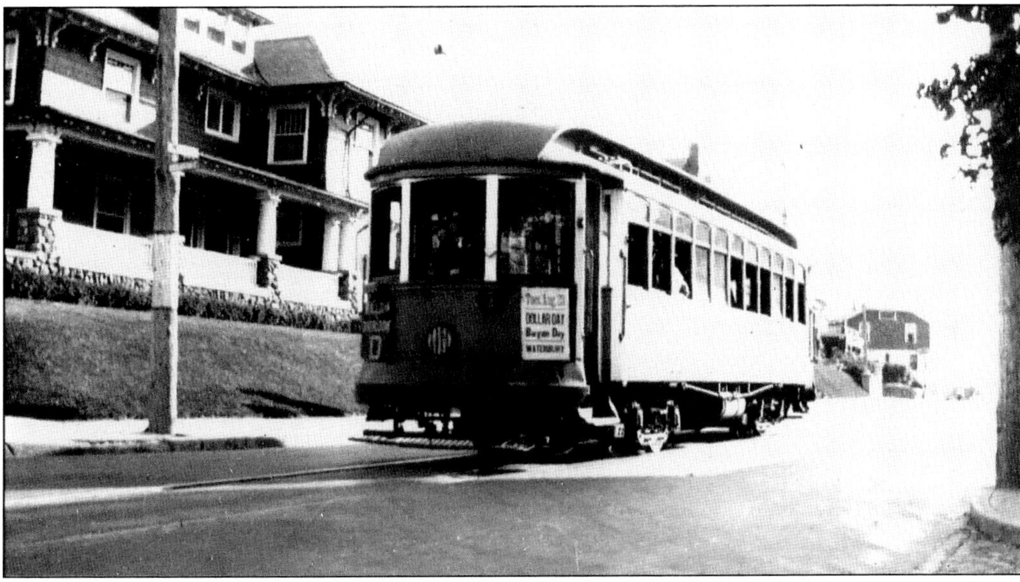

An older wooden car is shown running outbound on Willow Street en route to Waterville. In 1909 cars No. 45 and No. 79 collided on Willow Street. The accident was attributed to the fact that No. 45 only had hand brakes. This started the controversy over the need to install air brakes on the streetcars.

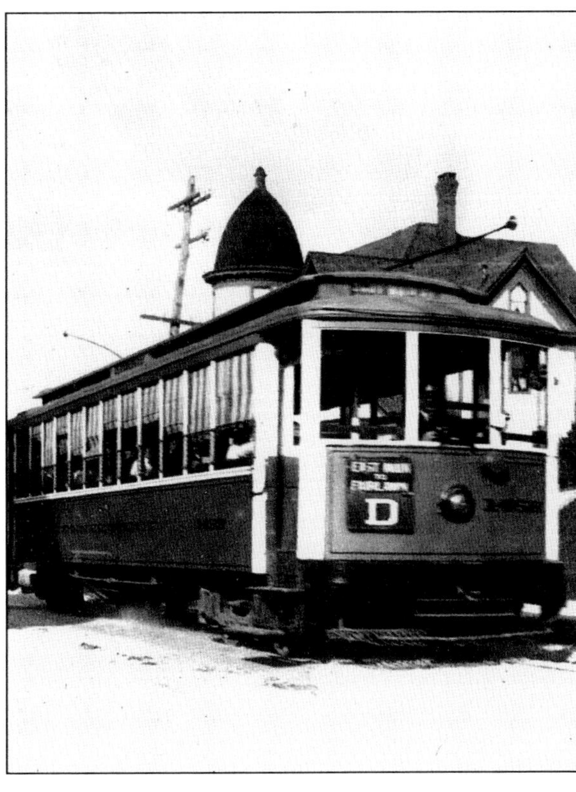

Car 1458 was originally an open car built in 1911. It was converted into a closed car by the Waterbury shops in 1920.

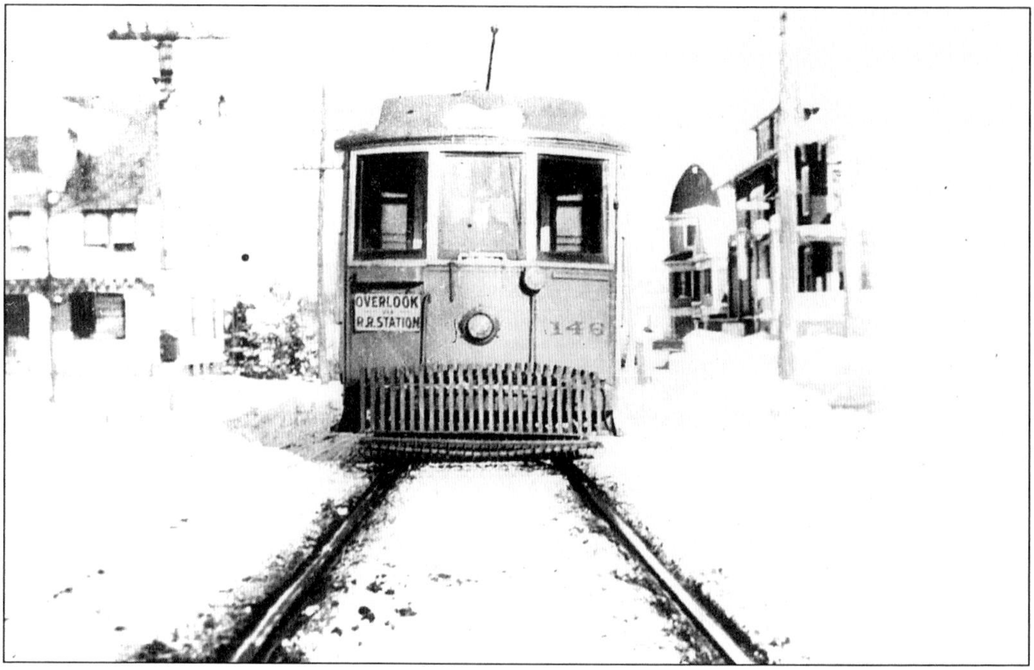

Here is a 1915 scene on the Overlook line.

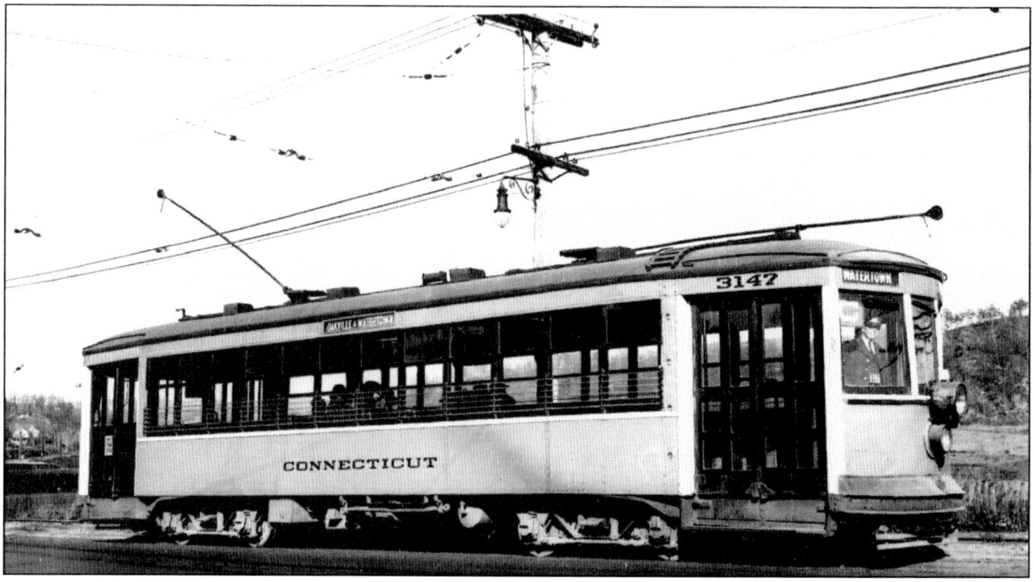

The 3100-series cars were the backbone of the Waterbury division in the 1930s. These cars had seating for 50 passengers and standing room for another 50 passengers; this was twice the capacity of the average bus in the 1930s.

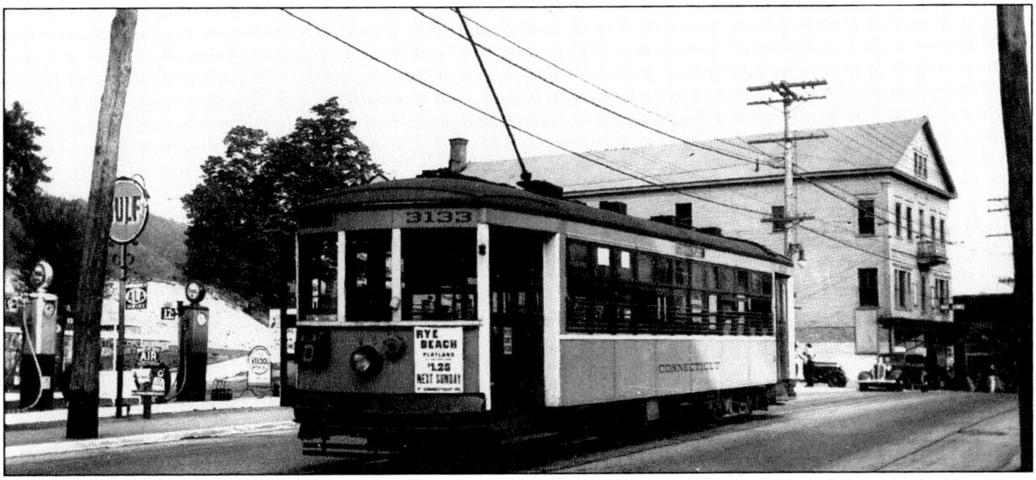

Car 3133 would soon get new lettering; on November 15, 1936, the Connecticut Company turned over all operations to the Connecticut Railway and Lighting Company that it had originally leased in 1906. Car No. 3133 was one of the cars sold to Third Avenue Railways in 1937.

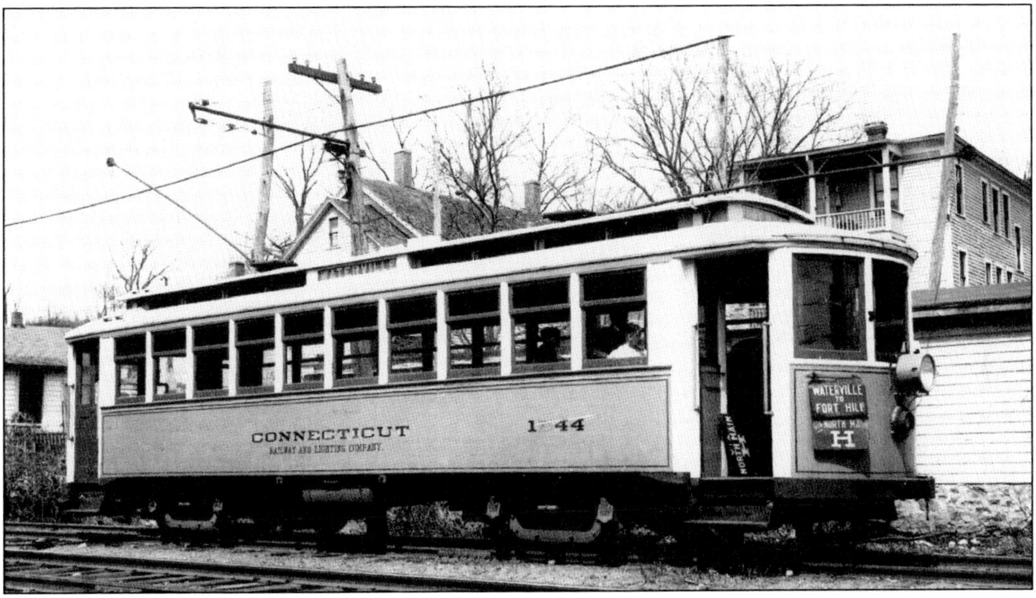

Here we see car 1544 lettered for Connecticut Railway and Lighting. By May 1937 the Waterville line was converted to motor coach.

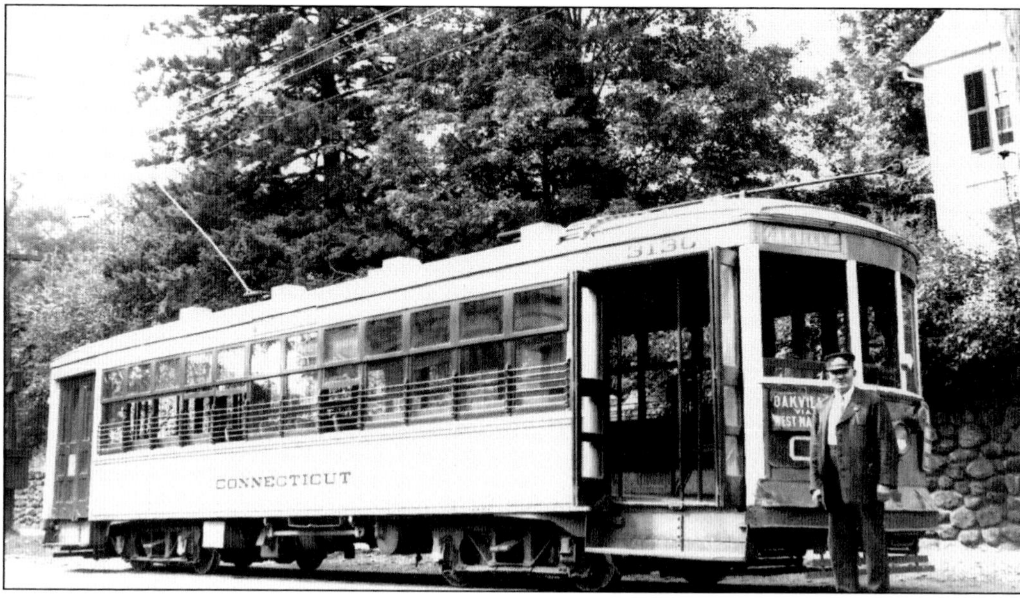

In the early 1920s the Connecticut Company began a program to convert all closed cars to single-man operation; the "operator" would perform the duties of both conductor and motorman. Open cars, when they were used, still required a two-man crew.

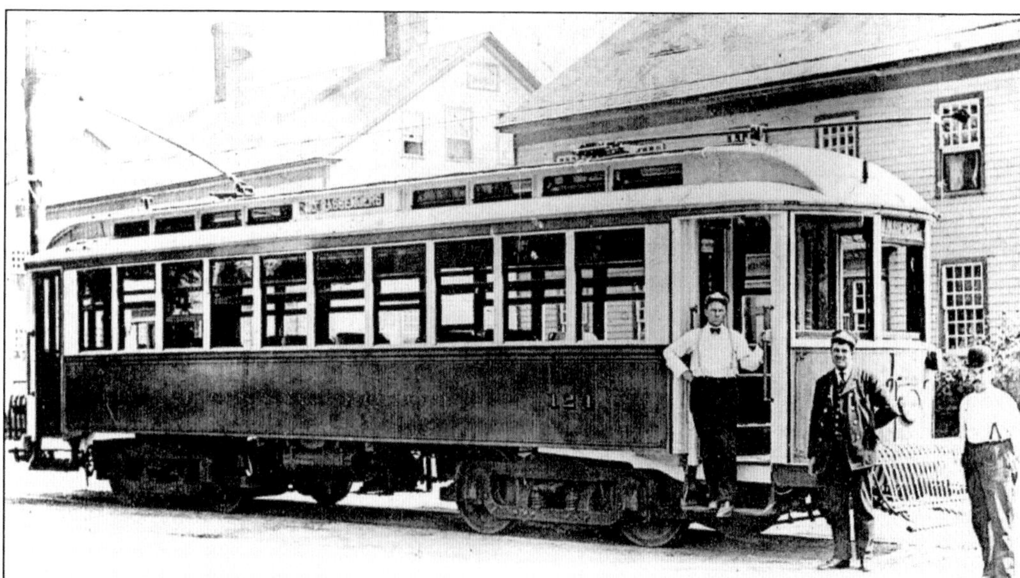

Here is a view of car 124 on the first trip to Thomaston on August 3, 1908. The line to Thomaston was an extension of the Waterville line. Hourly service was provided. This line was originally projected by the Thomaston Tramway Company, but was built by the Connecticut Company. The line ran up the Naugatuck Valley, through Waterville, to Reynolds Bridge and Thomaston. The contractor for the construction was F. T. Ley & Company of Springfield, Massachusetts.

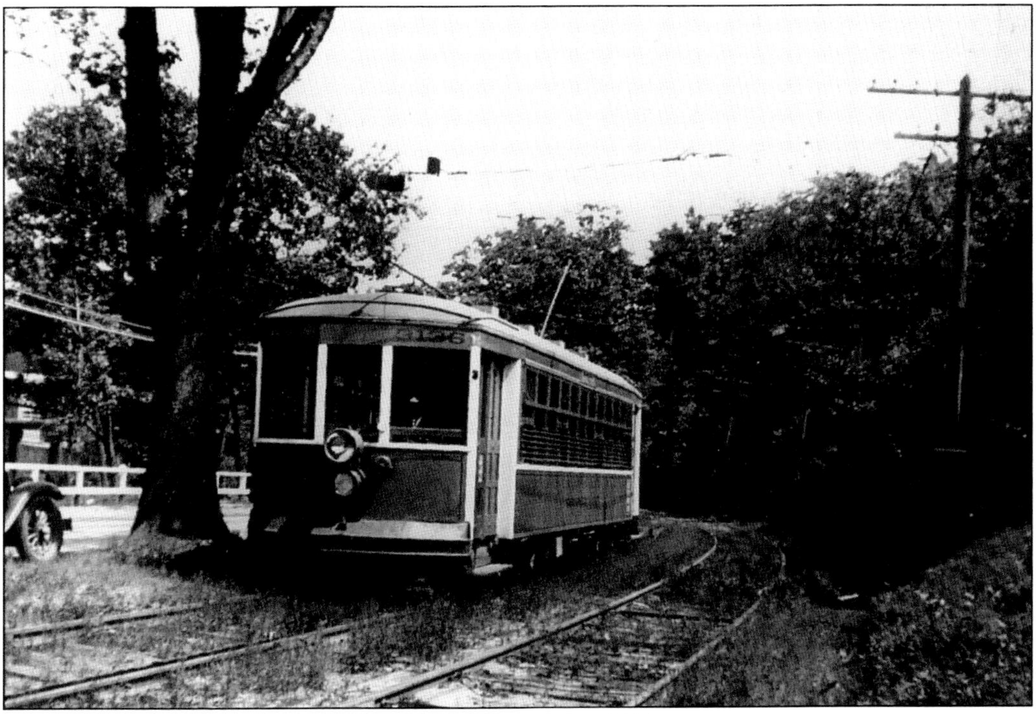

Here is Woodruff's Turnout, on the Waterville line, in 1931.

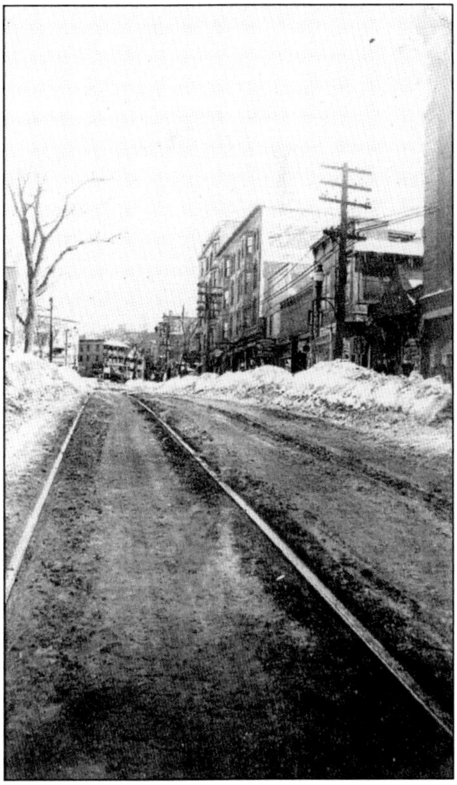

A 1914 view of North Main Street near Spark Street is shown here. Not a car in sight today.

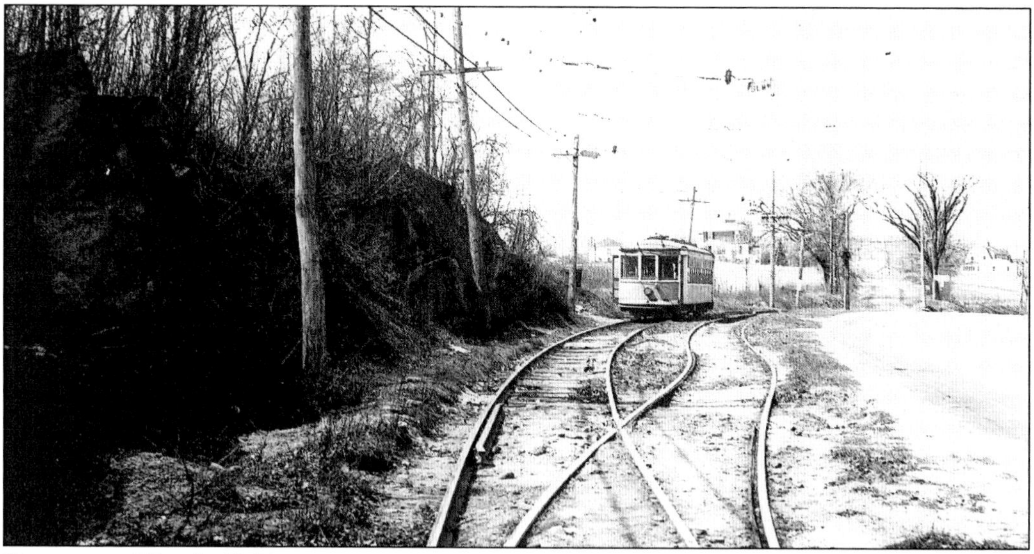

Here we see Woodruff's Turnout in 1937, just a month before the conversion to buses. Operating expenses to run streetcars climbed considerably after 1920; all the materials and services needed to run streetcars could not be offset with fare increases. By 1920 the fare for most rides had increased 50 percent or more; labor and coal costs had increased by 100 percent or more. Buses, on the other hand, did not require the vast infrastructure required for streetcar operation. Buses cost more per mile to operate, but they ran on public highways.

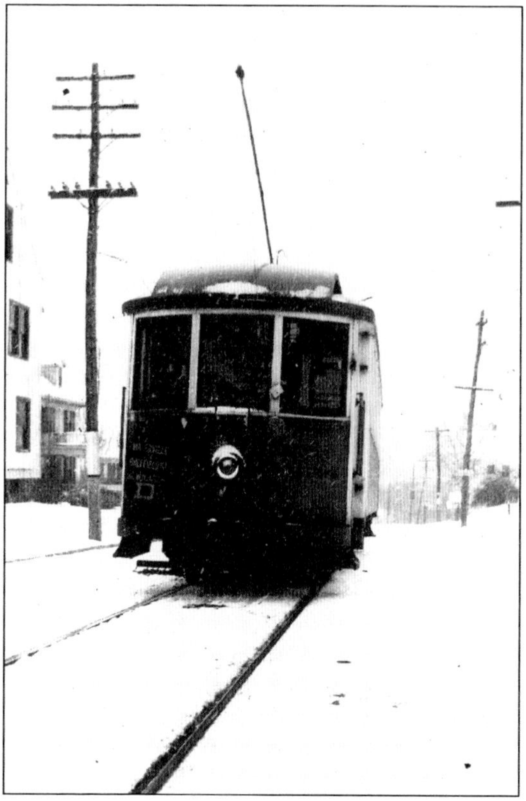

Here is car 1524 on the Waterville line in 1927. The old, heavyweight wooden passenger cars could operate even in deep snow, while the newer lightweight cars, such as the 2300 series, would get stuck in just two inches of snow.

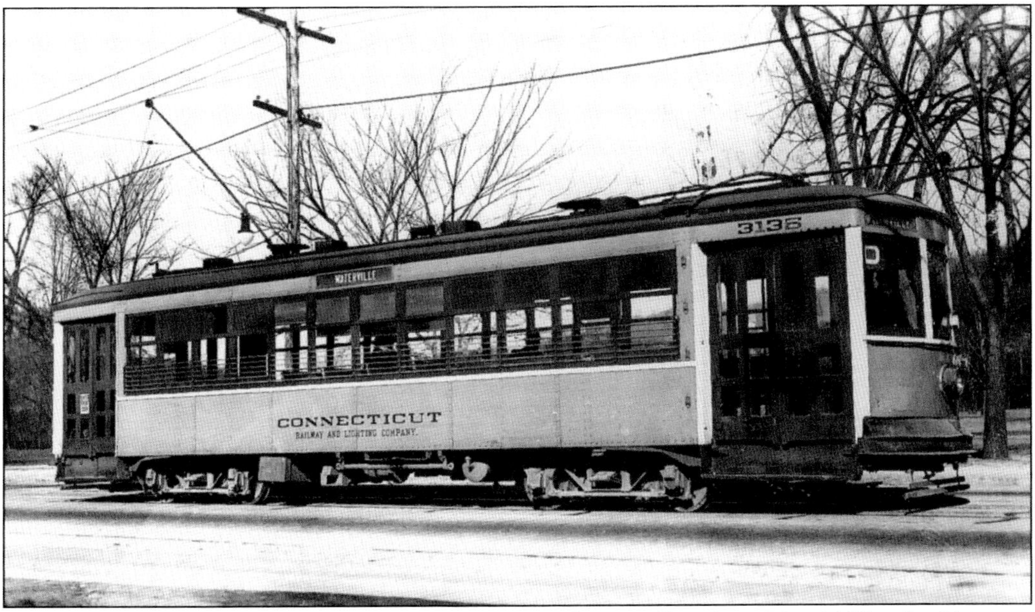

Third Avenue Railways used the trucks, motors, and controllers from No. 3135 to build a new car in its shops in 1937. Connecticut Railway and Lighting had no interest in operating a street railway. The company did not want to be in the bus business either, but the bankruptcy of the Connecticut Company in 1935 forced Connecticut Railway and Lighting to take back its transit properties in Bridgeport, New Britain, and Waterbury. This picture was taken in February 1937 on Thomaston Avenue opposite Waterville Green in Waterbury.

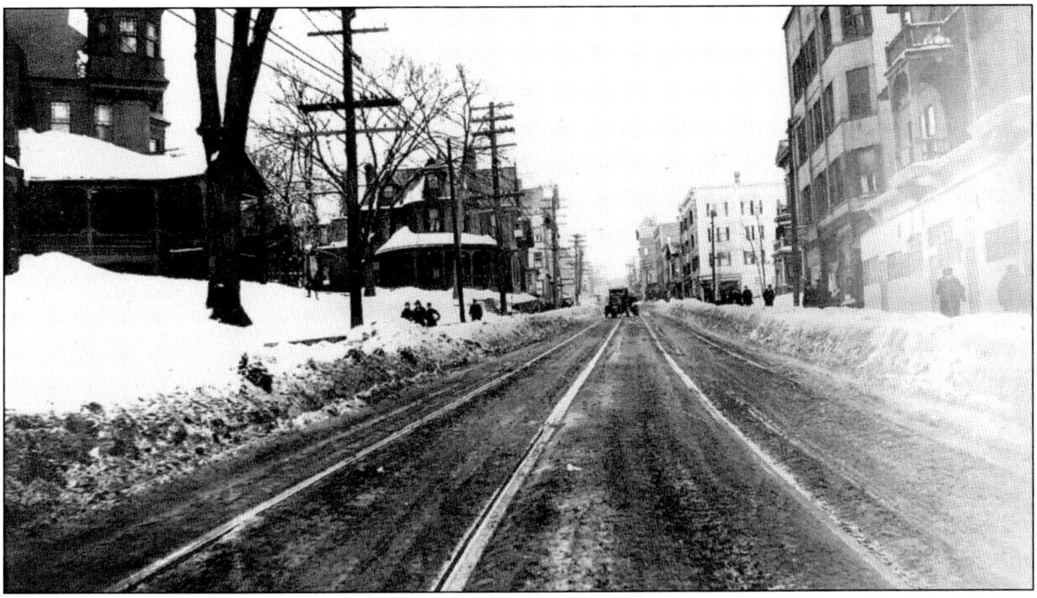

Here is a winter view of North Main Street near Spencer Avenue in 1914. The "bulldog" Mack truck in the distance is probably delivering a load of anthracite coal to one of the buildings in the picture. Coal was the primary heating fuel in the Northeast well into the 1950s.

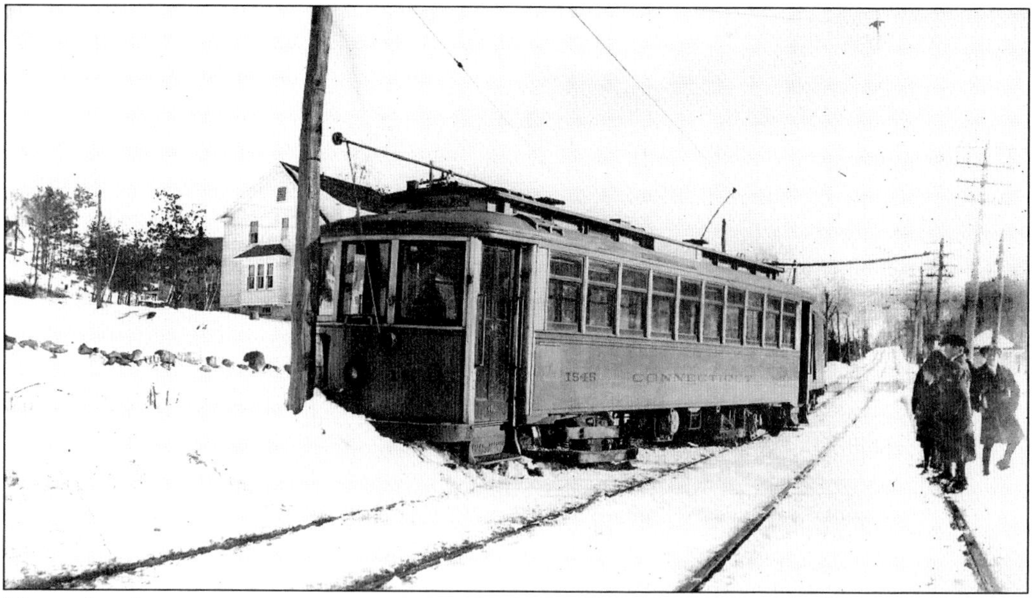
Minor derailments were a common event in the streetcar days, especially during the winter, when cars ran up on ice. In this scene from 1920, it looks like the wooden pole stopped the forward motion of car 1545 on the Overlook line.

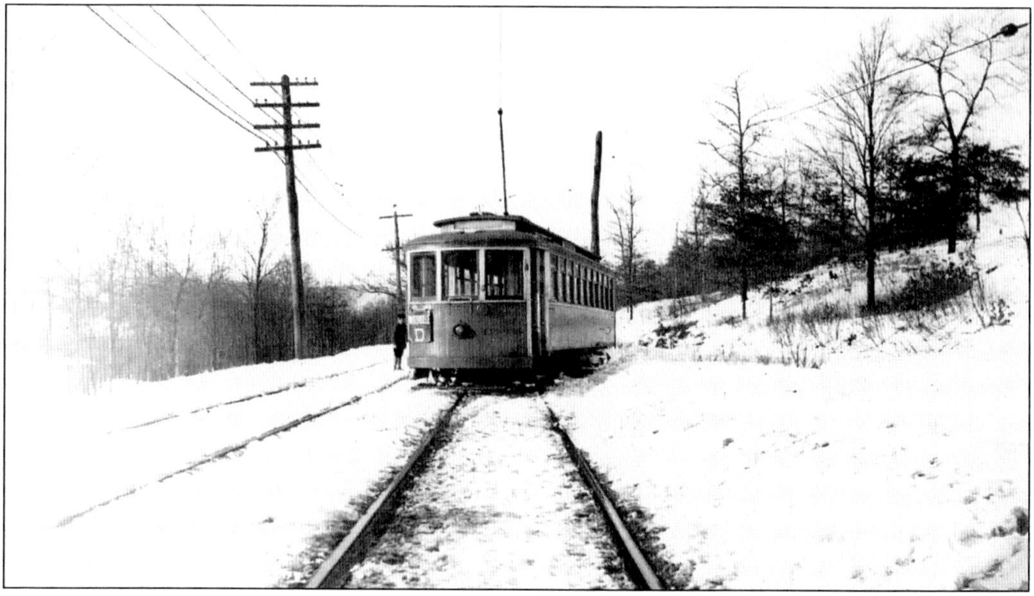
This view reveals how far off the track the car 1545 was. The shop crew from the Waterbury carbarn would make short work of this minor derailment. Typically a car like 0205, shown on page 54, would respond to such an incident with some of the car shop crew and all the jacks and other tools required for the job.

Here is an open car, traveling inbound toward Waterbury on the Woodbury line, in 1914. The line was completed on October 20, 1908, and passed through territory still of great natural beauty in 2005. Woodbury, with a 1908 population of 4,500, was six miles from the nearest steam railroad. The fare in 1915 was 25¢, and the trip took an hour from Exchange Place in Waterbury to the end of the line in Woodbury. The line was built to very high standards for a streetcar line and ran almost exclusively on private right-of-way.

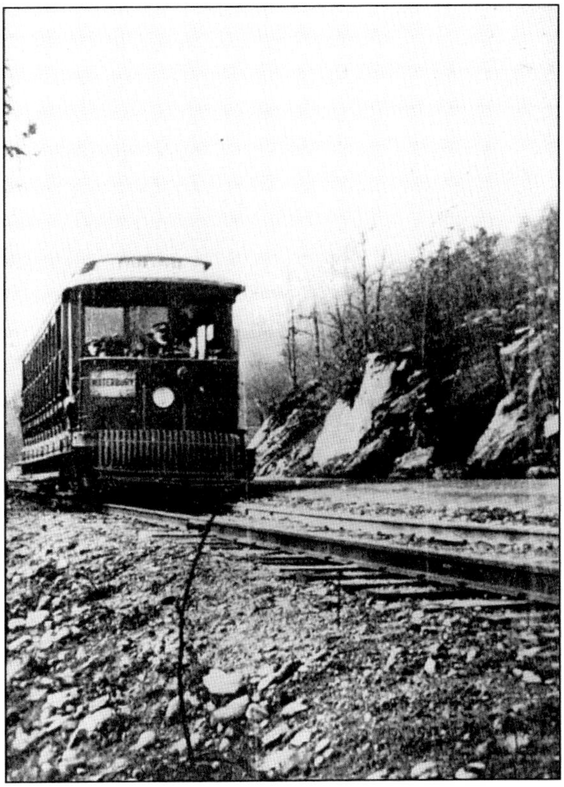

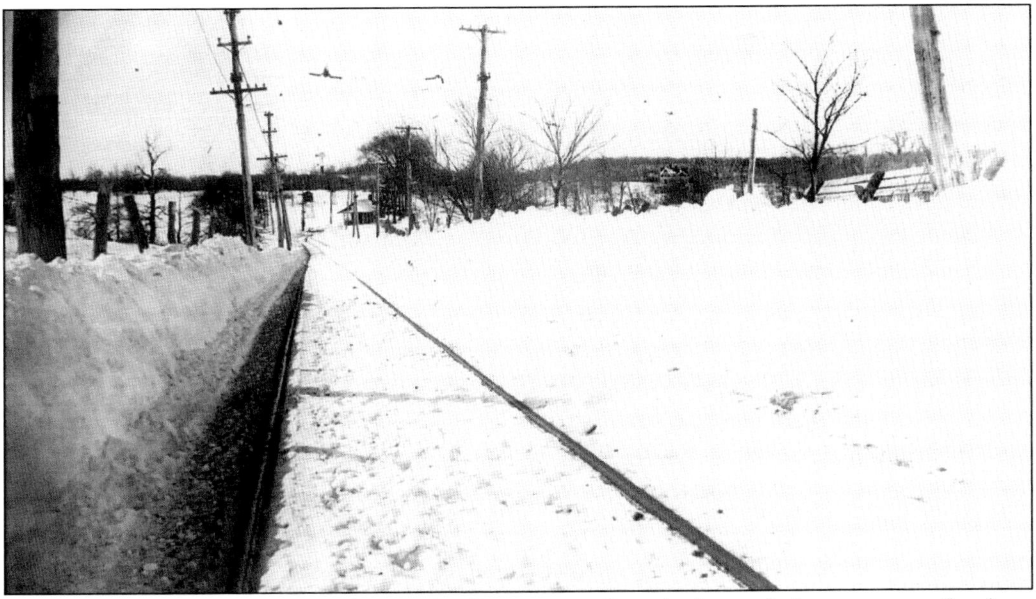

In this view we see the approach to Lake Quassapaug Switch, located about seven miles from downtown Waterbury. In the summer months cars operated from Waterbury every 30 minutes; winter months saw hourly service.

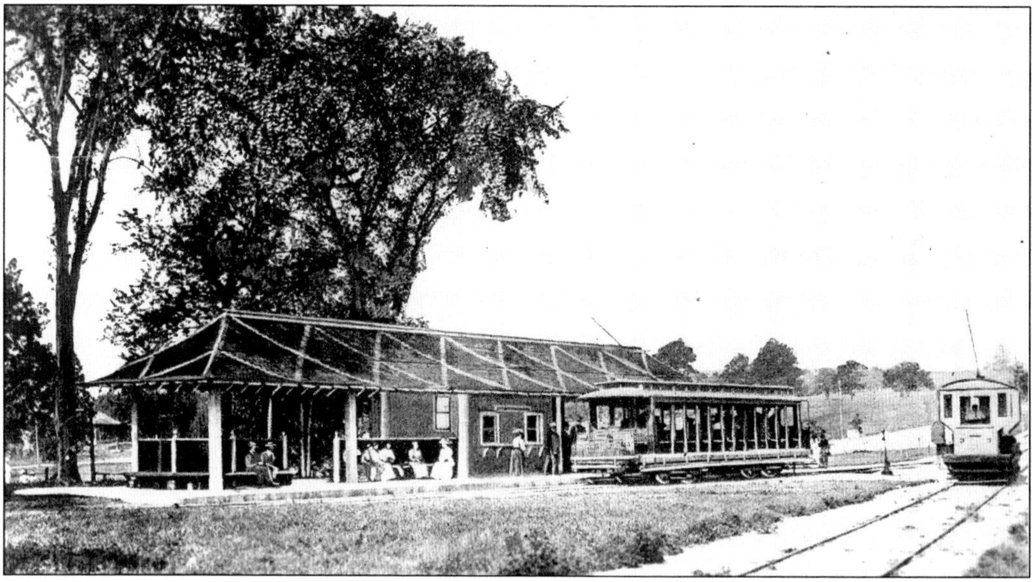

Here is a 1908 view of the Lake Quassapaug trolley station, with its unusual Japanese pagoda roof. The Connecticut Company developed the park here, which, with its famous lake (a mile square), was a welcome destination to Waterbury's population of 60,000 residents (in 1908). In 1910 a dance pavilion was built to supplement the picnic grove and swimming area. A loop was constructed in front of the park to handle the heavy traffic in the summer months. During the winter months hourly service was provided by two combination cars that could handle passengers, pouched mail, and small packages.

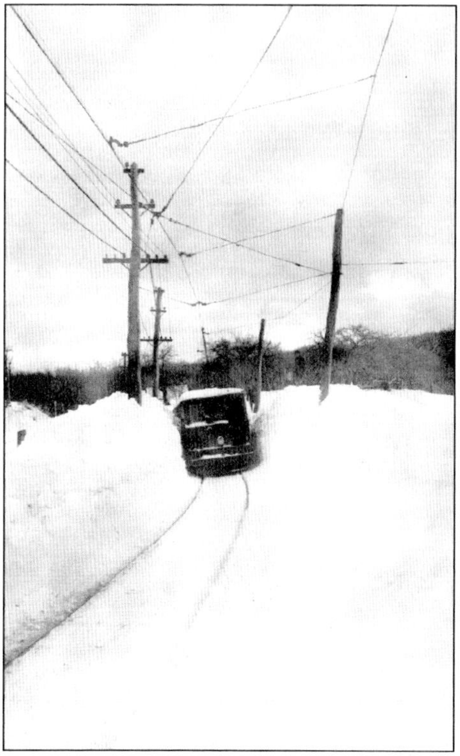

Here is an express car running on the Woodbury line in the winter of 1922. Note the height of the snowbanks. During the winter months, the lake provided a major source of income for the Connecticut Company in the form of block ice cut from the lake and shipped by streetcar to icehouses in Waterbury. In the summer months the ice was delivered to homes and businesses—this was before the days of refrigerators.

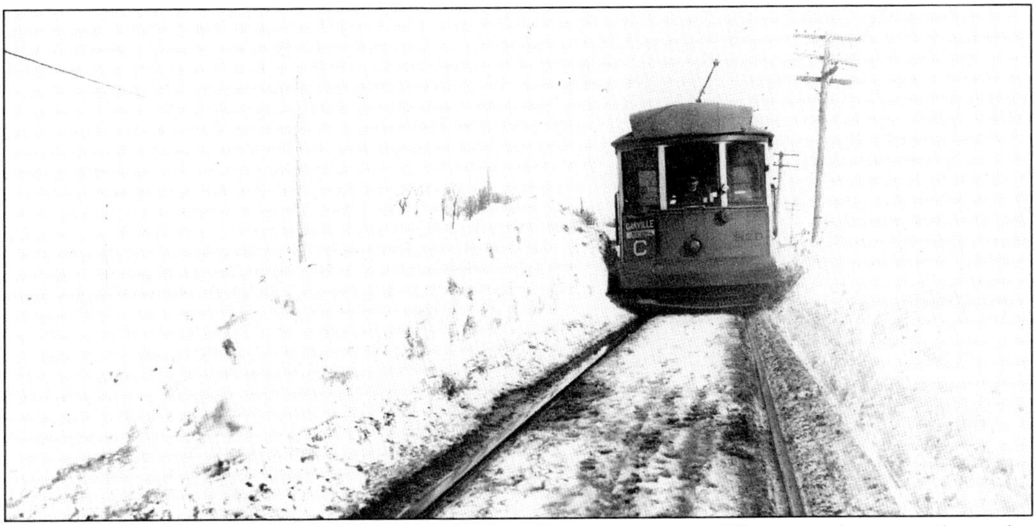

Car 970 is en route to Watertown in this 1922 winter scene. This car also served on the Bridgeport and Derby divisions of the Connecticut Company. Moving cars between divisions was a common practice.

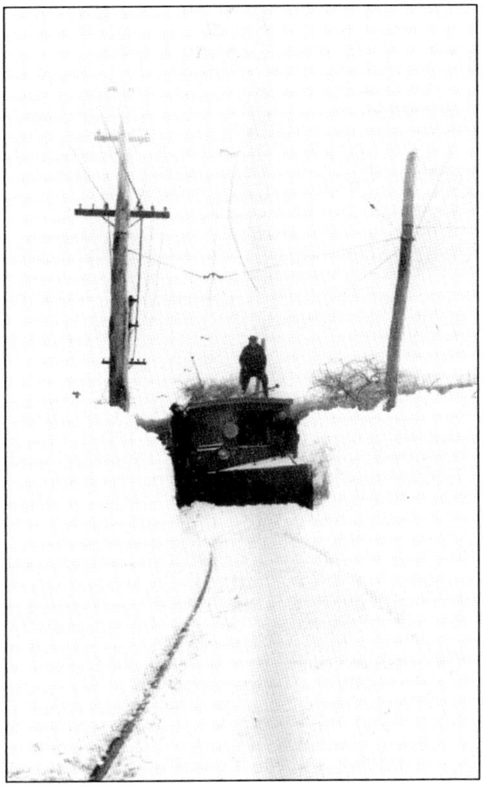

This snow crew is breaking through a snowdrift near Middlebury Station, on the Woodbury line, after the February 4, 1920 storm.

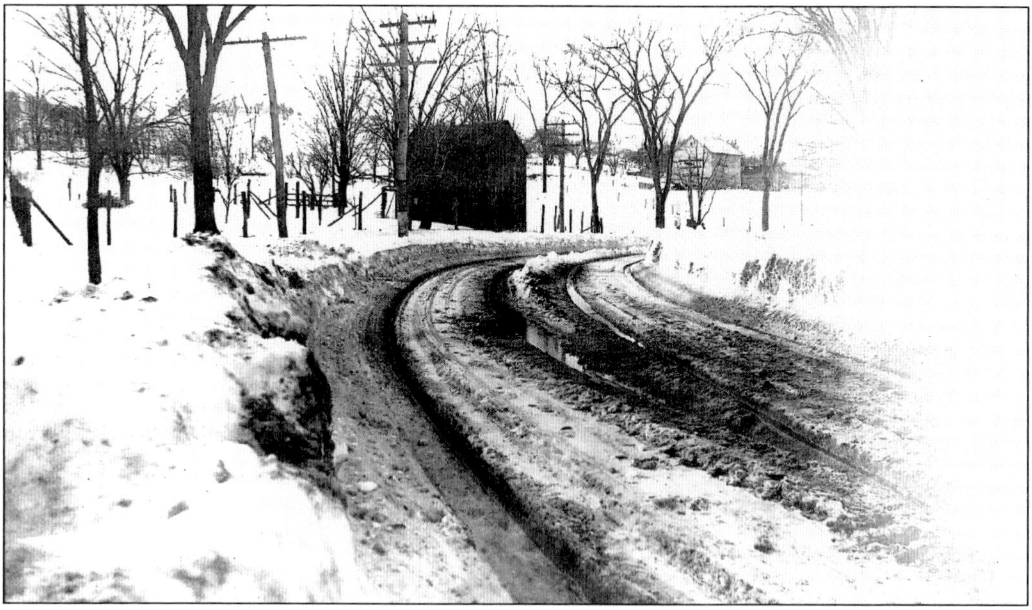

Here is a view of Adts Switch, on the Watertown line, just after the big storm of February 4, 1920.

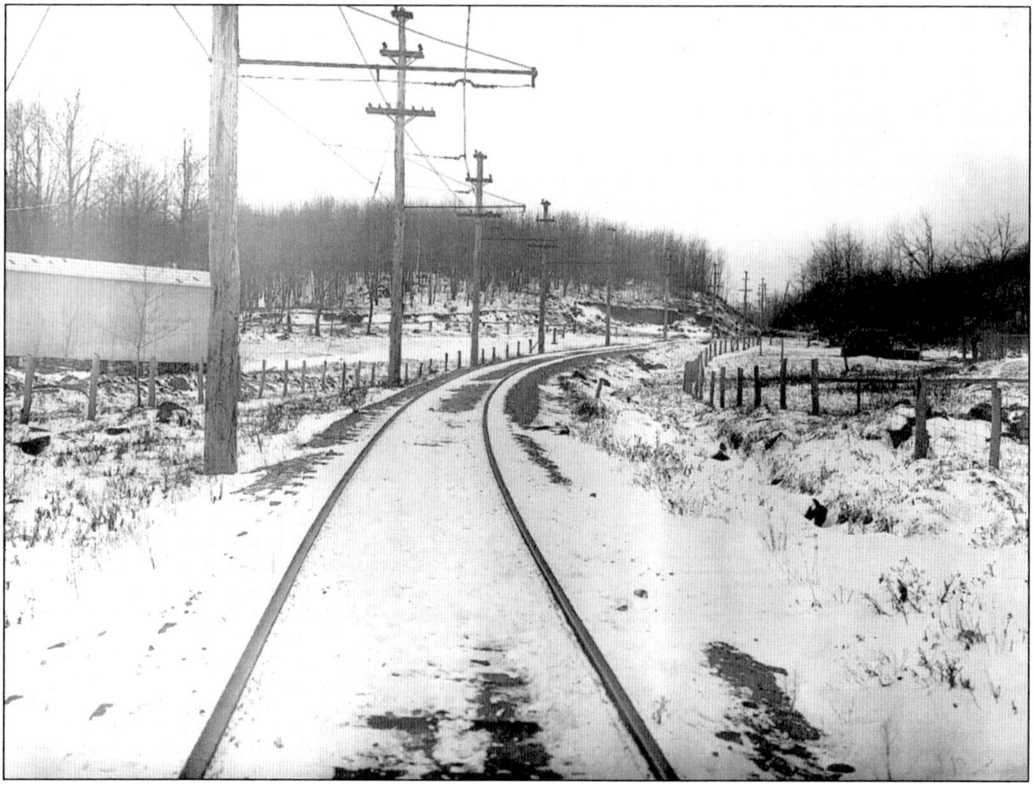

With few stops to be made, the streetcars always moved right along on the private right-of-way on the Woodbury line. A two-mile extension to Hotchkissville was planned but was never built. Public transportation did not come to Hotchkissville until the Woodbury line was motorized on September 28, 1930, and the bus route was extended to the village.

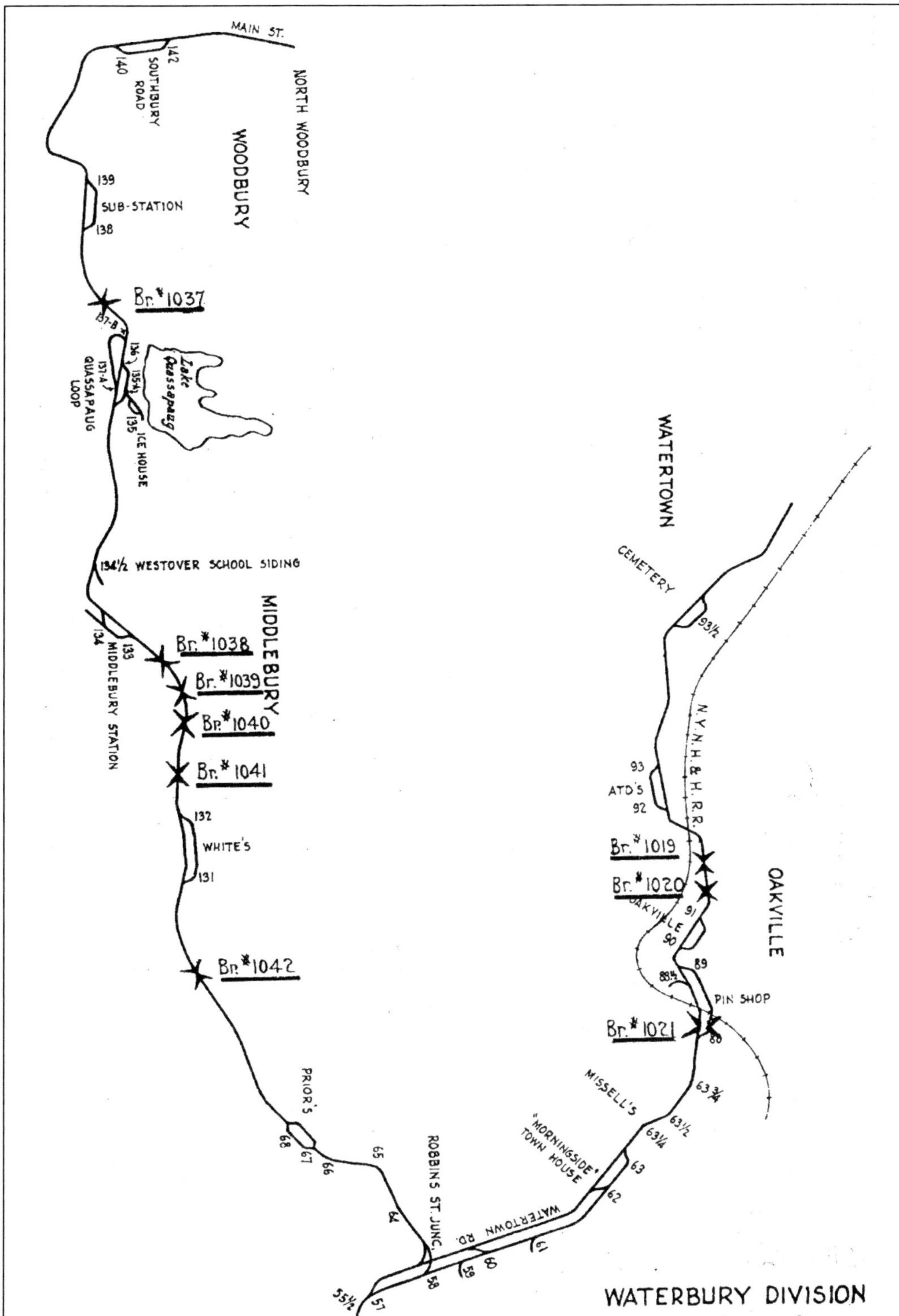

Shown here is a map of the Woodbury and Watertown lines in 1920.

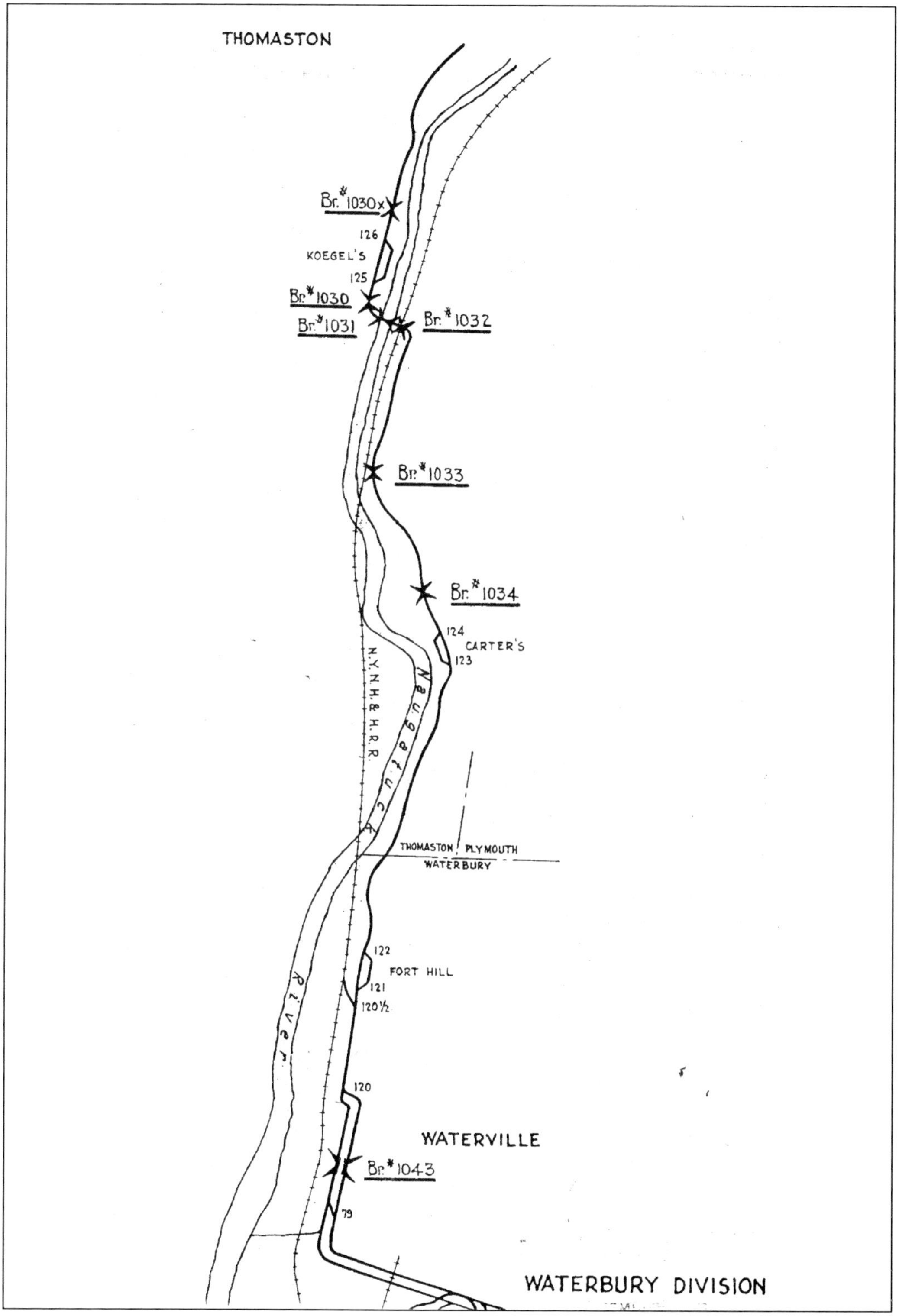

Here is a map of the Thomaston line in 1920.

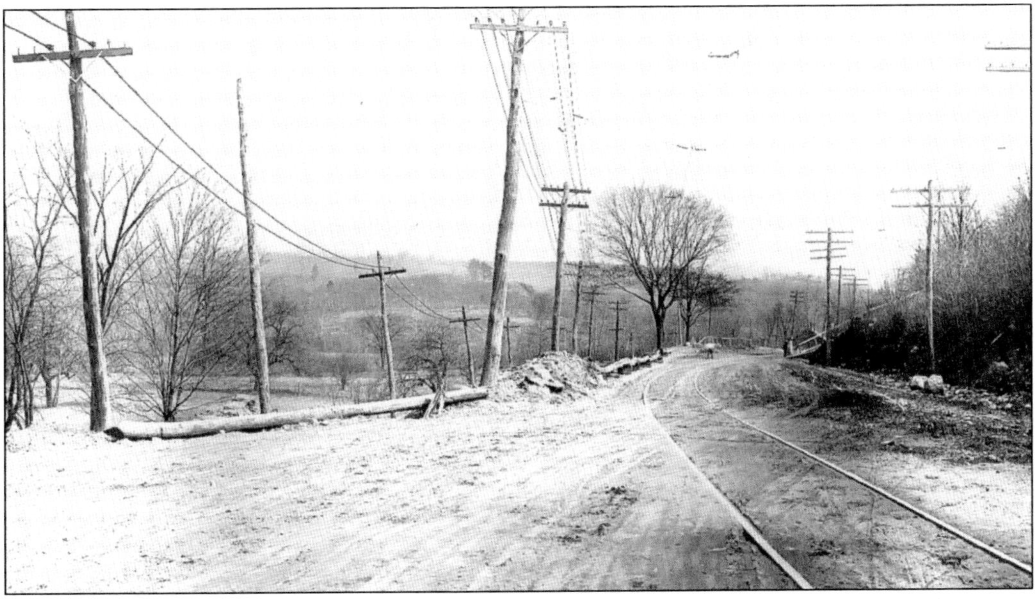

This April 4, 1913 view of the Woodbury line in Middlebury, close to the Waterbury city line, shows the rather primitive roads that early motorists were exposed to. By 1917 the street railway companies had 44,800 miles of track in the United States, employed 295,000 people, and carried 11.3 billion riders annually. In 1923 the ridership climbed to 14 billion annually; however, after 1923, the numbers began to steadily decline and never recovered. As early as 1925, many streetcar companies were looking at motorizing all the lines with low ridership, and leaving only the high-volume routes with streetcar service.

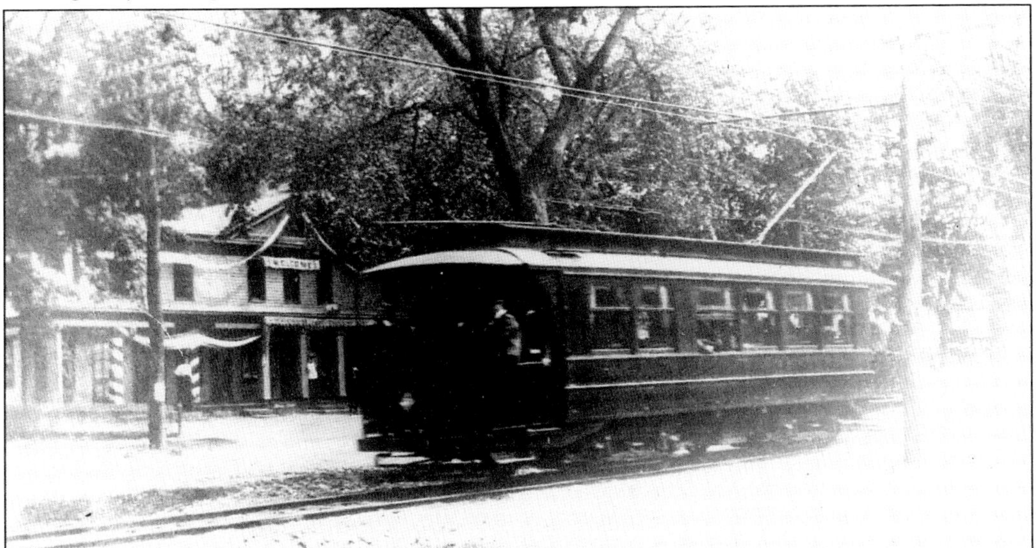

Connecticut Company parlor car 500 is shown in Woodbury in 1914. Note the open platforms; not long after this picture was taken, the car was sent to the Hartford shops to have the ornamental ironwork railings removed and the vestibules enclosed. This car was used all over the Connecticut Company system for line charters and the Public Utilities Commission's yearly line inspections (as required by Connecticut state law). Today car No. 500 is on display at the Shore Line Trolley Museum in East Haven, Connecticut.

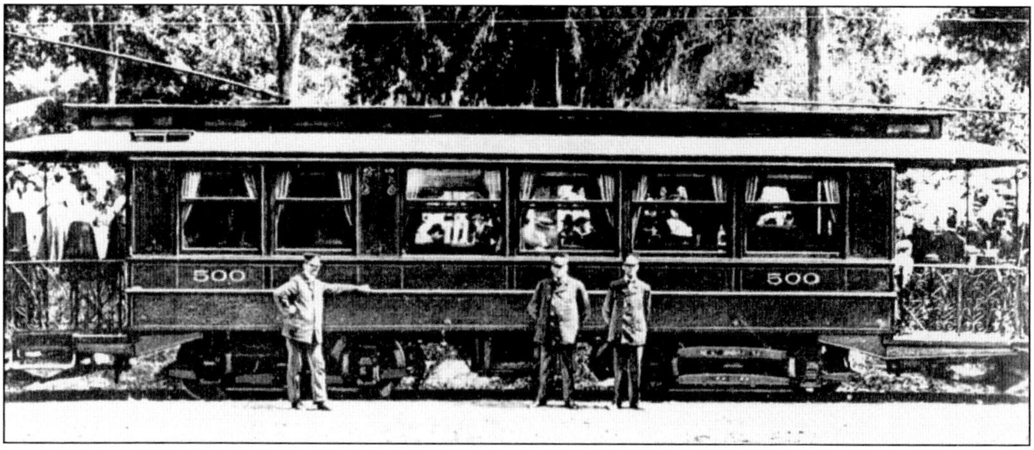

Here is a view of car No. 500 in Woodbury. This car was available for charters—one time it carried a wedding party from New Haven to Meriden. On at least two occasions car 500 transported coffins to the cemetery. The car was originally built in 1903 by J. G. Brill Company of Philadelphia, Pennsylvania, as an inspection car for the Connecticut Railway and Lighting Company, and was taken over by the Connecticut Company in 1907. Seating 35 on wicker armchairs amidst an interior finished in mahogany—this was riding in class 1900s style.

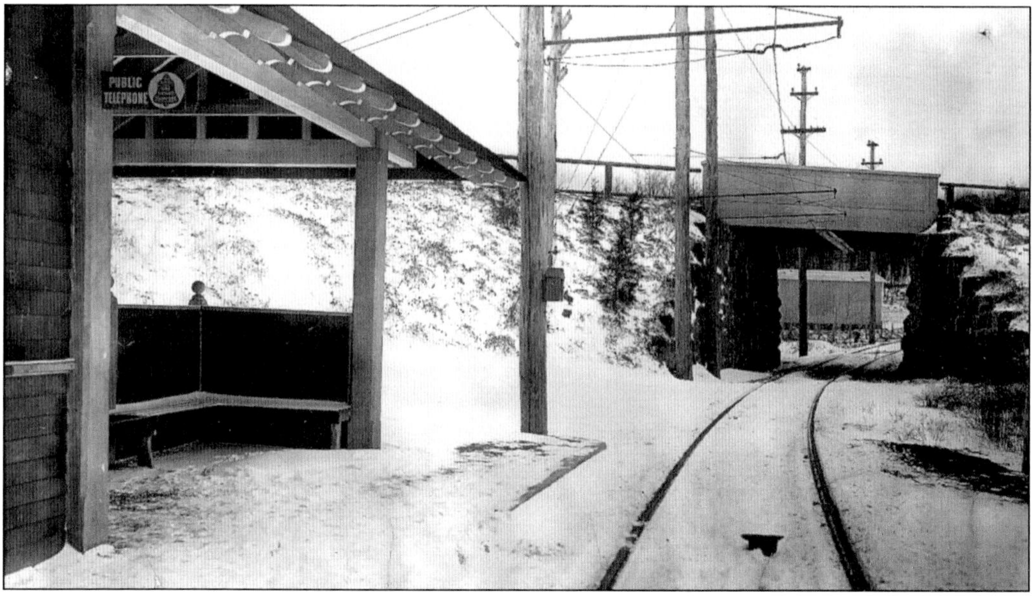

Here is Middlebury Station, on the Woodbury line, on February 8, 1911. There is a rather interesting story about this line, which concerns a streetcar that vanished for a few hours in 1910. It seems that at the end of the line in Woodbury the track stopped abruptly. One night a motorman was not paying attention and ran the car right off the end of the track into the woods! On the same night, another outbound car approached Southbury Road siding and waited there for the inbound car to appear. After waiting for a long time, the crew decided that the missing car must have broken down. They proceeded cautiously toward the end of the line, and were amazed to not find a streetcar when they got to Woodbury. As the second streetcar began to return to Waterbury, out of the woods came the crew from the missing car, who then explained their embarrassing situation. The two crews, using a very long chain, were apparently able to pull the missing streetcar back onto the rails and return to Waterbury.

Four

SOUTH TO DERBY

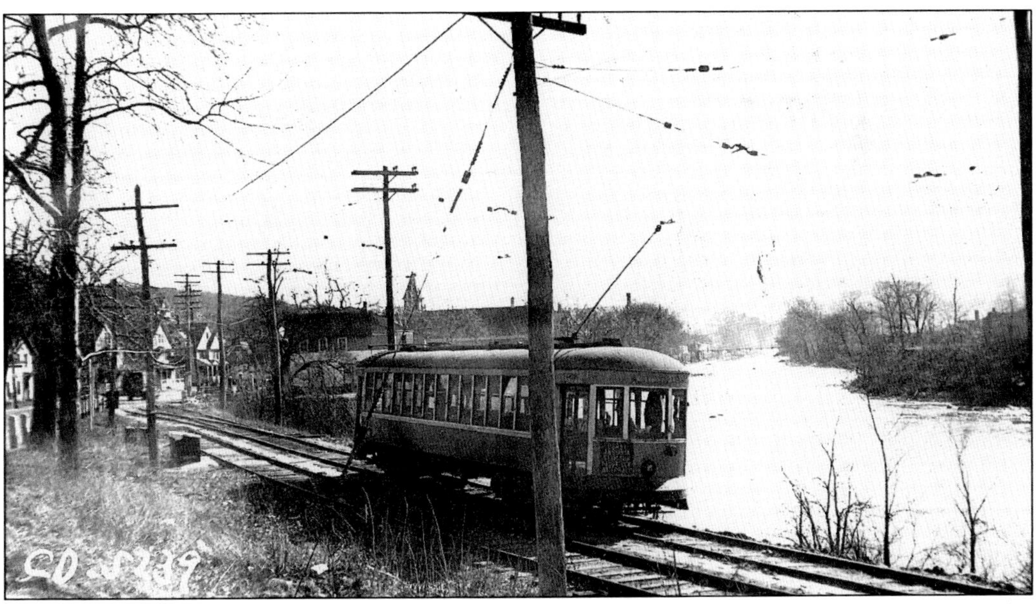

A 1900-series car is seen here going southbound through Bristol's Switch in Union City on the line to Derby. The fare to Derby from Waterbury was 30¢, and the ride took one hour. The car would continue on to New Haven with an additional 10¢ fare and another 45 minutes of travel. If one traveled via Cheshire Junction going to New Haven, the fare was 40¢ and the ride took one hour also.

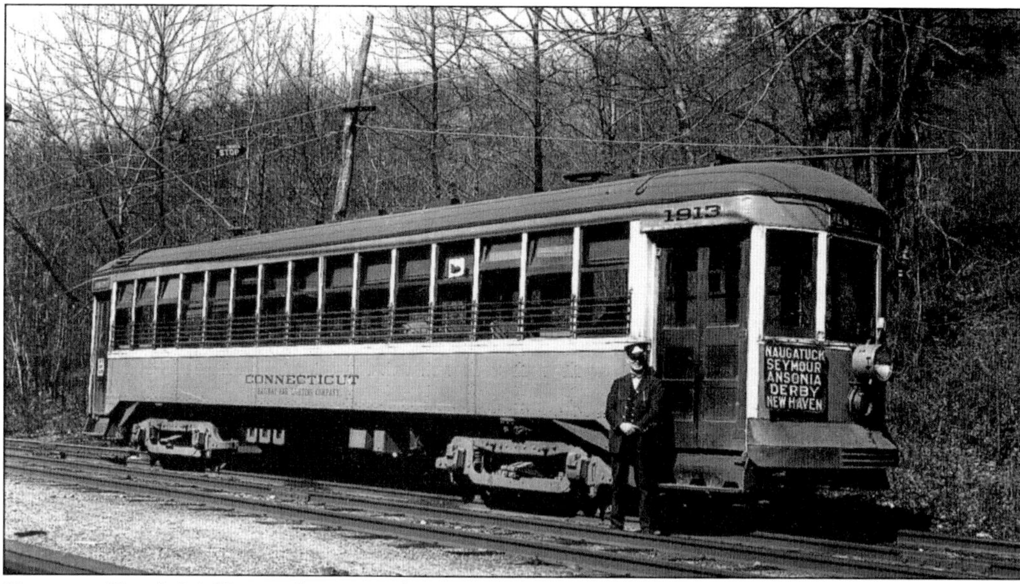

Operator Frank McKay is shown with Connecticut Railway and Lighting Company car 1913 running in Seymour in 1937.

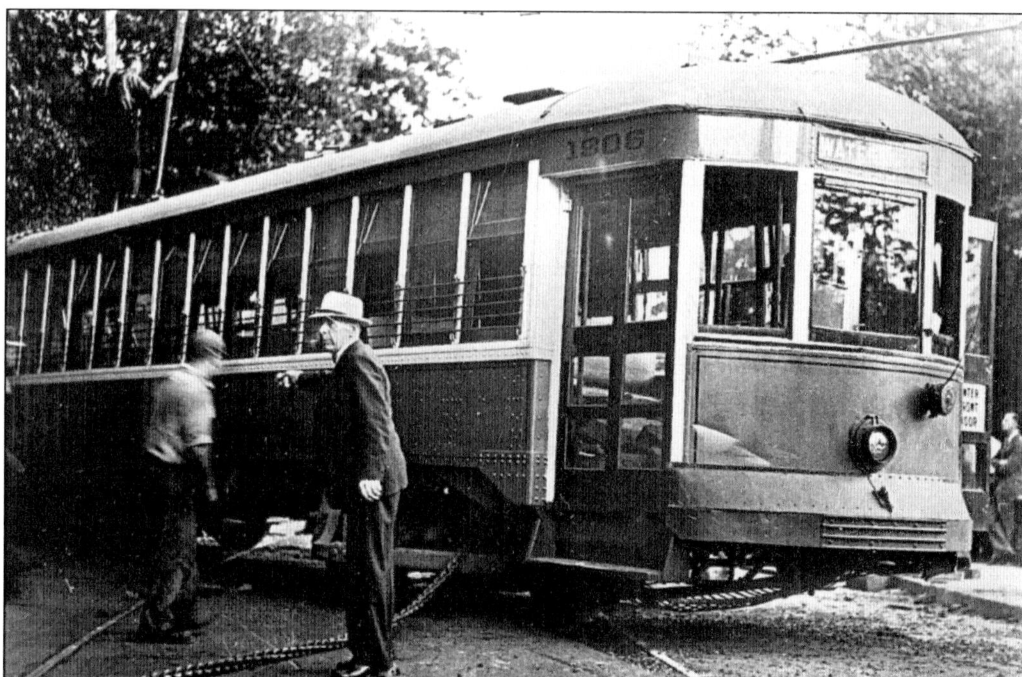

New Haven–bound car 1906 is shown here in Naugatuck after it jumped the track just north of Maple and North Main Streets. Today this area is under Route 8. The Waterbury car shop crew would have this car back on the rails in no time.

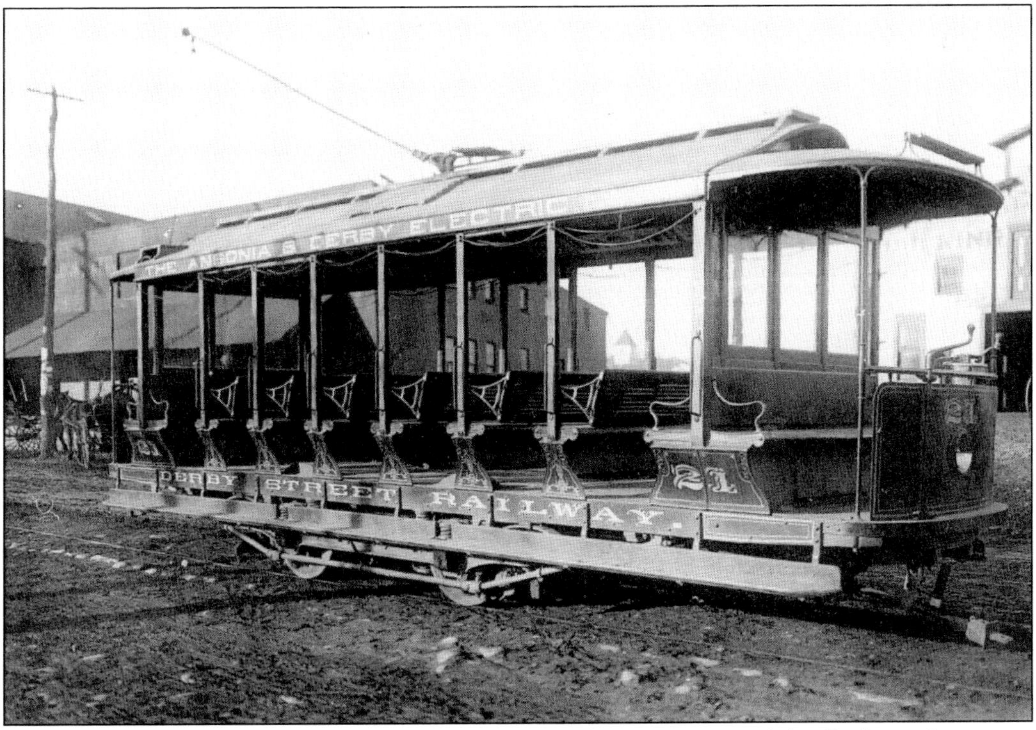

Derby Street Railway open car 21 is almost new in this 1899 view of the Derby carbarn, just off Main Street. Car No. 21 was built by Jackson & Sharpe Car Company of Wilmington, Delaware, in 1894. It later became Connecticut Company car 84; it was scrapped in 1916.

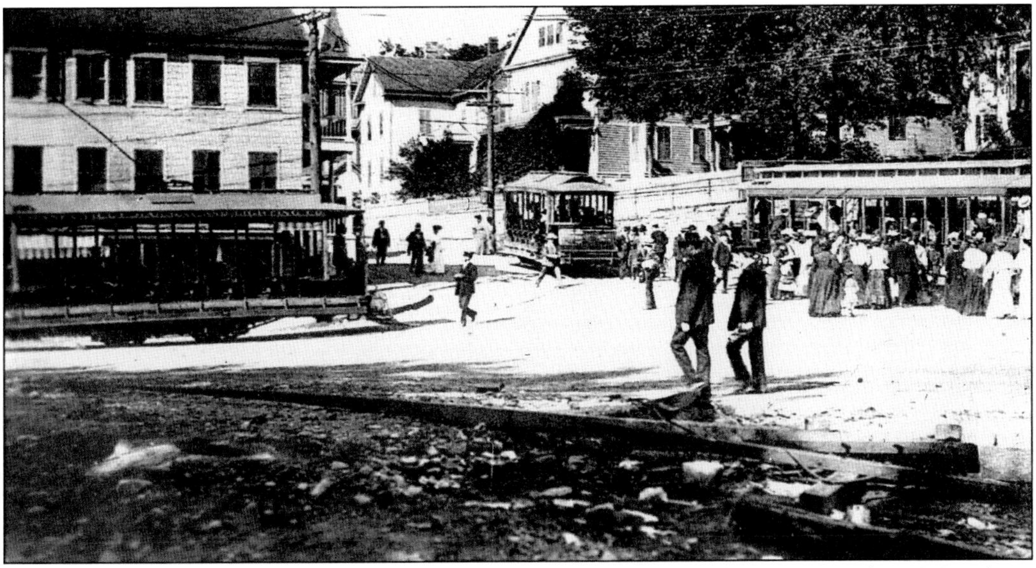

East Derby Junction is shown in this 1900 view. This was where the lines coming from Waterbury and New Haven connected with the Derby local lines. The open car on the left, coming from the Derby business district, has just crossed the Naugatuck River, while the large open car on the right has just come in from New Haven.

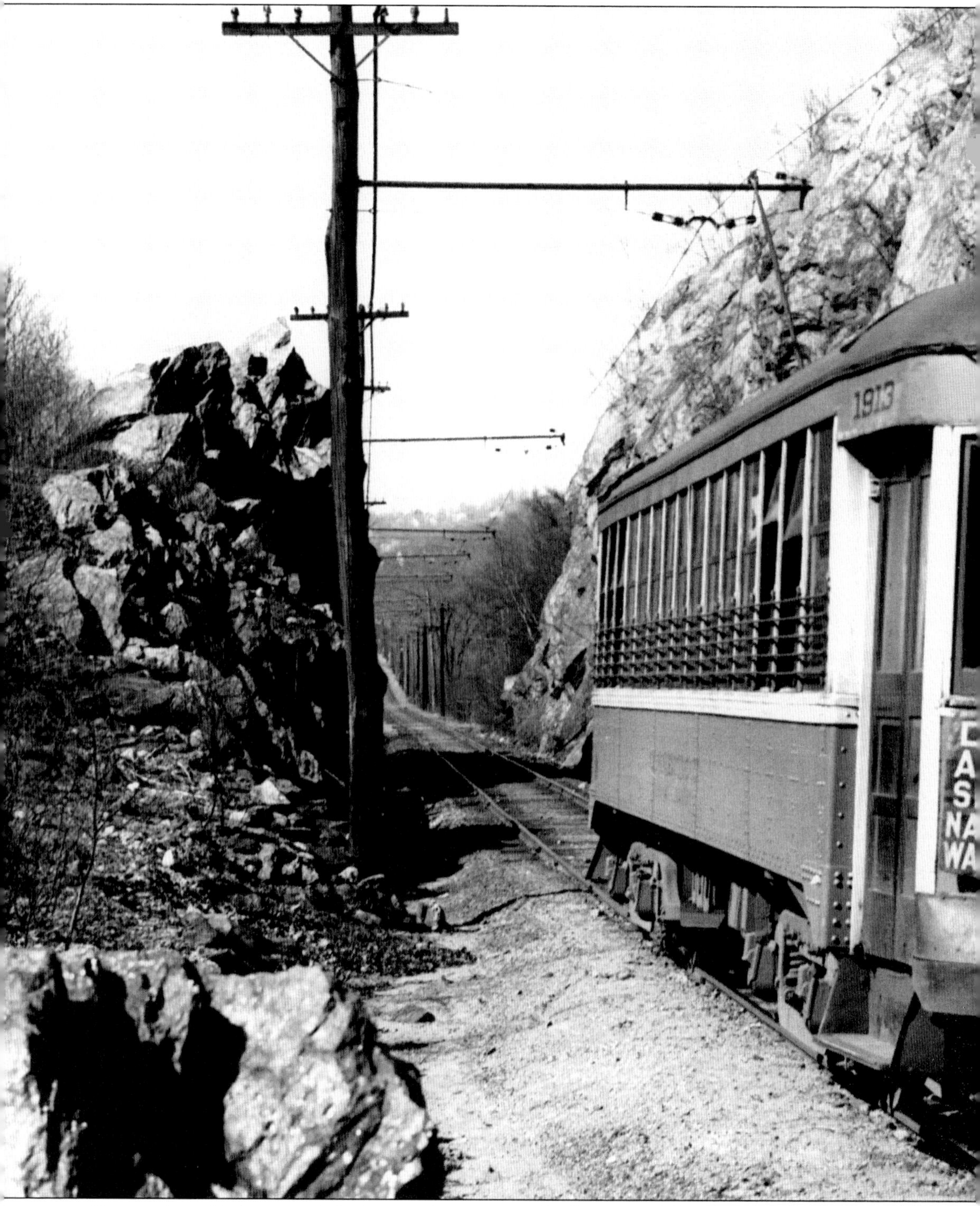

Connecticut Railway and Lighting Company suburban car 1913, proceeding inbound to Waterbury, is seen in this May 2, 1937 view at High Rock Grove in Naugatuck. The 1900-series cars were used all over the Connecticut Company system to serve the longer suburban lines.

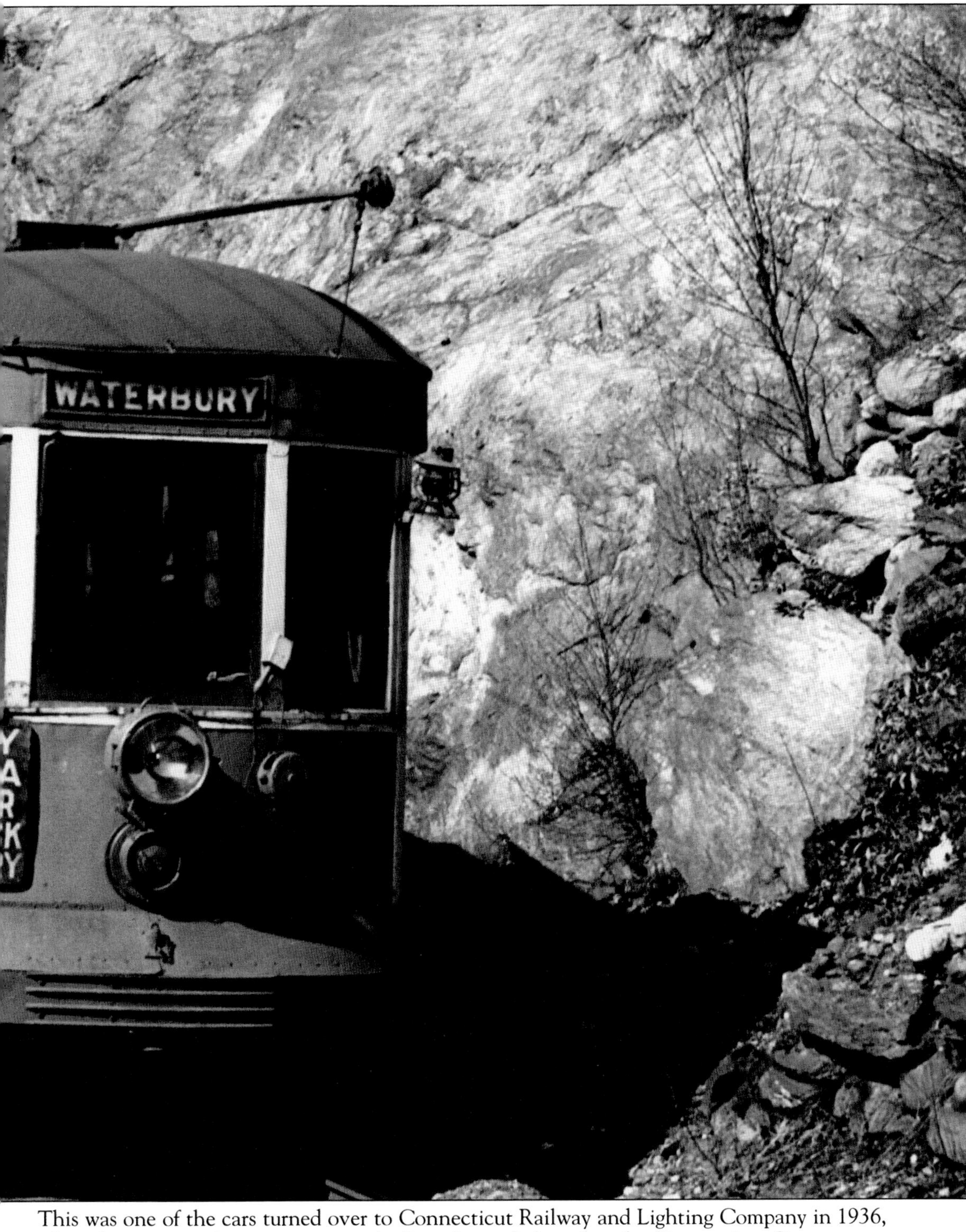

This was one of the cars turned over to Connecticut Railway and Lighting Company in 1936, when the company began to operate the lines formerly leased to the Connecticut Company.

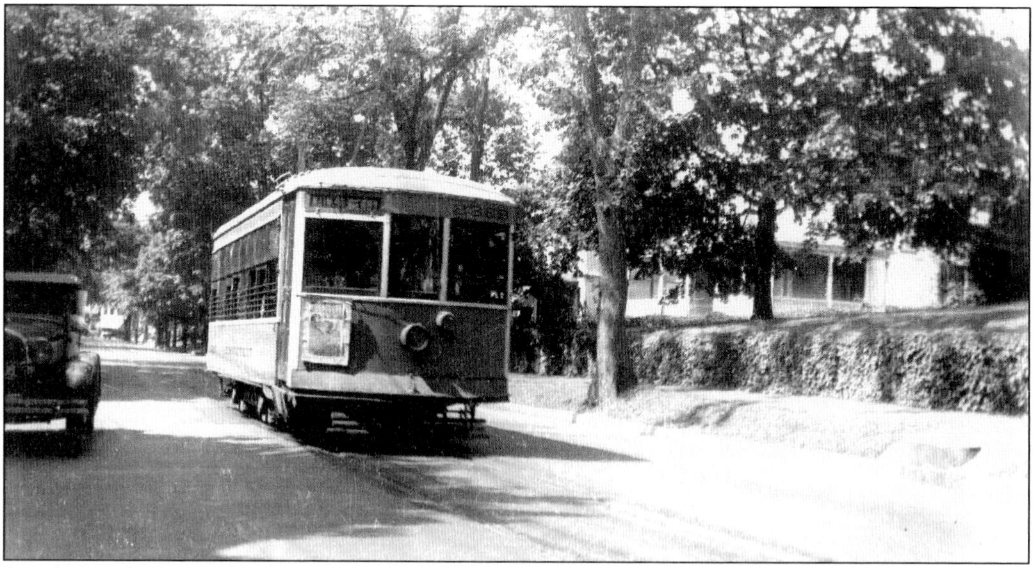

Single-truck Birney car 2365 is seen here operating on Main Street near Atwater Avenue in Derby. In 1916 Charles O. Birney, of the firm of Stone and Webster, designed a short single-truck car that was one-third the weight of the average streetcar of the era. These were designed to be one-man cars and were equipped with a "dead man" control that stopped the car if the operator was disabled for any reason. The cars had poor riding qualities and were very underpowered. Thousands were built though—the Connecticut Company had more than 160—as the Birney cars were inexpensive to run and helped keep marginal lines operating long after they would have survived using conventional streetcars.

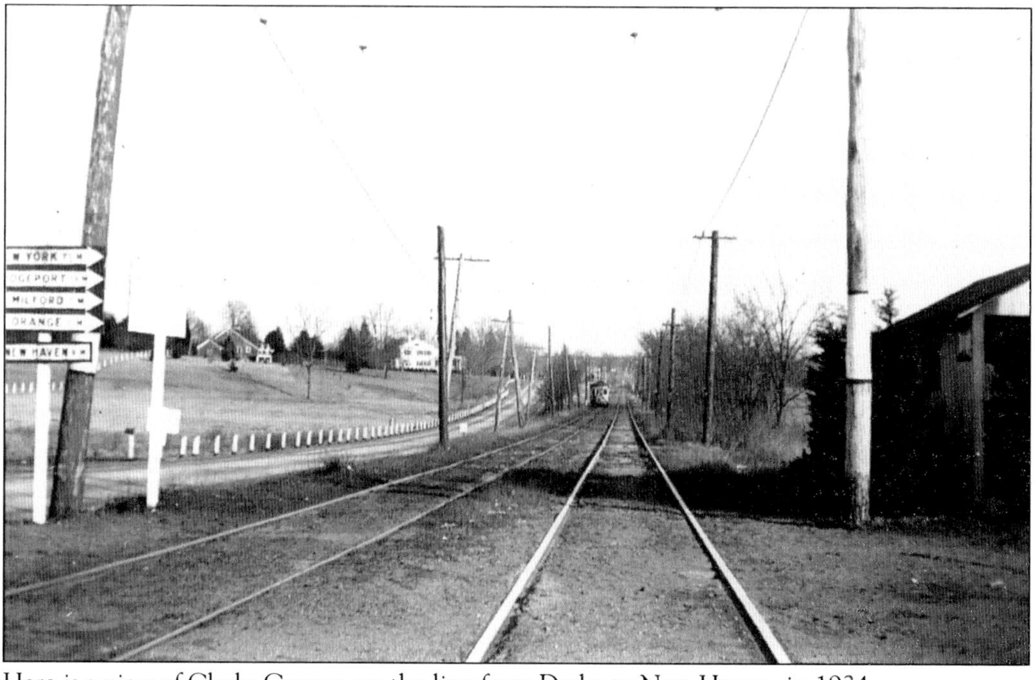

Here is a view of Clarks Corner, on the line from Derby to New Haven, in 1934.

New Haven–bound car No. 1927 is pictured at Chestnut Hill in Derby.

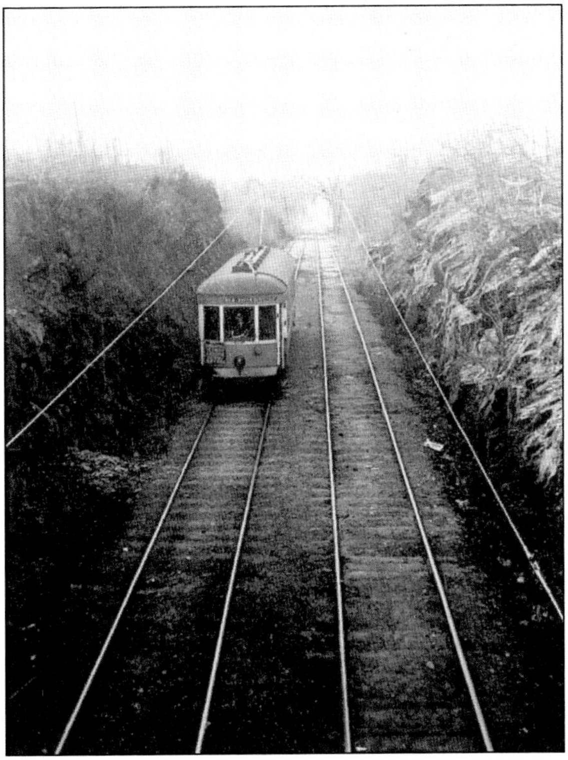

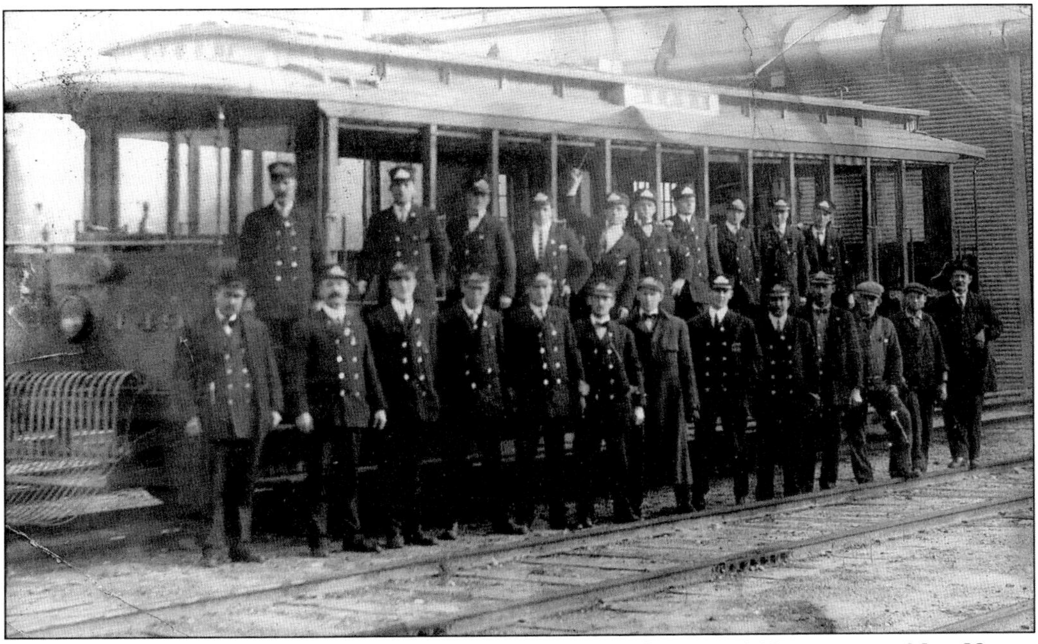

Here is a group picture taken at the Derby carbarn in 1912. Open car 149 was sent to New Haven in 1931 and renumbered 1459; it ran until all open cars were taken out of service in 1947.

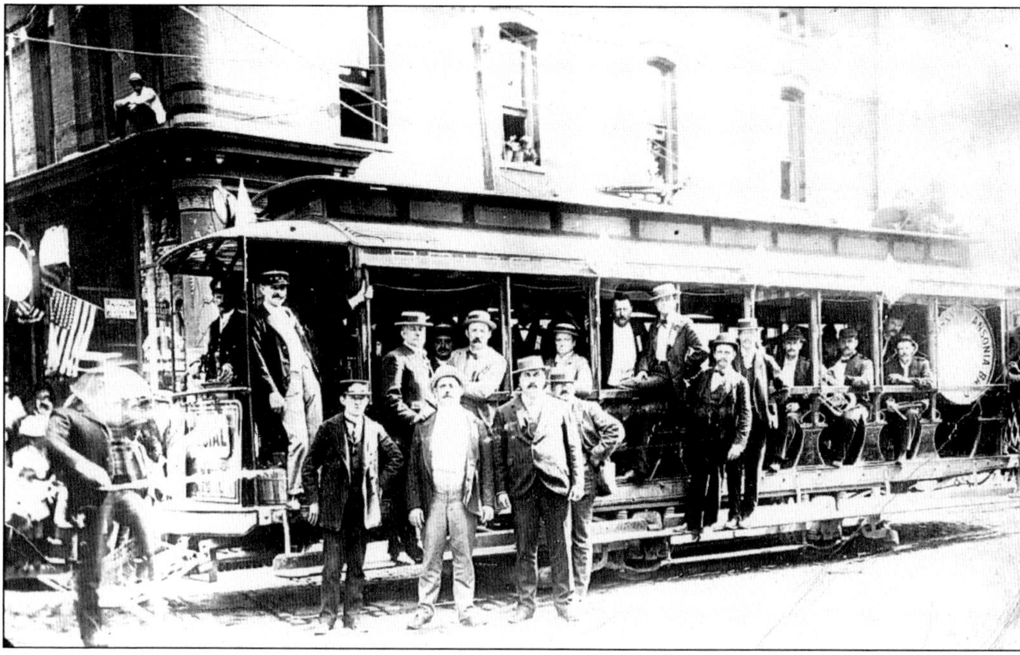

This photograph was taken in Derby at the Shelton Bridge. This was the first car to run from Bridgeport to Derby in 1898.

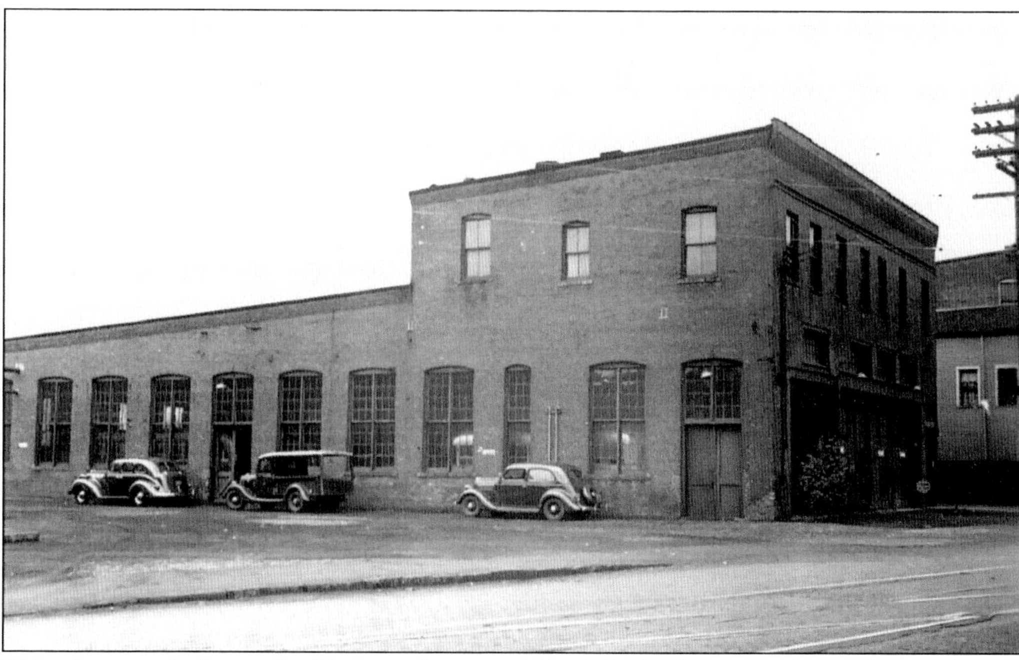

This photograph shows the Derby carbarn in 1934. The building was located just off Main Street. When this picture was taken, the structure was also used to house motor coaches. Power for the Derby lines was supplied by Derby Gas & Electric Company. In 1920 alone, the cost of electric current to run the streetcars was $74,352.28.

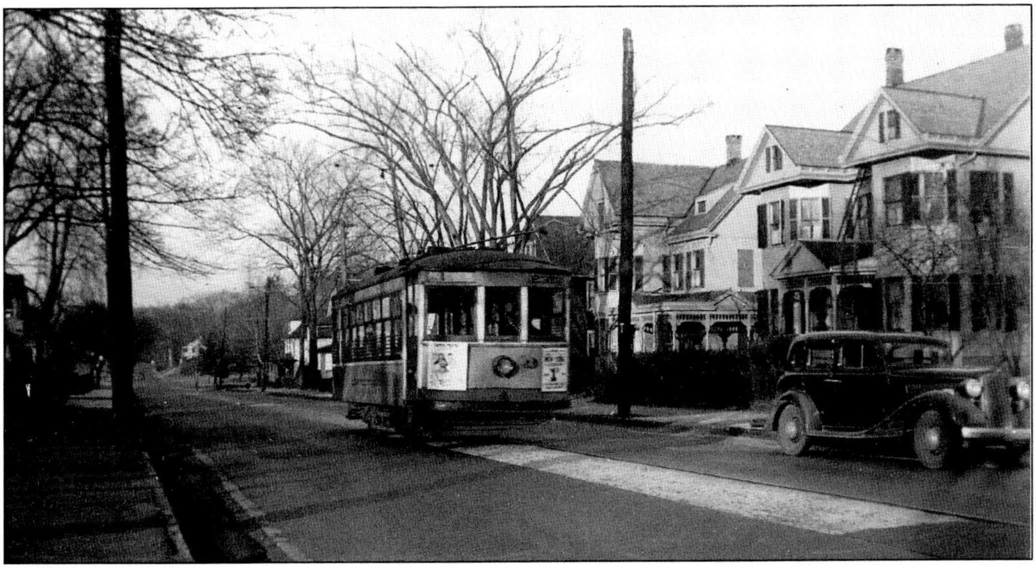

Here is a scene on Wakelee Avenue in Ansonia in 1937. By this time, most local service in Derby was provided by single-truck Birney safety cars. Those cars would be substituted with double-truck wood cars when there was snow on the ground because just two inches of snow would cause the underpowered cars to stall and derail. Derby was the last city in Connecticut to have the Birney cars in regular service.

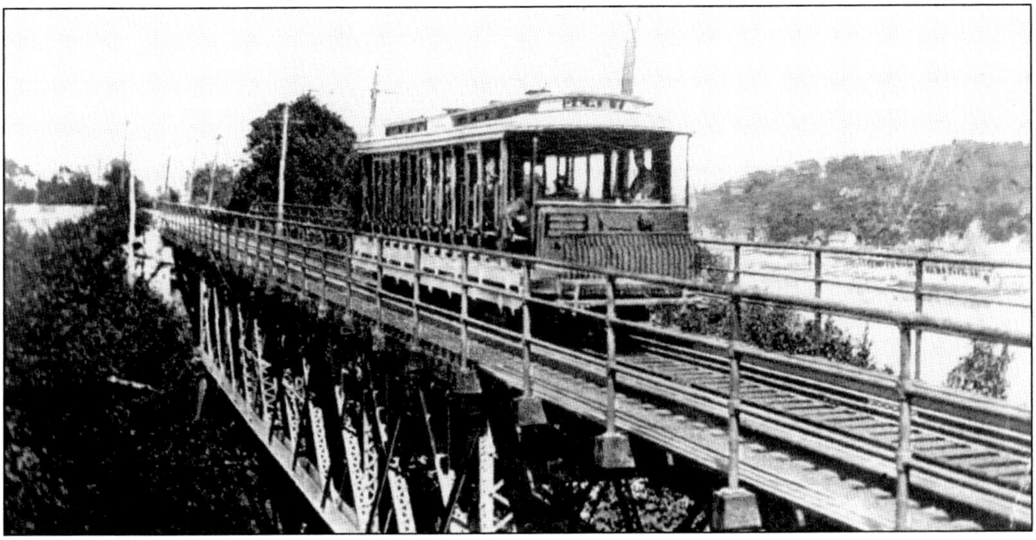

Here is a Derby-bound car crossing Pecks Mills trestle on the line from Bridgeport. On August 6, 1899, a single-truck open car jumped off the trestle and landed on its roof, which collapsed. In the accident, 29 passengers were crushed to death and 6 were hurt. The conductor was among those killed; the motorman jumped and was injured, but lived. No reason for the derailment other than high speed could be discovered, as other cars immediately following the doomed car had continued over the trestle without a problem. In 1921 this line had another fatal accident when two streetcars collided, killing 8 and injuring 25. A passenger was carrying a five-gallon pail of gasoline that turned the wrecked cars into a blazing inferno. Shortly afterward, the Connecticut legislature enacted a law forbidding smoking and the transportation of gasoline or kerosene in any bus or streetcar.

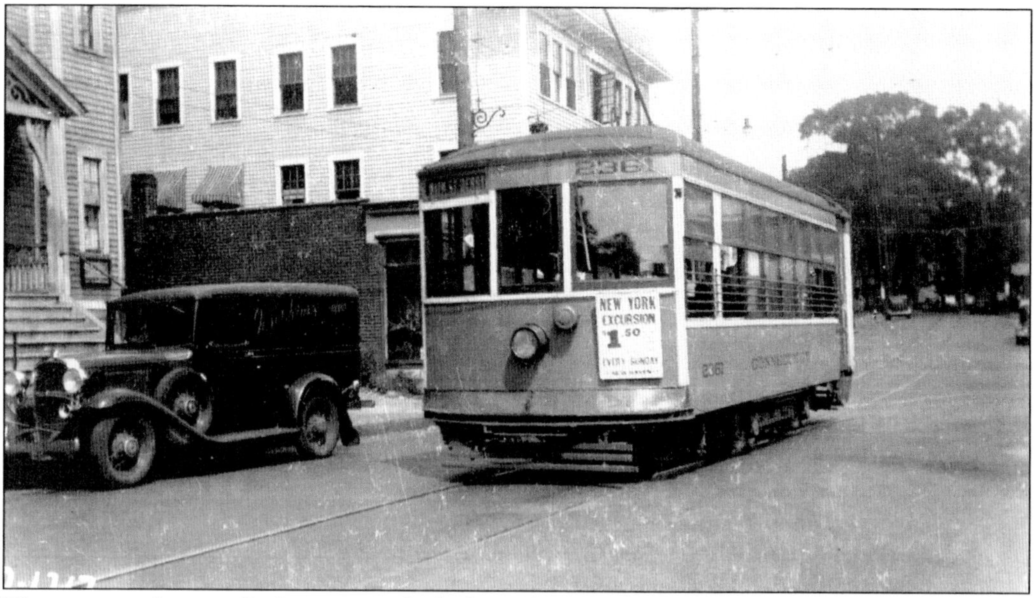

The streetcar lines in Derby consisted of a loop that ran on both sides of the Naugatuck River, running through the centers of Derby and Ansonia. Branches were operated on Housatonic Avenue and across the Housatonic River to Howe Street in Shelton. The Derby division was one of the smallest divisions of the Connecticut Company, with only 24 miles of track—about 3 percent of the company total—as compared to Waterbury with 88 miles and Hartford with 165 miles. Car 2361 is shown on Main Street in Derby.

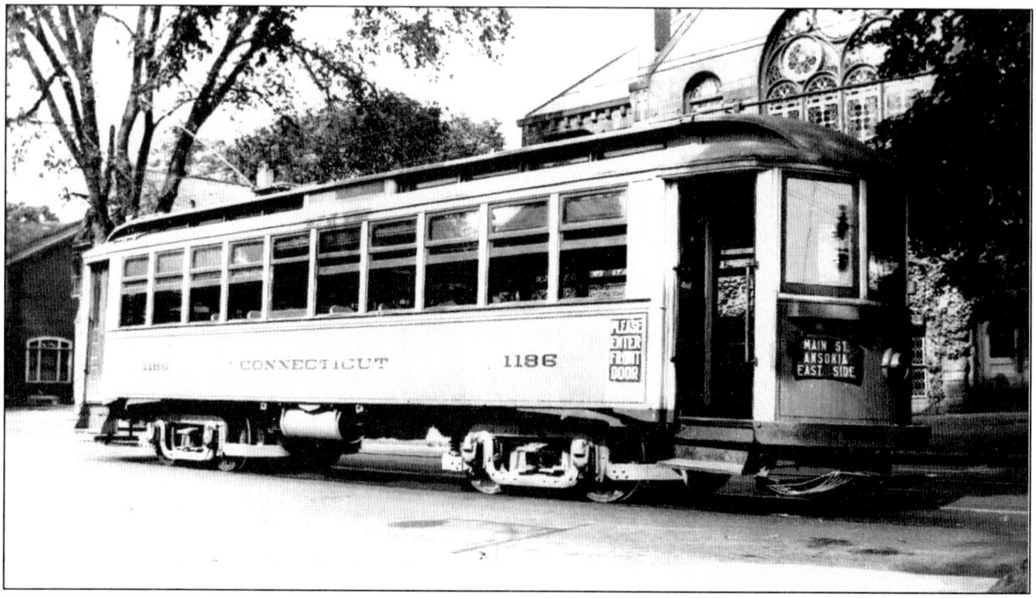

Older heavyweight wood cars like 1186, shown here, were used for rush-hour service and in the winter months to replace the lightweight Birney cars that had difficulty in the snow.

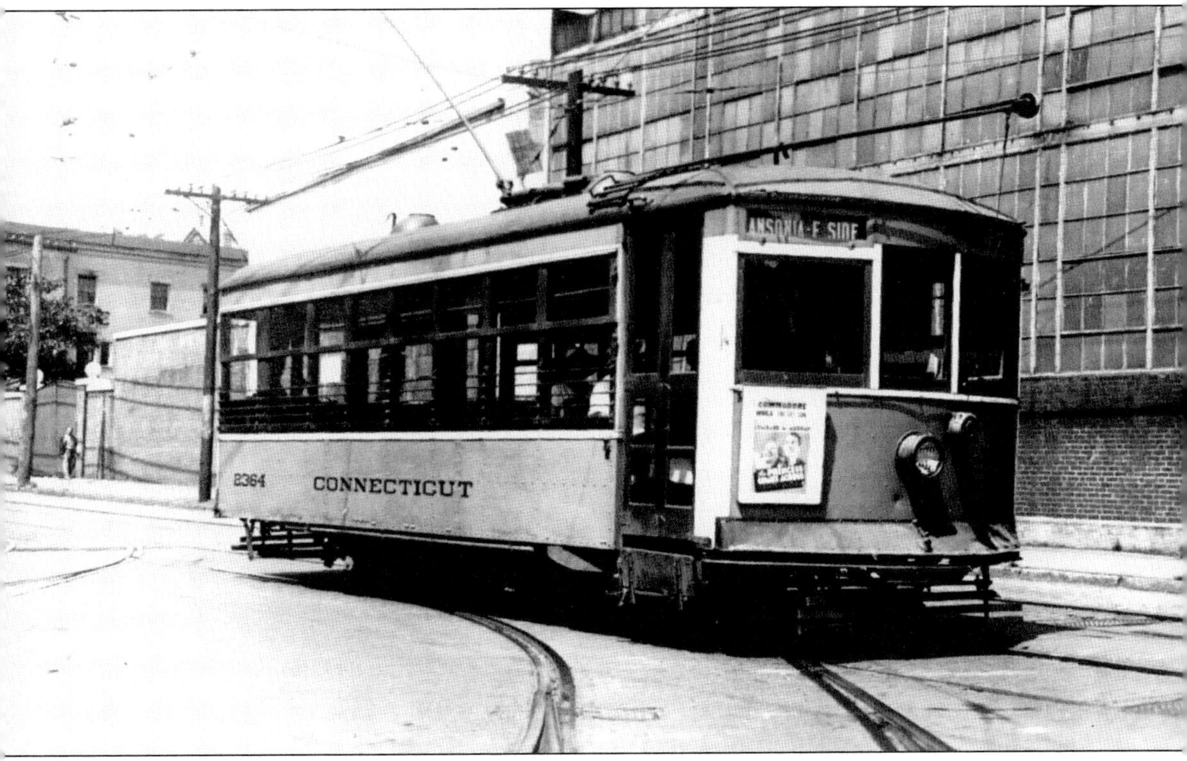

Here, car 2364 waits its turn to enter the carbarn on Main Street in Derby in 1934. This car was built by Wason Manufacturing Company in 1920.

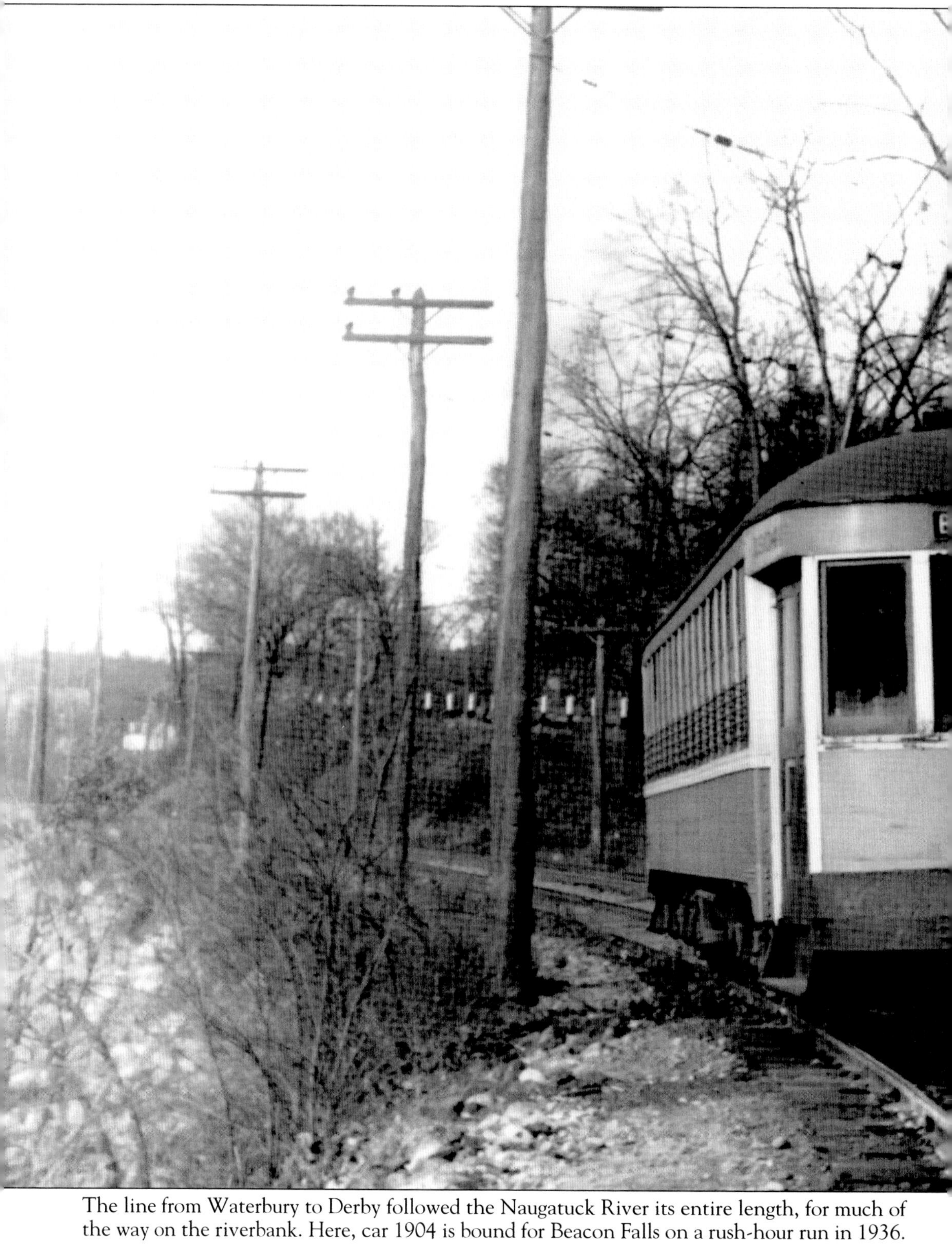

The line from Waterbury to Derby followed the Naugatuck River its entire length, for much of the way on the riverbank. Here, car 1904 is bound for Beacon Falls on a rush-hour run in 1936.

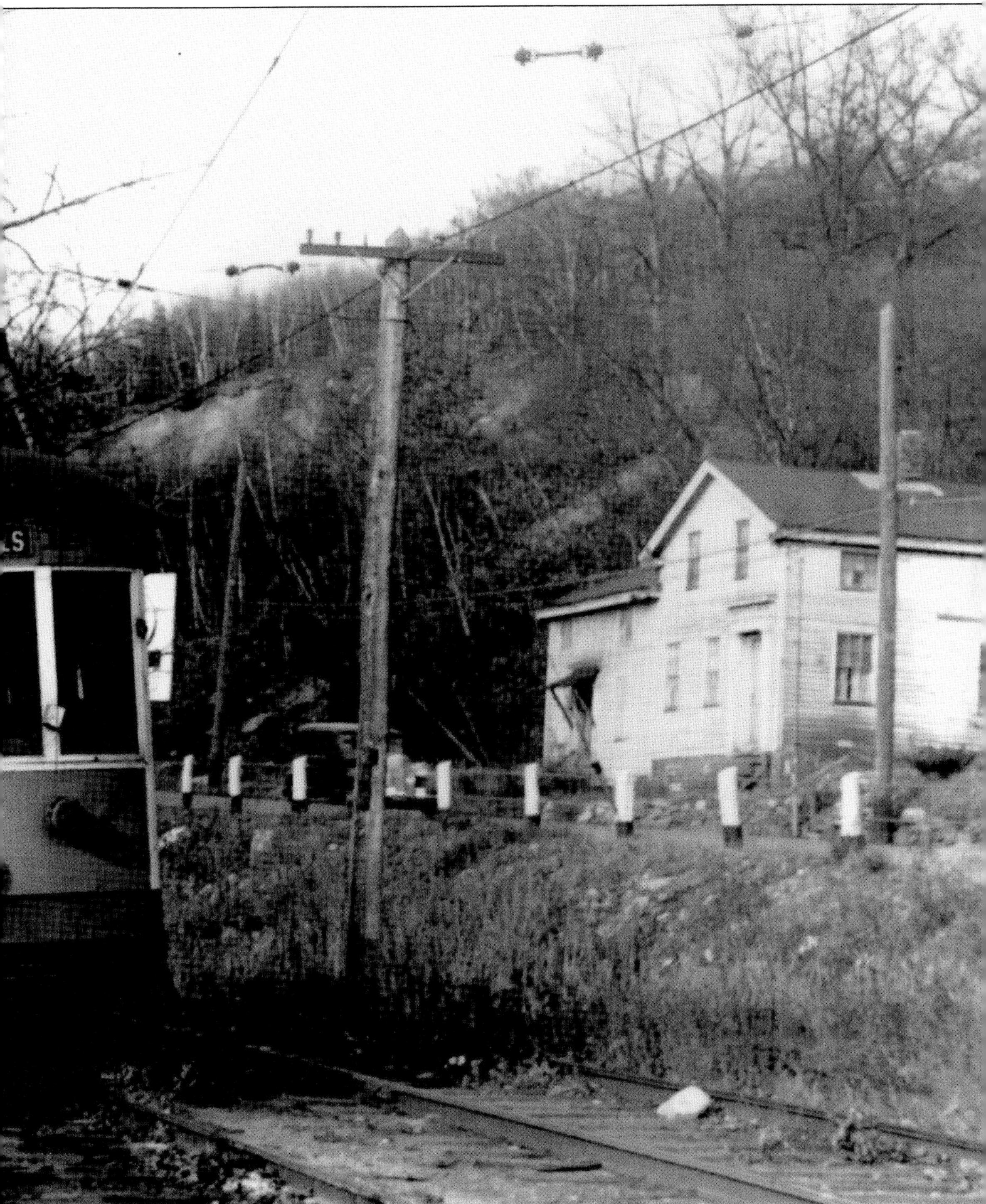

The 1900-series cars could seat 56 people and hold 100 or more standing passengers. These cars were real "crowd swallowers."

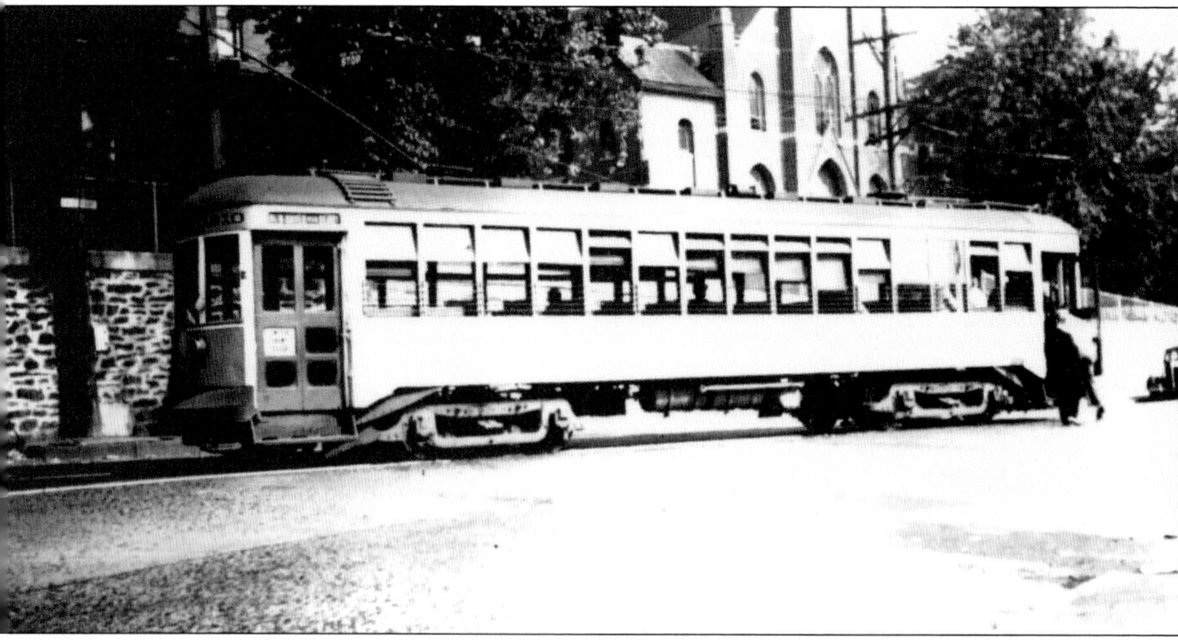

A New Haven–bound 1900 car stops at East Derby Junction en route from Waterbury.

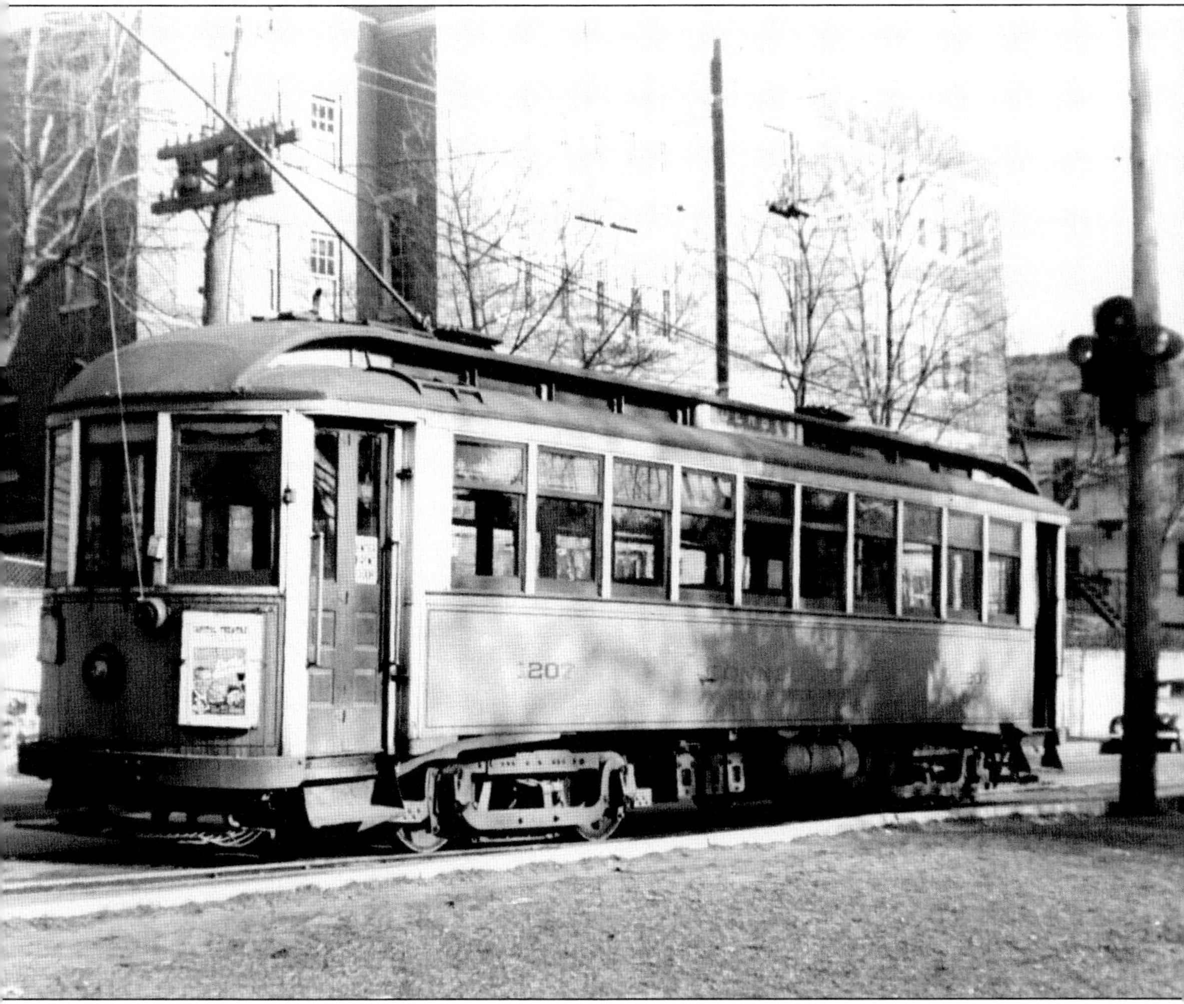

Here is a view of Connecticut Railway and Lighting Company car 1207 in Derby in 1937. On page 82 there is another picture of this same car from 1908, when it was Connecticut Company No. 124.

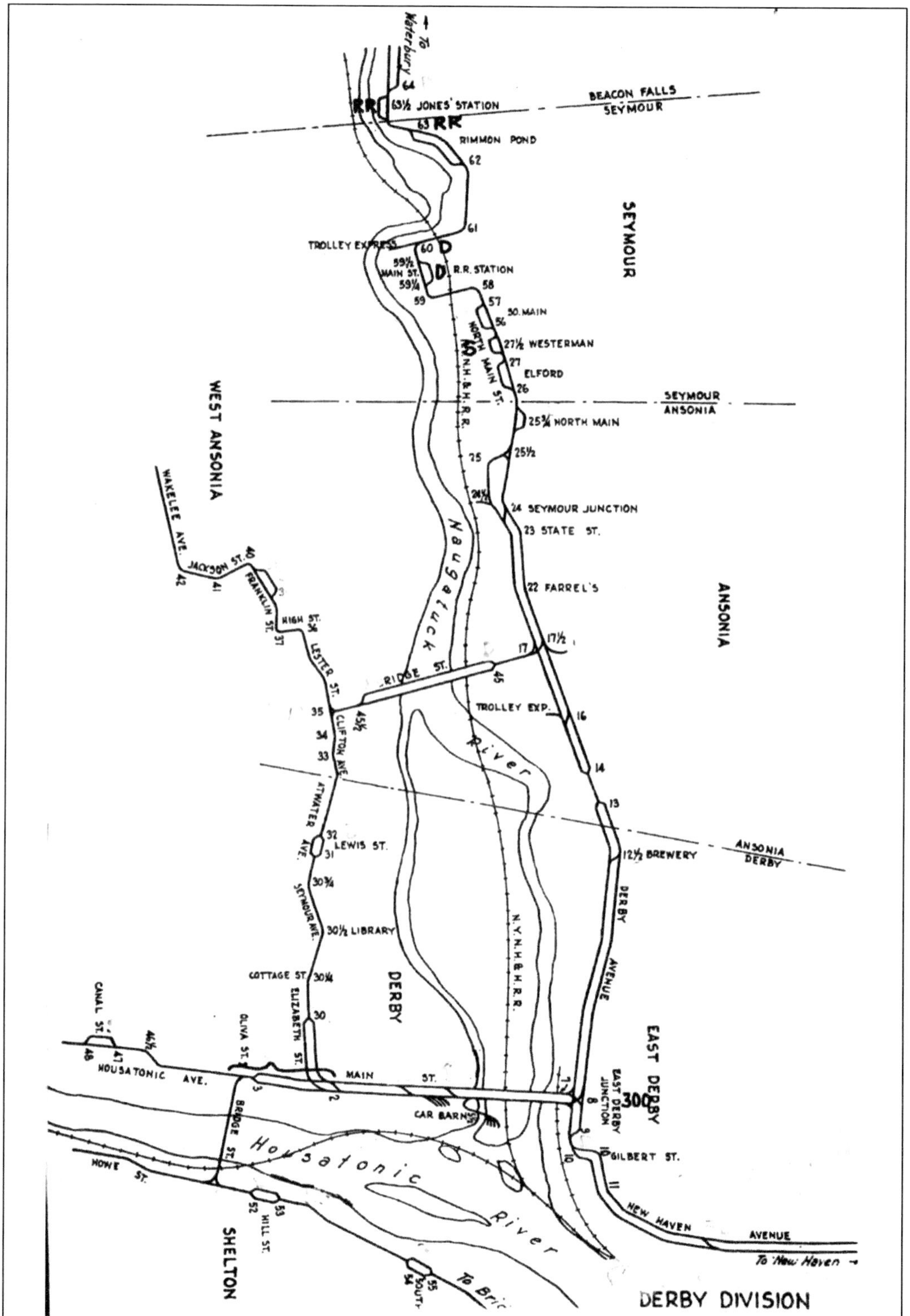

Here is a map of Derby division lines in 1920.

Five

Torrington & Winchester Line

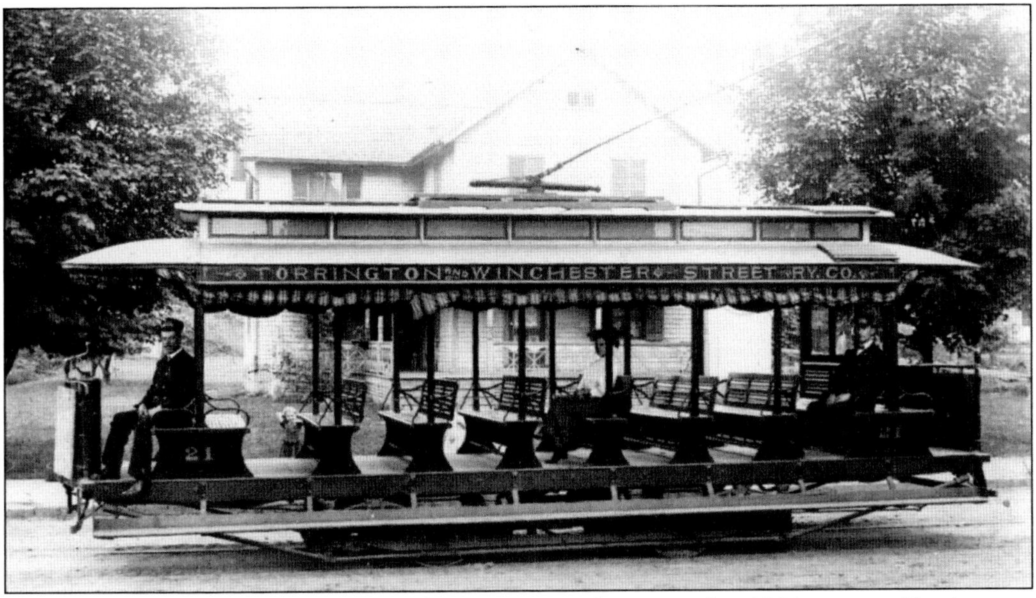

Torrington & Winchester Street Railway car 21 is shown in this 1901 view in Torrington. Car 21 was built in 1897 by the Massachusetts Car Company, and subsequently became Connecticut Company 415 in 1915. It was scrapped in 1916, along with 400 other single-truck cars that had become obsolete by that time.

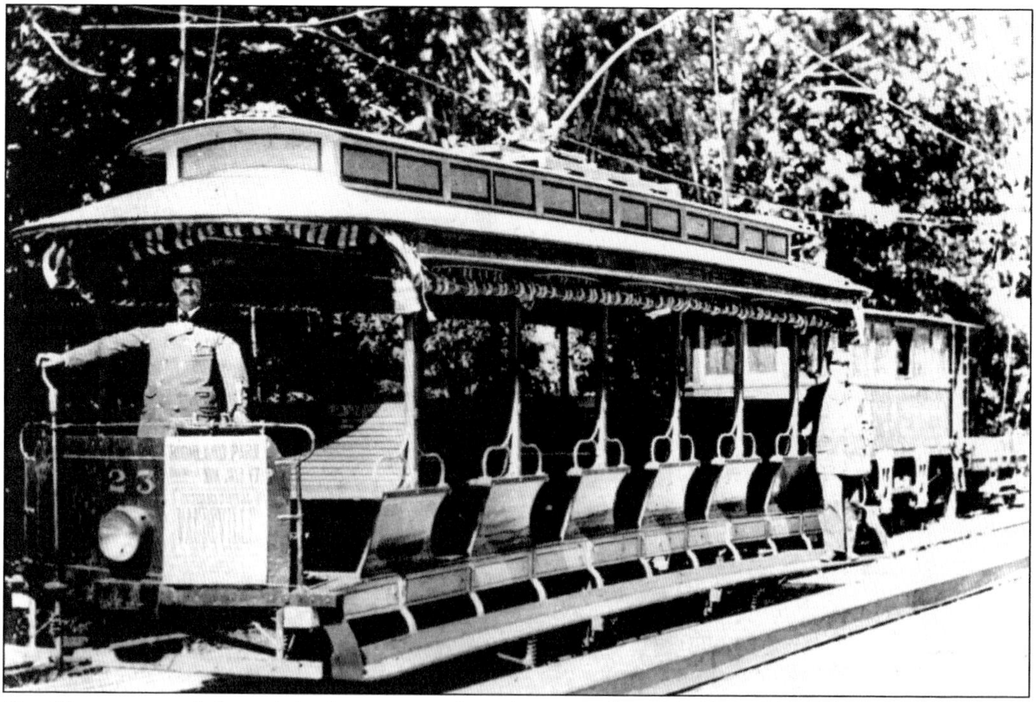

Car 23 was one of the original open cars bought new when the line opened in 1897. The car lasted until the line was abandoned in January 1929.

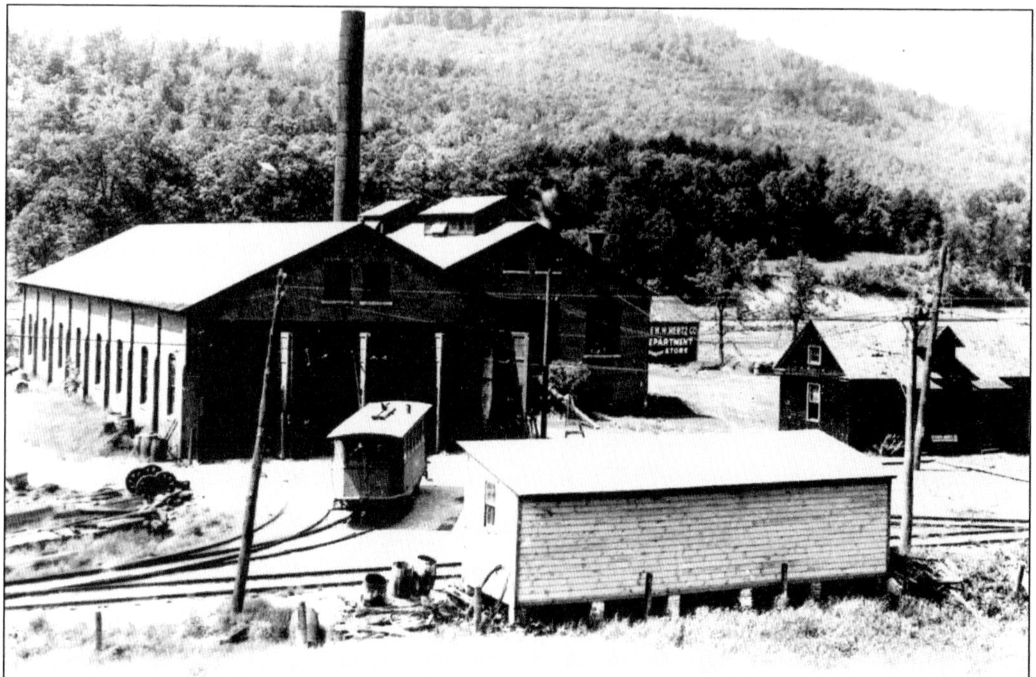

Here are the carbarn and powerhouse of the Torrington & Winchester Street Railway, located in the Burrville section of the town of Winchester.

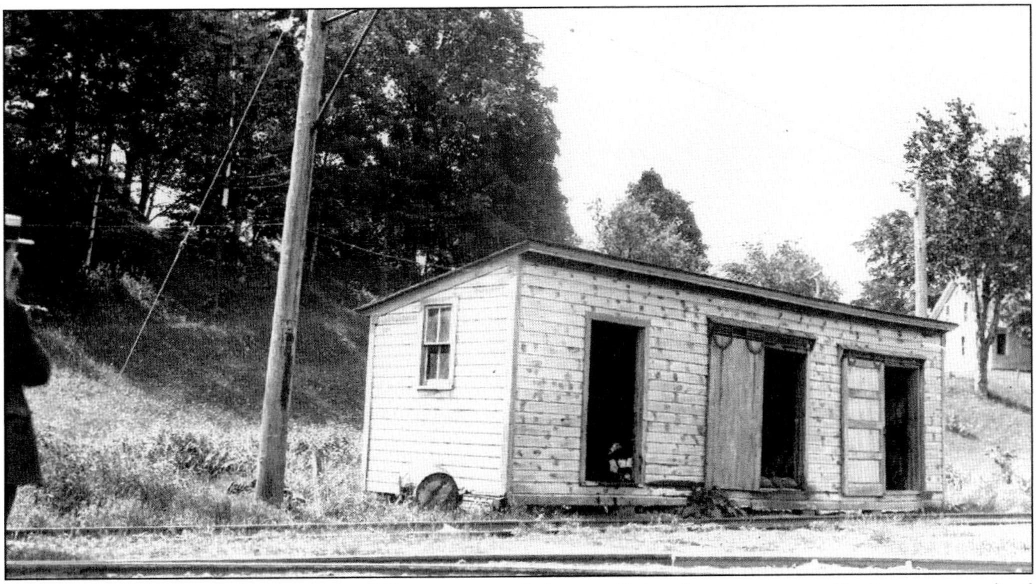

Here is the building that was used for storage of dry sand for the streetcars. Each streetcar had a hopper that would dump sand on the rails in slippery weather in order to help stop the car or prevent its wheels from slipping. (F. S. Bennett Collection.)

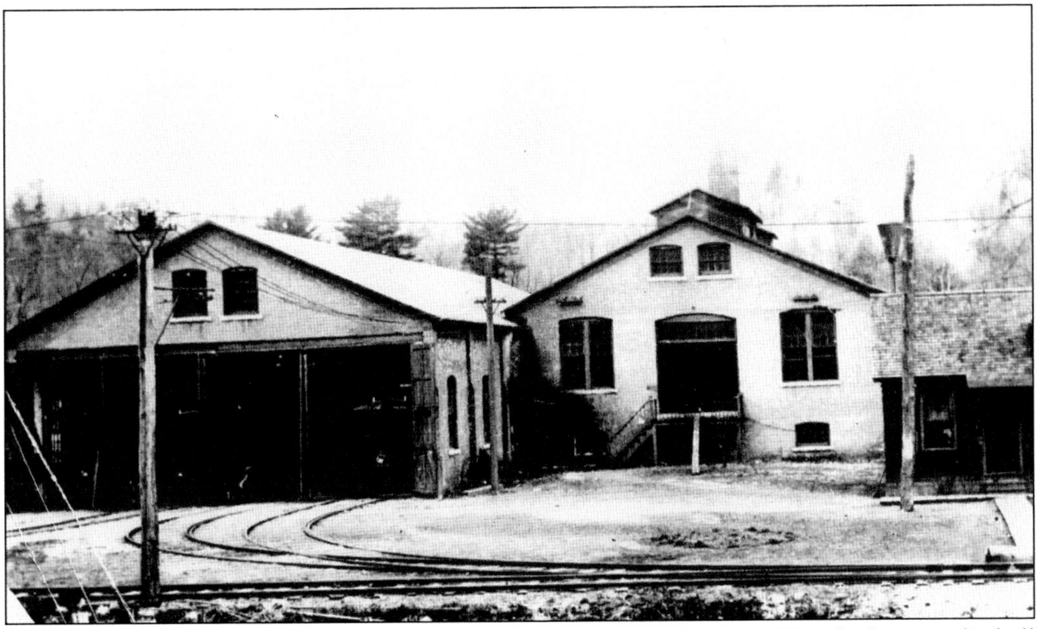

Shown here is the Burrville power station on the Torrington division. This facility supplied all the power for the entire line from 1897 until the plant was closed in 1920. There were three boilers and 175-kilowatt DC generators connected to 250-horsepower condensing engines. Following the plant's closure in 1920, the equipment was sold to a scrap dealer. After that time, electric current for the operation of the streetcars was supplied by Winsted Gas Company, as it was the provider of both electricity and gas for greater Winsted. (F. S. Bennett Collection.)

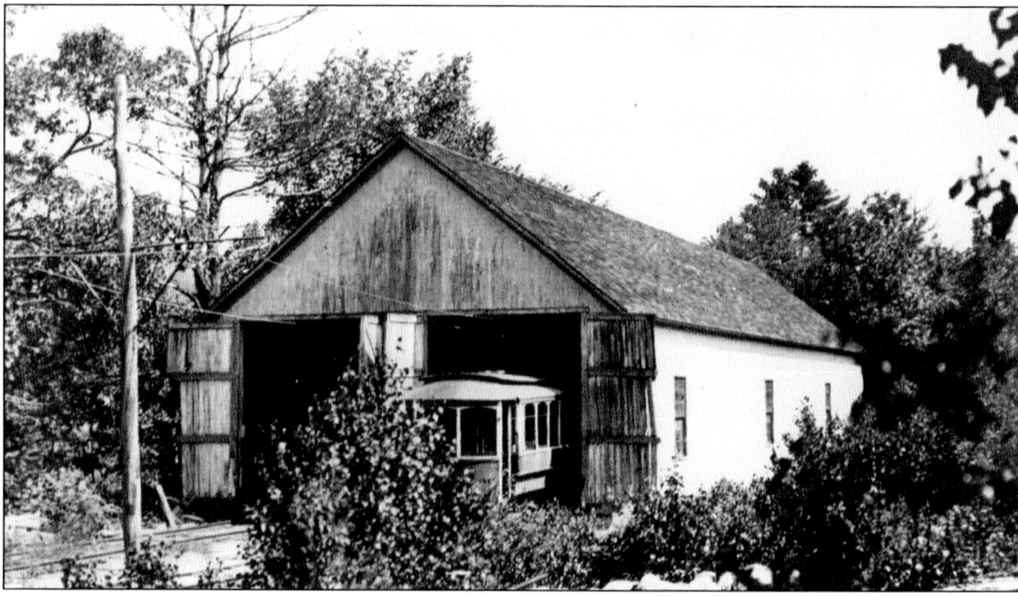

In addition to the main carbarn, the line also had a smaller building for storing the open cars in winter and closed cars in summer. The Torrington division facilities were rather modest compared to those of other divisions. (F. S. Bennett Collection.)

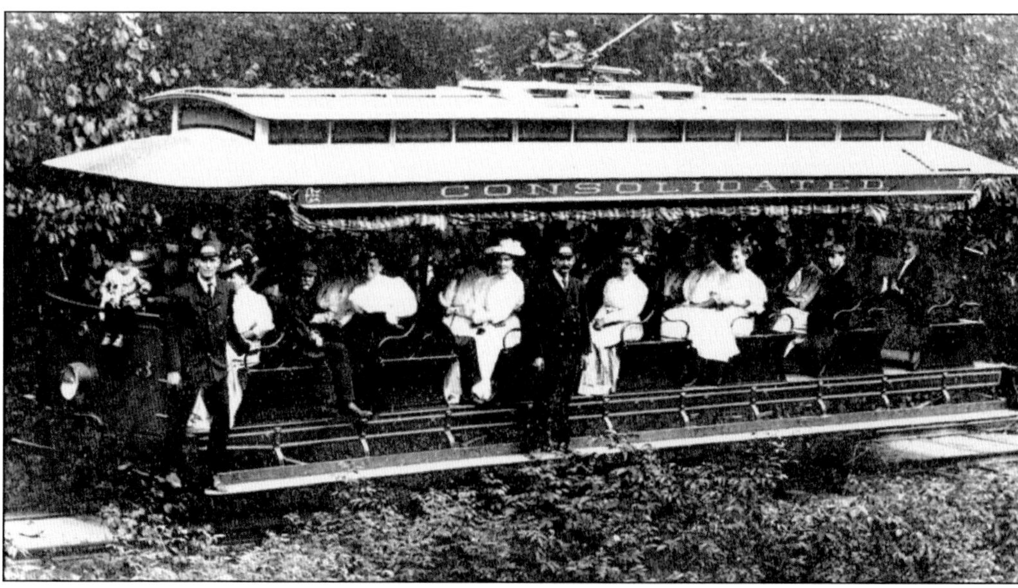

A trolley car outing to Highland Lake was a popular diversion for Torrington and Winsted citizens in the years before World War I. In this view, car 23 has a full load of passengers en route to Highland Lake *c.* 1907. (F. S. Bennett Collection.)

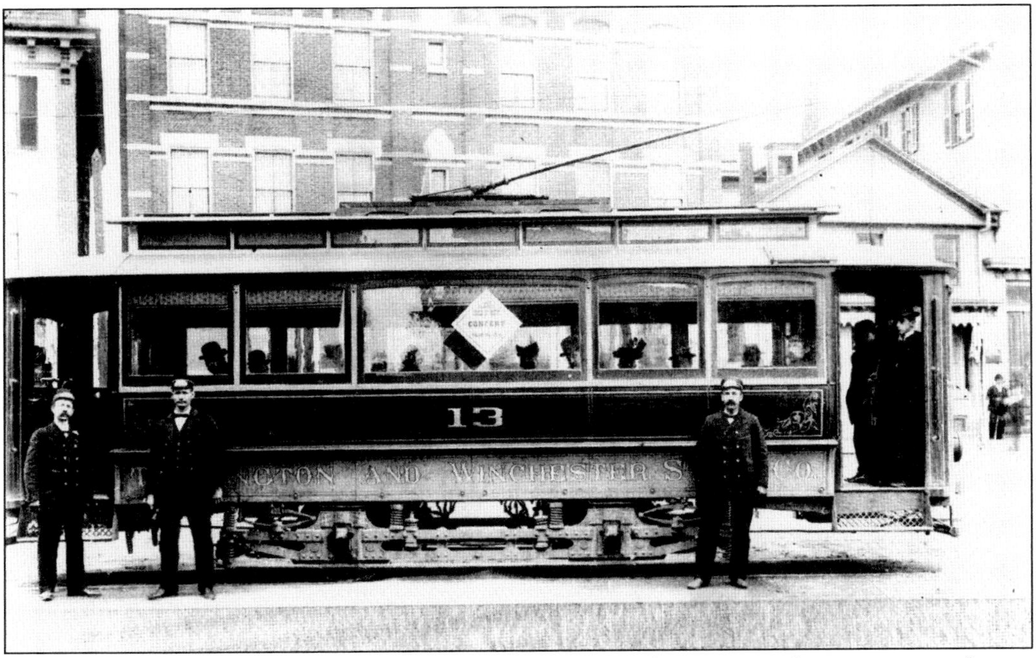

Torrington & Winchester car 13 is seen here in its original maroon-and-cream paint scheme. The large picture window in the middle of the car is a rather unusual feature.

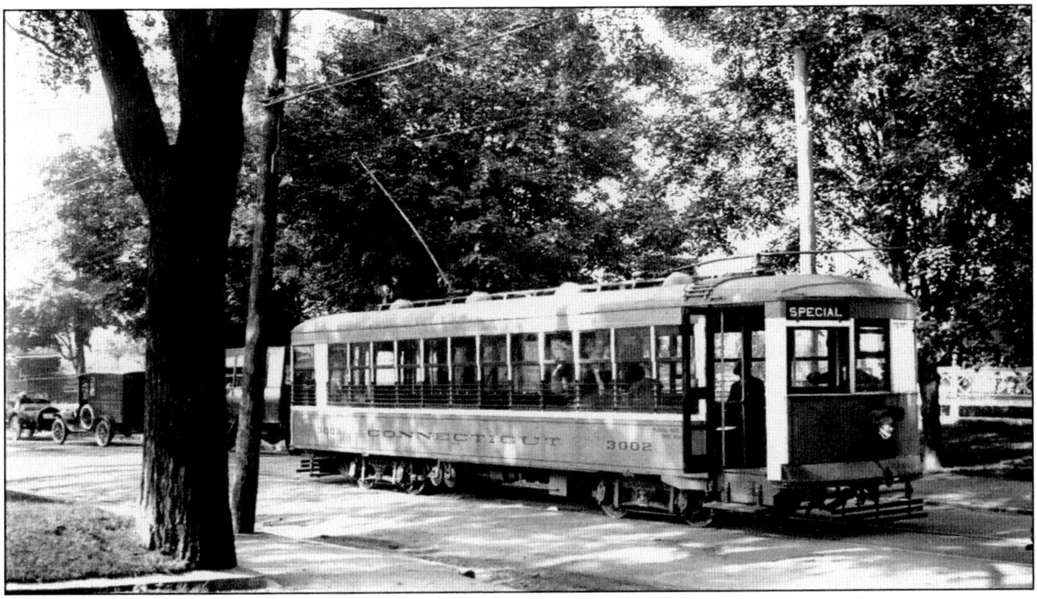

Here is a view of Birney safety car 3002 in Torrington in June 1922. The Connecticut Company purchased three double-truck safety cars from Wason to help upgrade service and increase ridership.

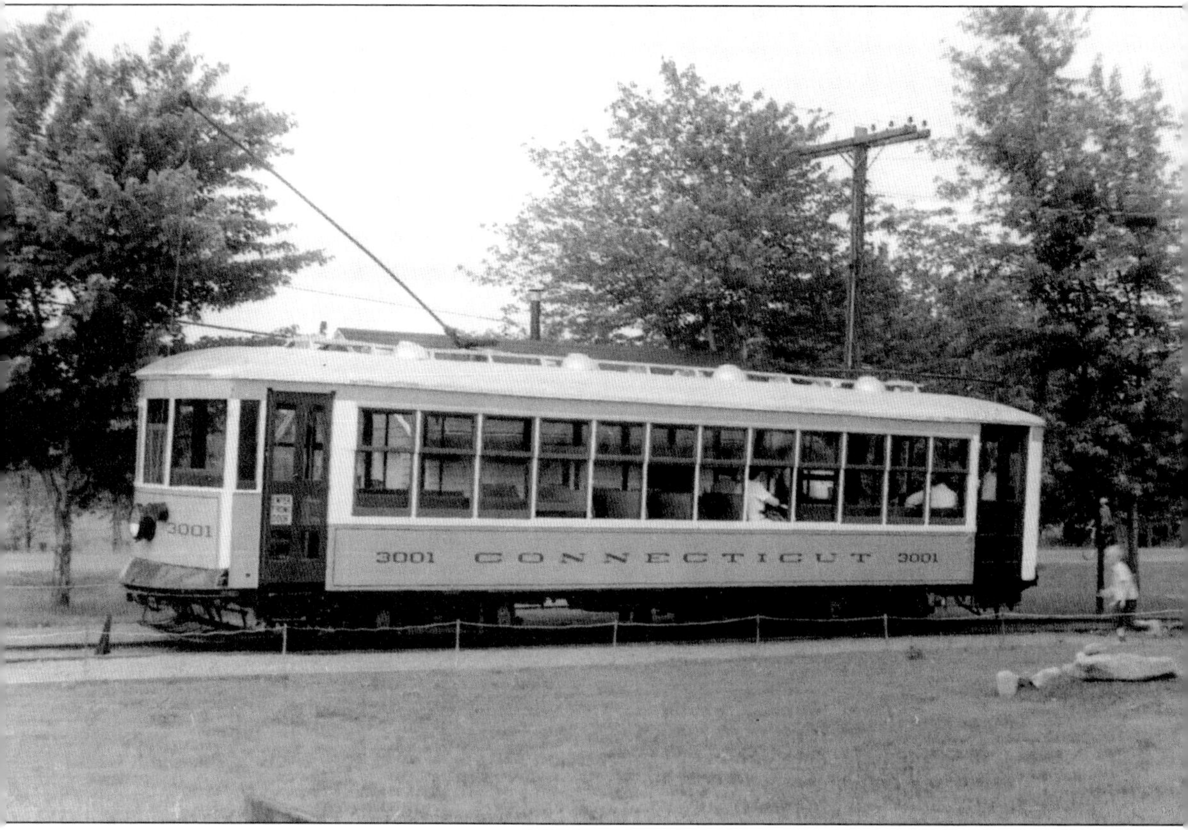

All three 3000-series cars were taken to New Haven when the line closed in 1929. The rest of the equipment was scrapped in Burrville that same year. Car 3001 ran in New Haven until the streetcars were replaced by motor coaches in 1948. The car was then acquired by the Connecticut Trolley Museum in East Windsor, and is seen here running on the museum's line in 1963.

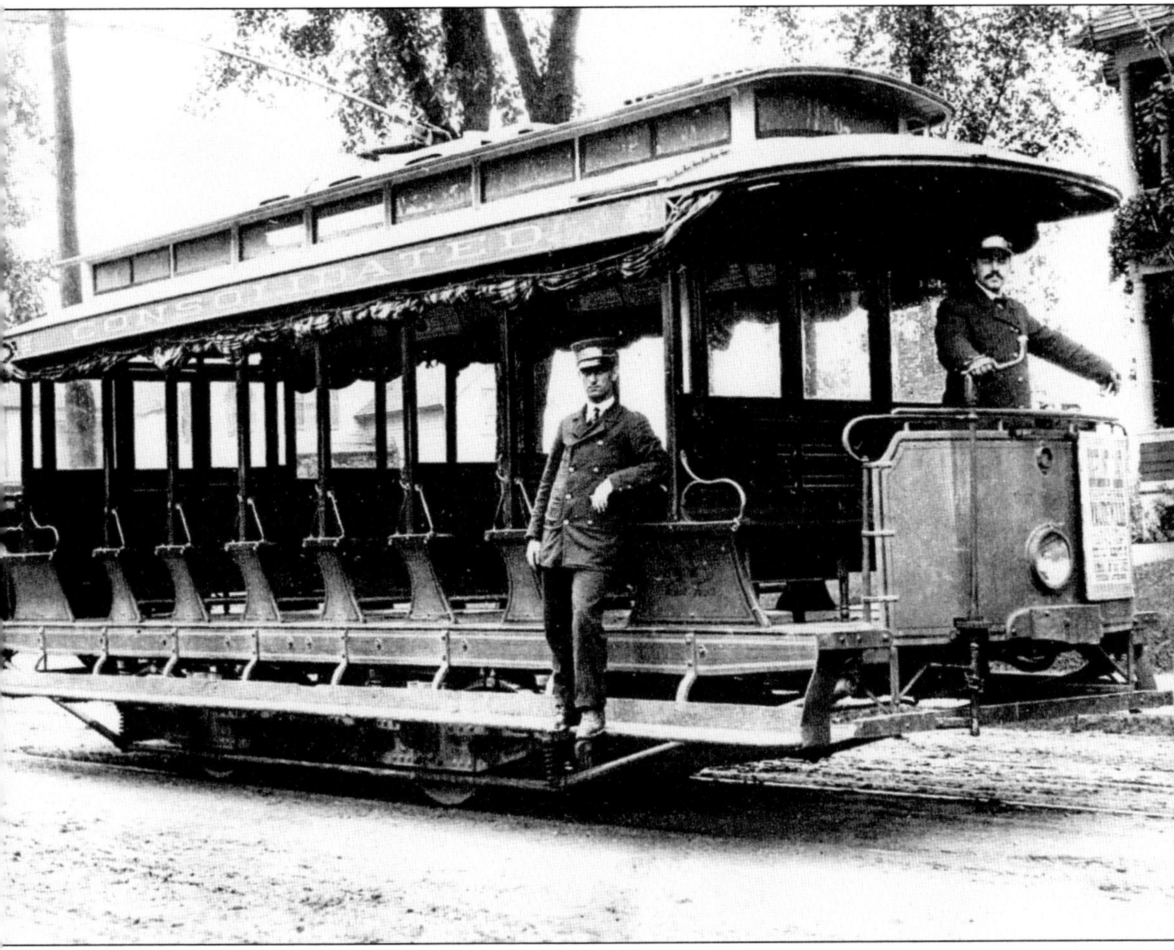

One of the original cars from 1897, No. 22, ran until it was scrapped in Burrville in April 1917. The Consolidated Railway name was only used for three years; in 1910 all the cars were relettered with the Connecticut Company name. (F. S. Bennett Collection.)

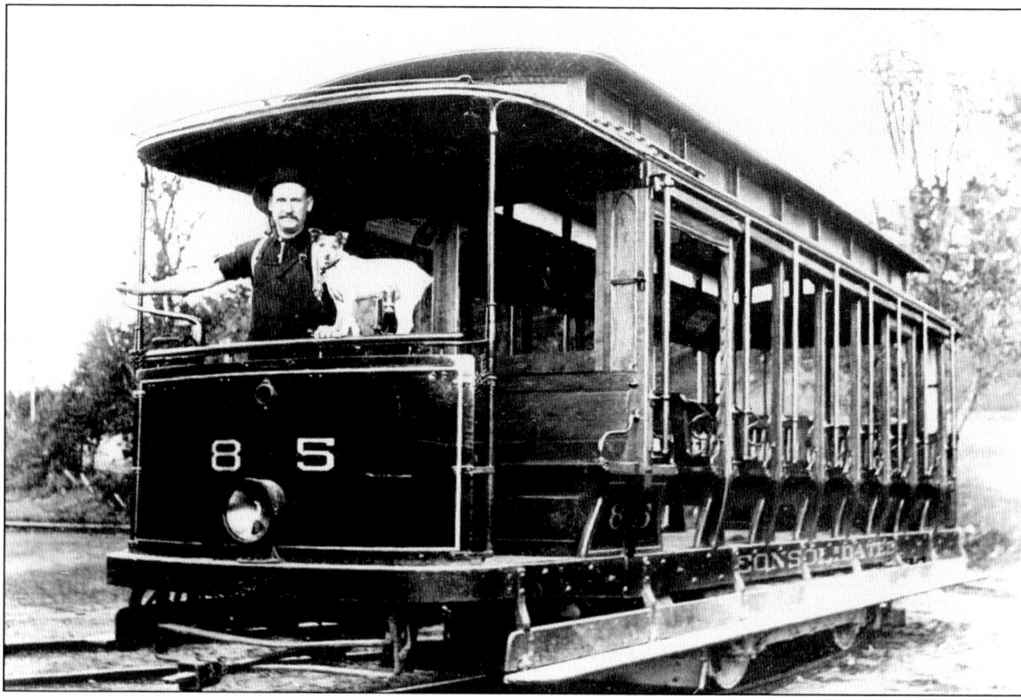

Car No. 85 of the Greenwich Tramway came to Torrington in 1907. It was built by the St. Louis Car Company in 1901. This photograph was taken in 1913; the dog was not a regular member of the crew!

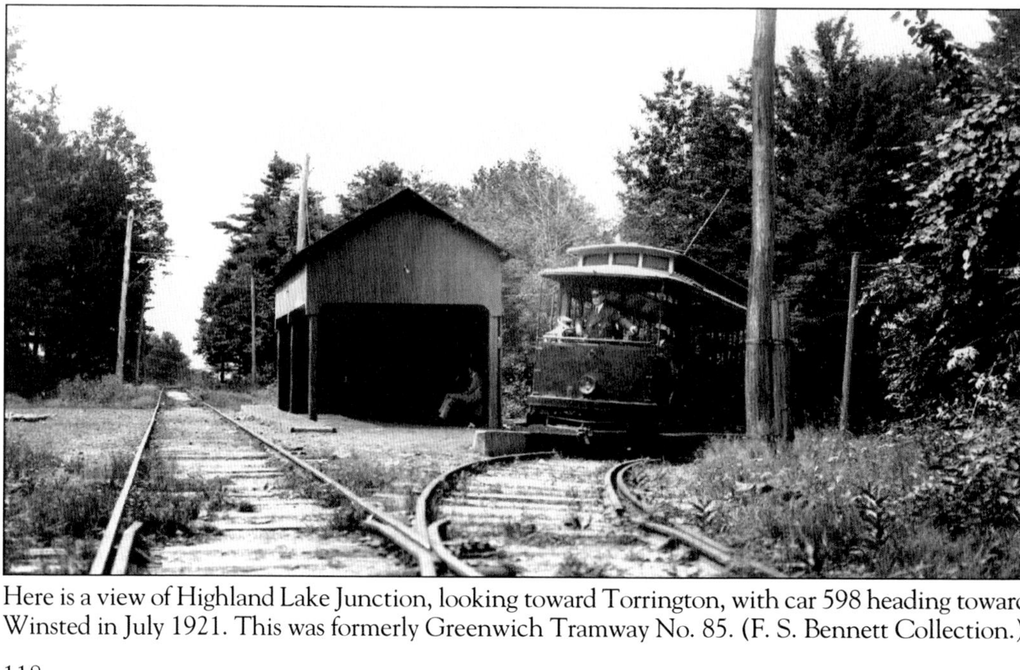

Here is a view of Highland Lake Junction, looking toward Torrington, with car 598 heading toward Winsted in July 1921. This was formerly Greenwich Tramway No. 85. (F. S. Bennett Collection.)

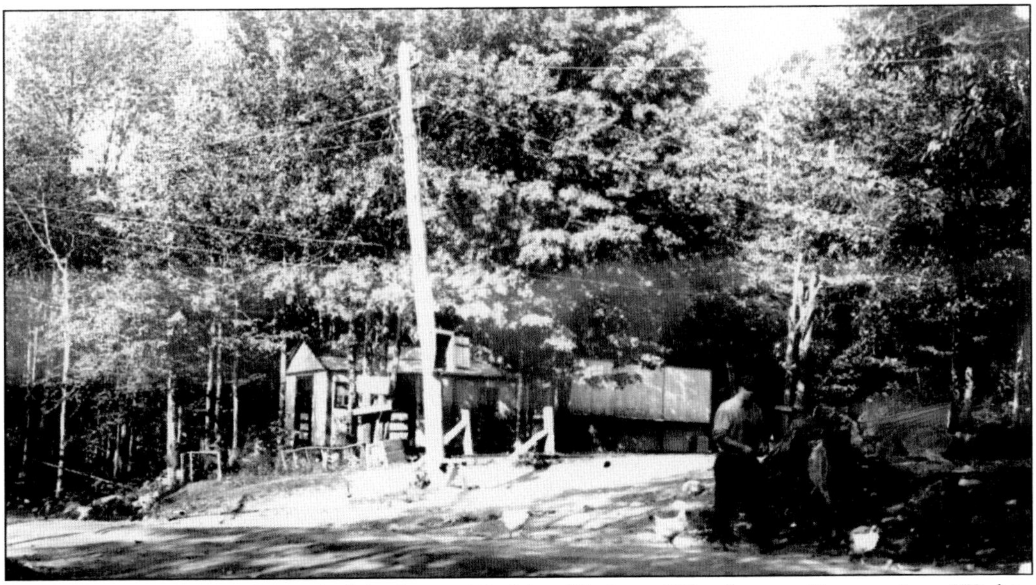

Here is a 1919 view at the end of the line at Highland Lake in Winchester, Connecticut. Within only a few years paved roads and automobiles would capture most of the traffic to Highland Lake. (F. S. Bennett Collection.)

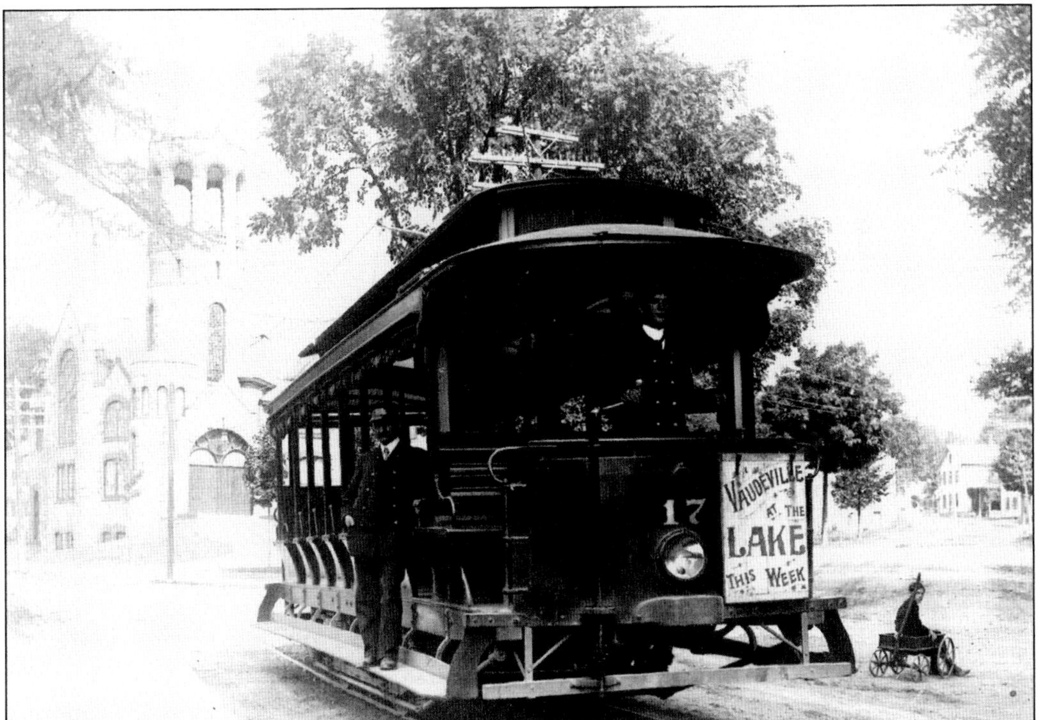

Here is open car 17 in Winsted *c.* 1899. There was little in the way of vehicular traffic at that time, and the trolley would reign as the primary mode of transportation for a few more years. (F. S. Bennett Collection.)

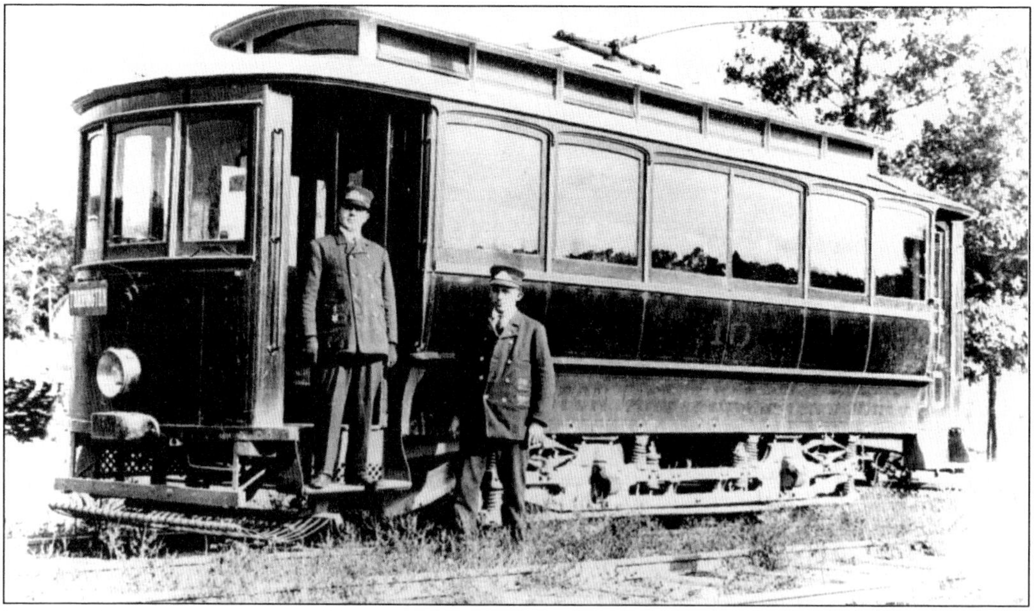

Here is closed car 10 at Burrville in 1906.

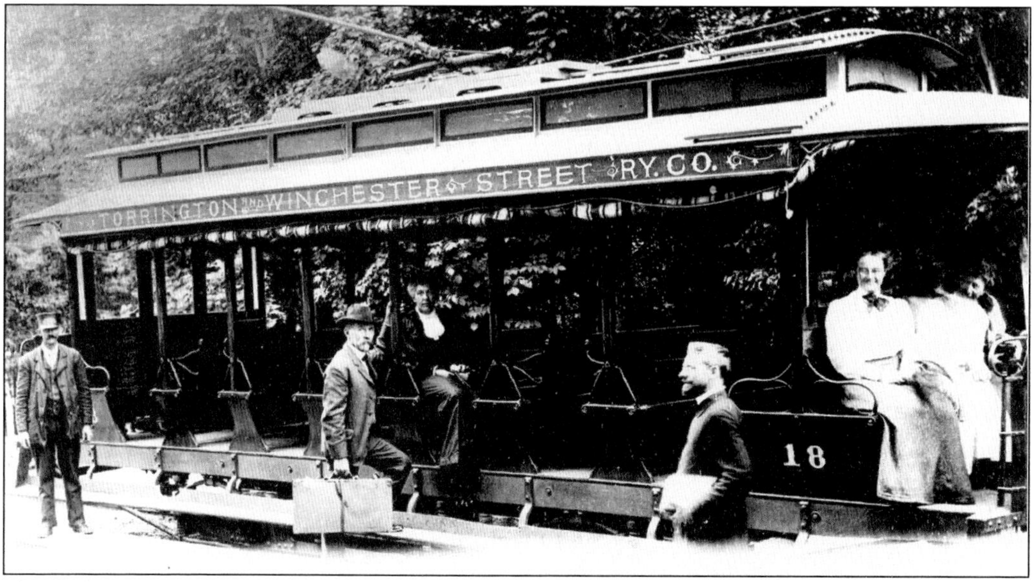

Shown here is an open car with a very distinguished group of passengers, who are dressed up in their best clothes. Notice the single running board, a feature that was later outlawed because it was deemed dangerous to the riding public. All open cars in the state of Connecticut had to be refitted with double running boards after the legislature enacted a law in the early 1900s. (F. S. Bennett Collection.)

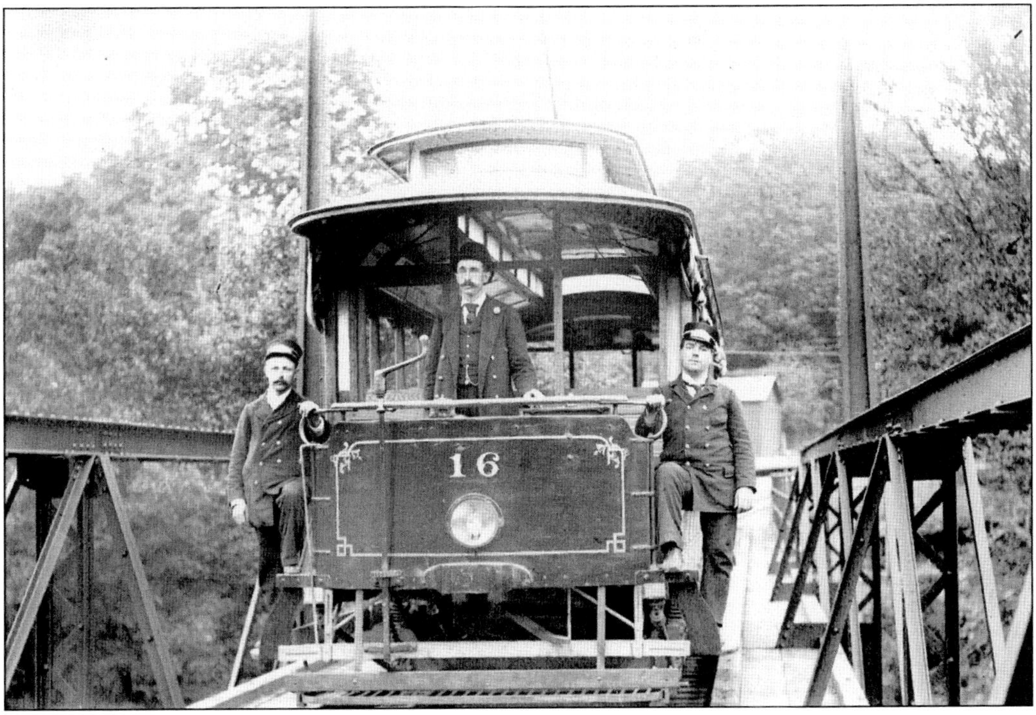

Torrington & Winchester Street Railway car 16 is shown on the bridge over the New Haven Railroad on the Highland Lake branch. This car met all cars from Winsted and Torrington at Highland Lake Junction. (F. S. Bennett Collection.)

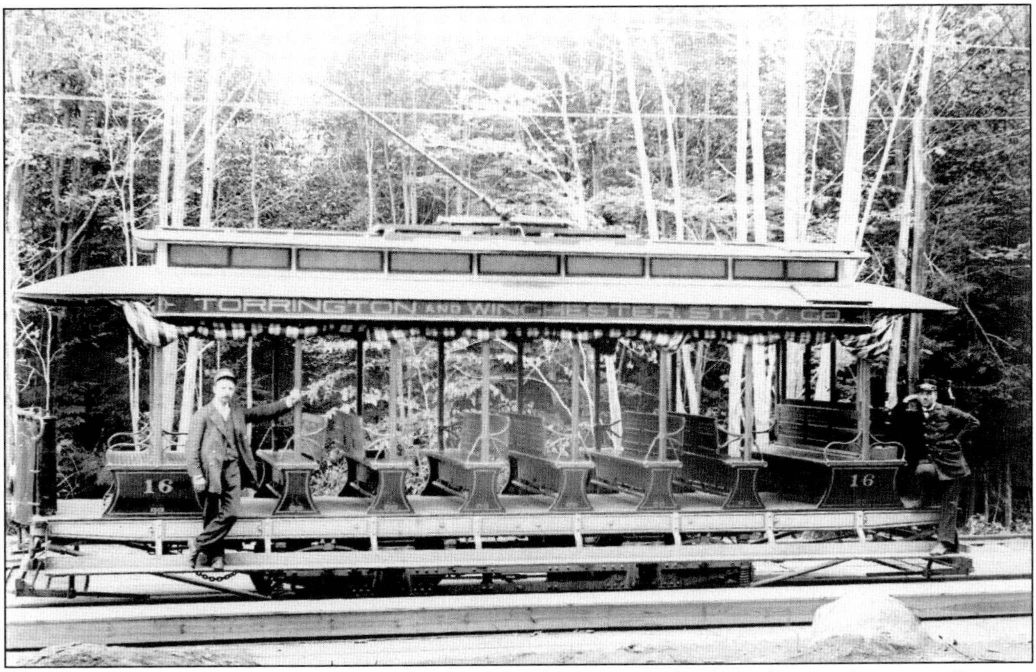

Here is a view of car 16 laying over at Highland Lake *c.* 1900. The New England open trolley was a tradition from May through October until after World War I. (F. S. Bennett Collection.)

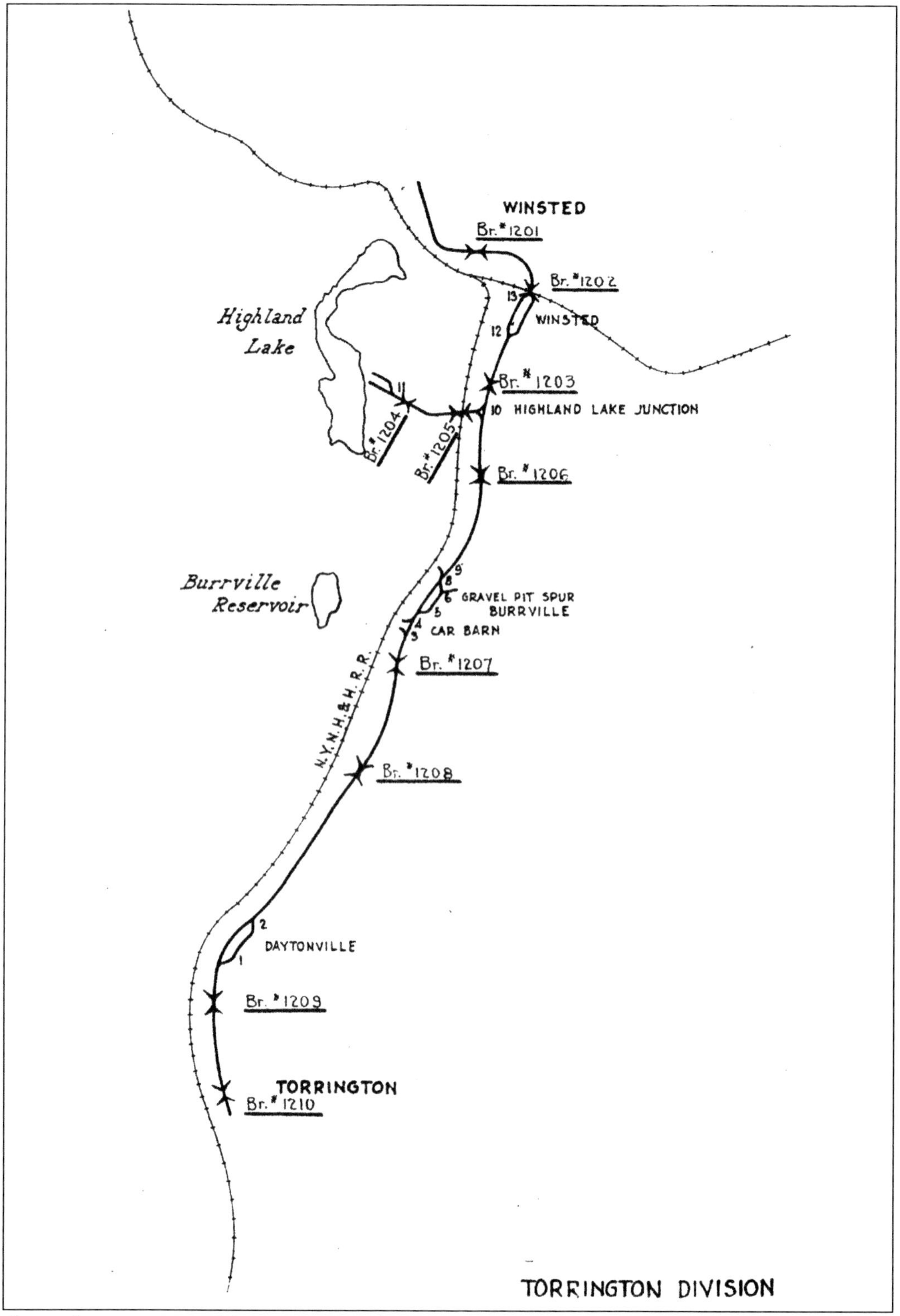

Shown here is a map of the Torrington division in 1920.

Six

WATERBURY & MILLDALE TRAMWAY LINE

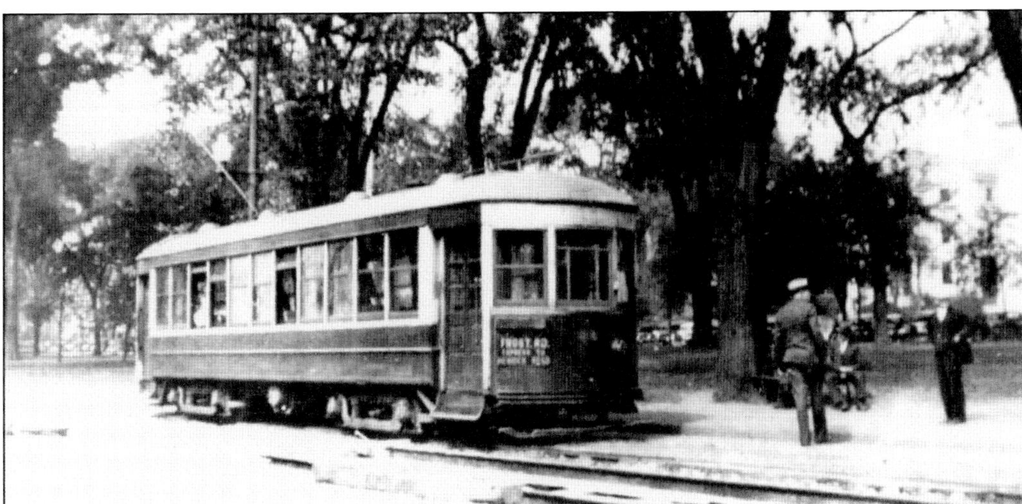

Here at the Waterbury Green in 1929 is Waterbury & Milldale car 102, bound for Frost Road. The car house and repair shops were located on Meriden Road in Waterbury. Frost Road was a turn-back point for rush-hour cars. A Waterbury & Milldale car followed Connecticut Company New Haven cars from Meriden Road and East Main Street to the green. On the outbound trip, the Waterbury & Milldale car would lead until it turned off on Meriden Road. Both cars would run express, not stopping except to pick up passengers going outbound.

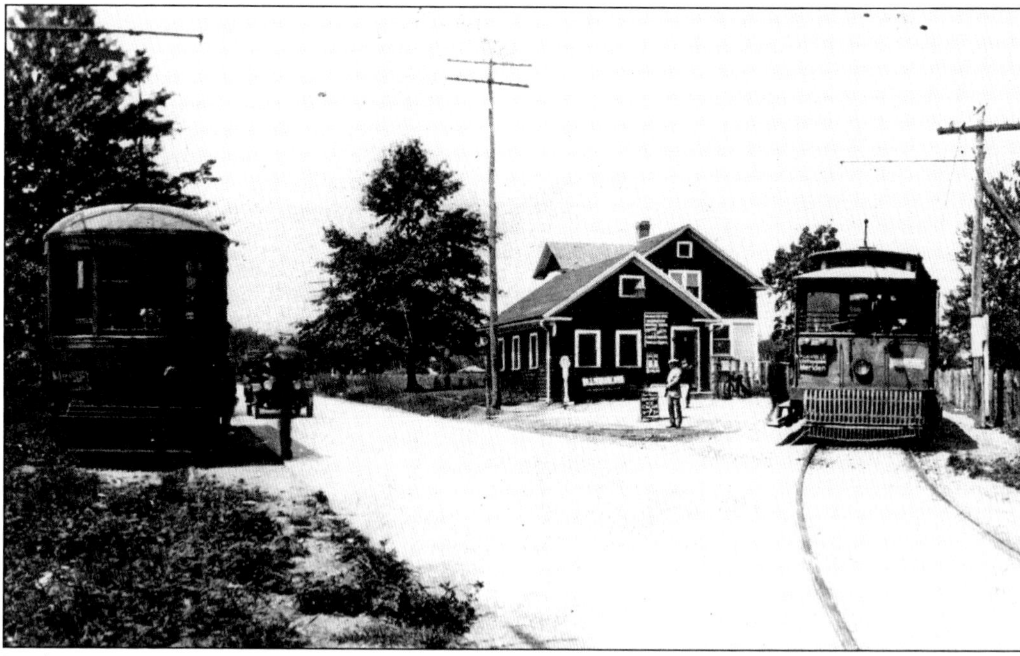

In this 1920 view at Milldale, we see a Connecticut Company open car en route to Meriden from New Britain, and on the left, a Waterbury & Milldale Tramway car at the end of the line in from Waterbury. The Connecticut Company also had a line that ran eastward from Waterbury that connected further south, at Cheshire Junction. At Milldale, passengers could board cars for Waterbury, Meriden, New Britain, or New Haven. (F. S. Bennett Collection.)

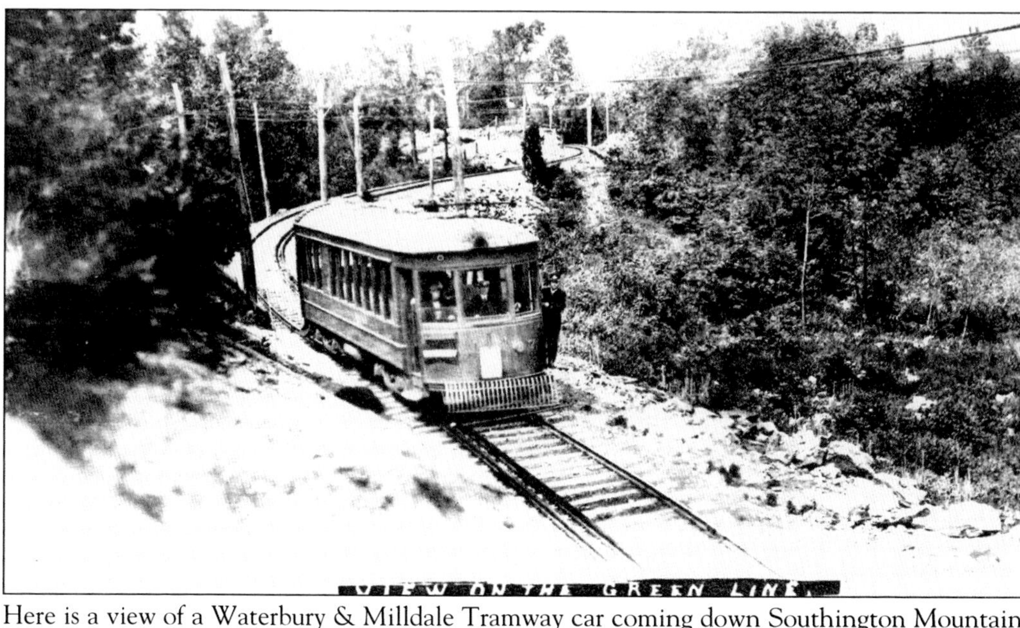

Here is a view of a Waterbury & Milldale Tramway car coming down Southington Mountain. The line was also called the Green Line. The line from Waterbury to Milldale was completed on December 4, 1914. In 1927 the line was abandoned from Hitchcock Lakes to Milldale.

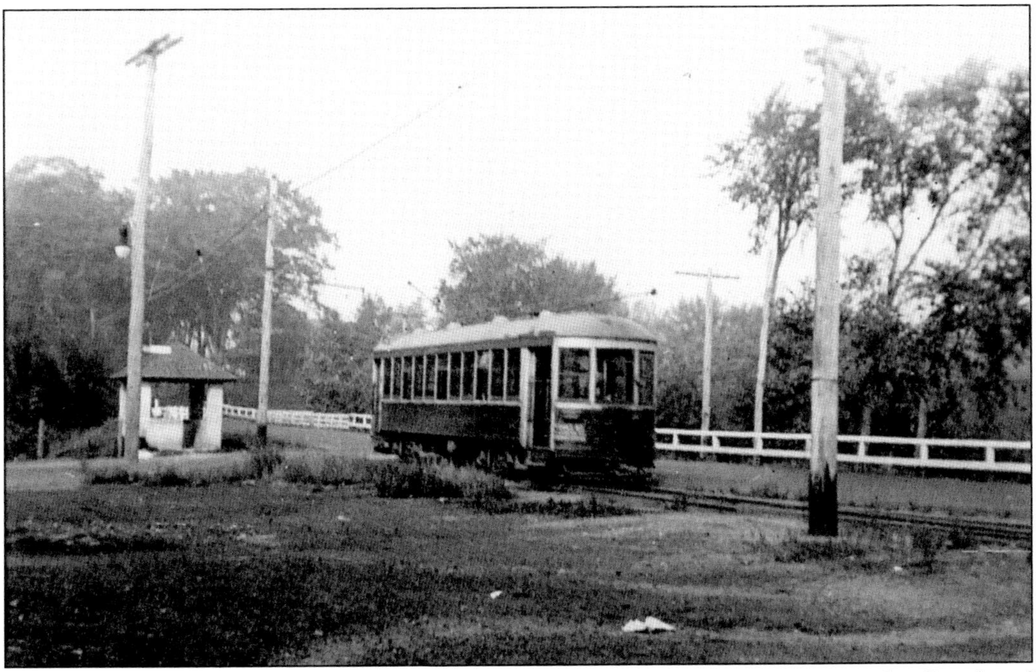

Here a car approaches a stop, which includes a small waiting station at Meriden Road and Woodland Avenue. In 2005 this structure still stands as a memorial to the long-departed Green Line. The line's car house is just behind the photographer.

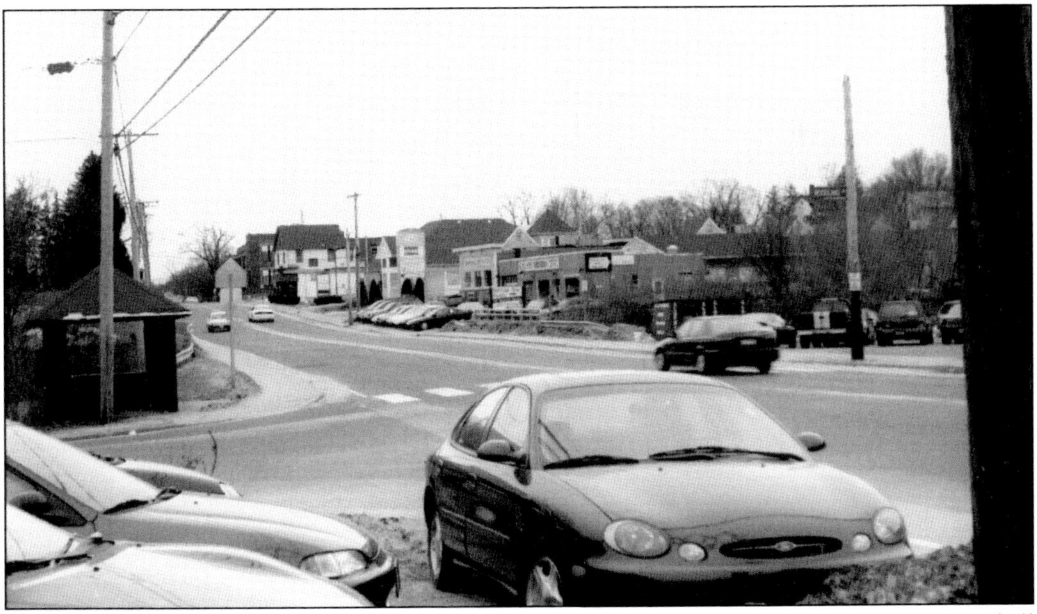

Here is a view of the trolley waiting station on Meriden Road in 2005. The Green Line ceased all streetcar operations on October 29, 1933, when the Connecticut Company abandoned its East Main Street line because of street repaving. The Green Line had trackage rights to Exchange Place in Waterbury, and it was not practical to operate without access to downtown Waterbury. On the following day, the Cooke Street Bus Line began operating motor coaches to serve Green Line riders; the bus line later would also be known as the Green Line to East End patrons.

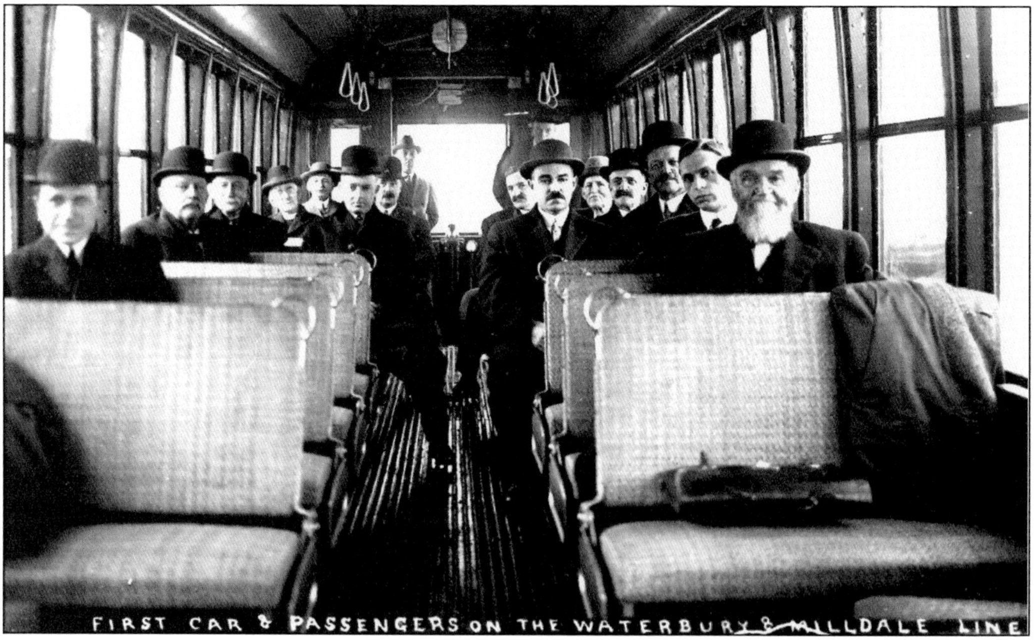

This picture shows the first trip on the Waterbury & Milldale Tramway on November 17, 1913. The bearded gentleman on the right is Charles H. Clark, president of the company.

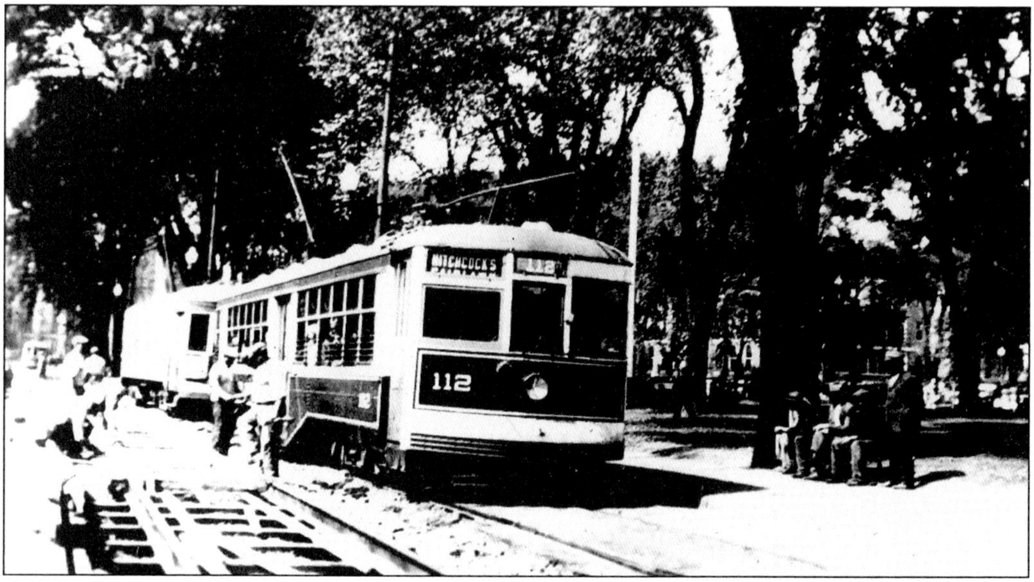

As it leads a Connecticut Company steel car past a track gang on its way east, Green Line center-door car 112 is shadowed by stately chestnut trees on the Waterbury Green. The "Hitchcocks" destination sign indicates that it will not be going past Hitchcock Lake down Southington Mountain to Milldale.

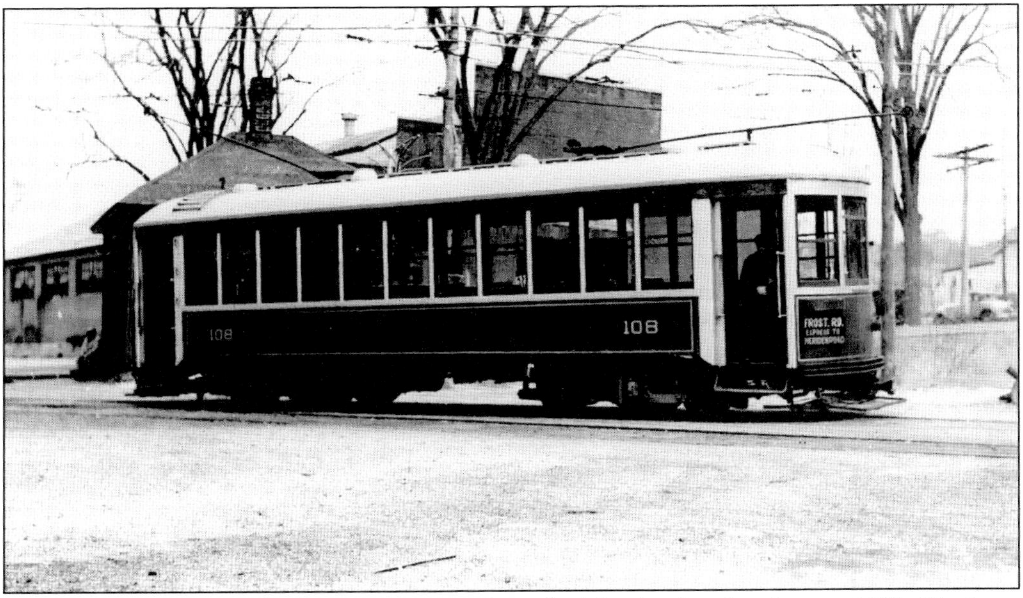

Here is Waterbury & Milldale Tramway car 108 at the Meriden Road carbarn in 1931. The large brick building behind the car, originally a trucking terminal, is today still in use as a church.

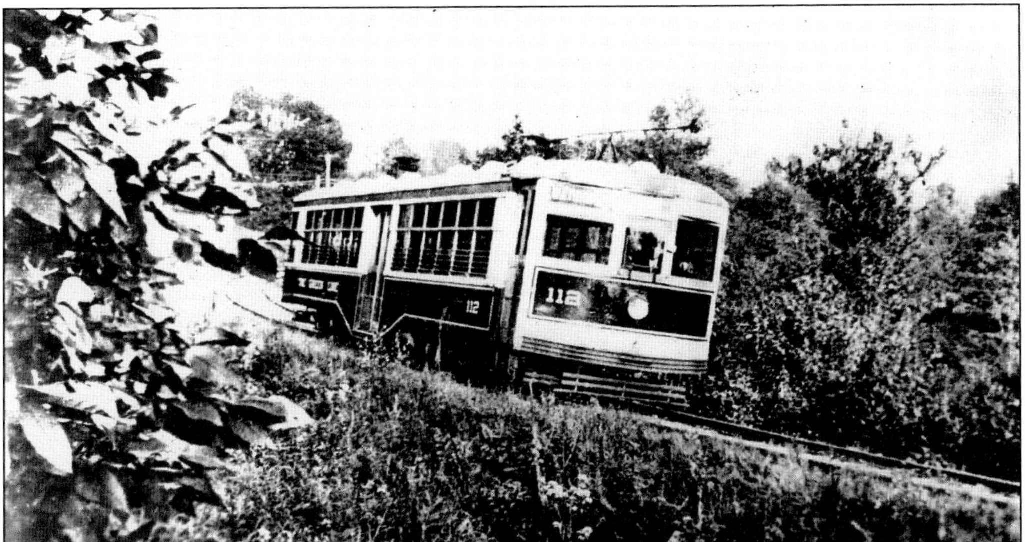

In a more bucolic setting, car 112 is seen heading west toward Waterbury on a summer day. In 1921 the Waterbury & Milldale Tramway purchased two center-entrance, double-truck Birney safety cars, the only two ever built, from American Car Company in St. Louis, Missouri. The cars had originally been ordered by the Cape Breton Tramways in Nova Scotia in 1918, but the order was cancelled before they were delivered. These were actually the first double-truck Birney safety cars ever built. Later-model double-truck Birney cars that ran in Torrington, such as 3000, 3001, and 3002, were of similar design but did not have the center door.

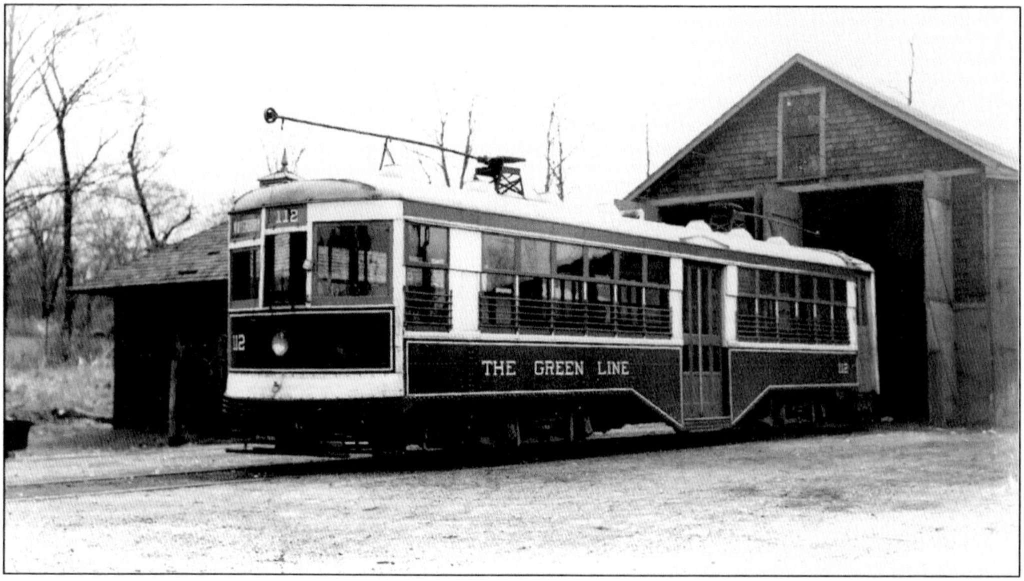

Here is center-entrance Birney car 112 at the Meriden Road carbarn in Waterbury in 1933. Both 112 and its twin, 114, were scrapped when the line ceased operations in October 1933.

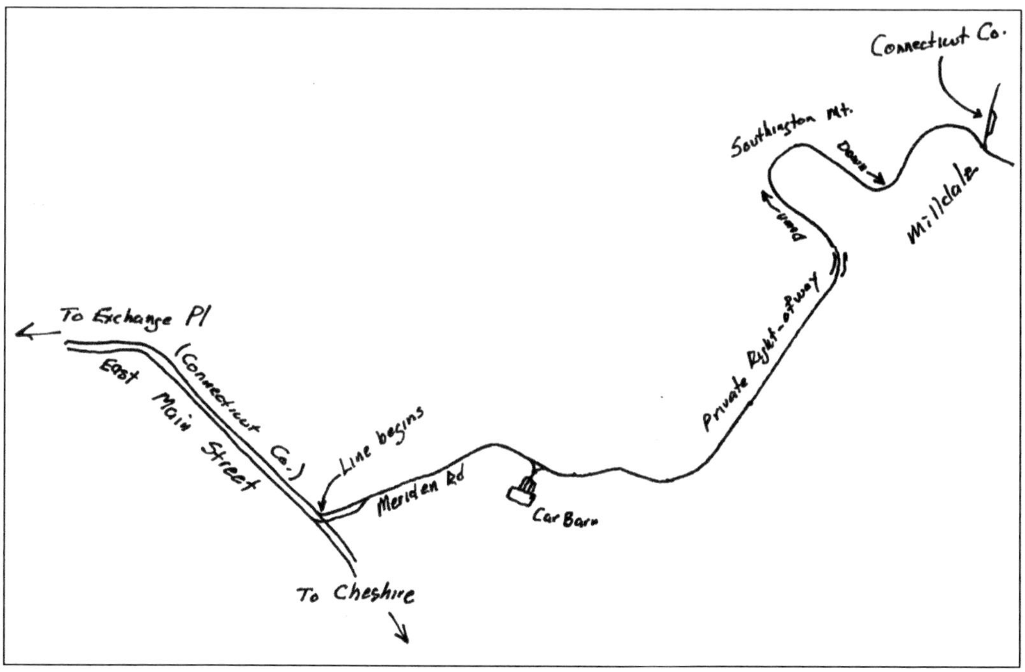

Shown here is a map of the Waterbury & Milldale Tramway line in 1925.